CW01457113

All change

The years that rocked the Cradle of the Railways

Mike Amos MBE

Front cover: Enniskillen Fusiliers on Shildon station during the railwaymen's strike of 1911.

Back cover: the Great Gathering, A4 steam locomotives at Locomotion, Shildon, in 2014.

For Sharon, incomparable
(and not even from Shildon).

All change

Text & cover © Mike Amos 2025

First published 2025

Mike Amos has asserted the moral right to be identified as the author of this work.
Apart from any fair dealing for the purposes of research or private study, or criticism or review, as permitted under the Copyright, Designs and Patents Act 1988, this publication may not be reproduced, stored or transmitted in any form or by any means except with the prior permission in writing of the publisher, or in the case of reprographic reproduction, in accordance with the terms of licences issued by the Copyright Licensing Agency. Enquiries concerning reproduction outside those terms should be sent to the publisher.

Published by Mike Amos
8 Oakfields, Middleton Tyas, Richmond, North Yorkshire
Email mikeamos81@aol.com
Blog: www.mikeamosblog.wordpress.com

Designed and typeset by County Print
using Adobe InDesign and Adobe Photoshop.
Text set in 11pt Times New Roman.
Printed by County Print, 11 Collingwood Court, Riverside
Park Industrial Estate, Middlesbrough TS2 1RP
01642 225867
sales@countyprint.co.uk

Most of the illustrations in this book have been used with kind permission of Alan Ellwood and The Northern Echo. If any other illustration is in copyright but not been acknowledged, the author will be grateful for information and will happily make amends in future editions.

ISBN:
978-1-8380404-4-4

Contents

Home truths

As would be expected from a long serving foot soldier in HM Press Corps, let's have honesty from the outset. This isn't really a book about the Stockton and Darlington Railway, not even on its bicentenary. There've been plenty of those already and, goodness knows, likely to be wagon loads more cascading imminently down the track. Neither is it a history or, properly, an autobiography.

Rather it's an account of how Shildon, Cradle of the Railways, has changed – changed hugely – since my long-gone formative years there. Right from the top, the bottom line may be that the 1921 census put the town's population at 17,659, that in 1941 it was 15,640, in 1951 14,510 and in 2021 – getting on 40 years after the wagon works closed with the loss of 2,500 jobs - a few dozen below ten thousand.

All Change isn't just aimed at Shildon folk, however, nor solely at those who know the dear old place. It's for all those who enjoy their social history lightly served, who appreciate an anecdote – any amount of those – and perhaps for those for whom social media meant Radio Luxembourg with the troops beneath a dimly illumined lamp post, who recall hanging out of carriage windows, who remember when smut was nothing more than a speck of soot in the eye and now perhaps resist a small tear for different reasons entirely.

Twenty minutes ahead of my twin brother Dave, and thus heir to the family misfortunes, I was born in October 1946 at Hardwick Hall in Sedgefield, then a maternity home and now a posh hotel. Shildon was ten miles and for our dad a sit-up-and-beg bike ride away, denying the claim that we arrived within earshot of the wagon works buzzer though such geographical authenticity seldom worries the millions who suppose themselves Bow Bells Cockneys. We finally came home, to a rented terraced house with an outside netty out the back, a week or so later.

Lots of houses had outside toilets, some the once familiar two-holers and multiples thereof, a sort of backyard community centre. The 1951 census further recorded that 12 per cent of Shildon's homes had no WC at all, 17 per cent hadn't a kitchen sink and 64 per cent either hadn't a bath or had to share one (presumably one at a time) with a neighbour. Probably the census takers didn't count the blackclocks, which was just as well, though they did record that nearly ten per cent of homes had no hot water. In 1947 the infant mortality rate equated to 63 per 1,000 births. The twins got away lucky.

The wagon works were still going hammer and tongs, of course, The pits were still in full vigour, as *A Christmas Carol* supposed of the workhouses and, like the workhouses, there were an awful lot of pits and an awful lot of hard labour. Unusually for a male resident of Shildon, our dad worked at neither.

He was a Londoner, Muswell Hill man, improbably joined the Queen's Own Cameron Highlanders and was posted before the war to Catterick where he met my mum who (of course) was a Shildon lass. They married in 1937 on condition (of course, of course) that they live not in Muswell Hill but in Shildon.

Demobbed a sergeant, would have been more senior save for an unfortunate incident with a wheelbarrow, he became a GPO telephonist by night, collected club money by day – firstly for Howards Stores in Bishop Auckland, then the Provident – and, clearly with time on his hands, managed a couple of allotments. More of digging for victory a little later.

Though he regularly claimed to have eyes like a hawk, and probably a 20-20 hawk at that, he never learned to drive. Though he's been dead 40 years, there are still old folk around the town who remember my dad's old bone shaker bike. Sadly, significantly, good eyesight isn't hereditary.

However hazardous, employment at the wagon works or down the pit had perks. Wagon workers and their families were annually given a number of free passes for the railways and thereafter travelled at substantial discount. Privvies, they called the tickets – as indeed they did the netties – and some of us felt under-privileged. Miners past and present had regular deliveries of concessionary coal, tipped onto the narrow back street without regard for the fact that it was our football pitch and thus compelling the match to be abandoned, We'd have shovelled the coal ourselves, if they'd have let us, just to start biffing a ball about again.

The Albert Street back alley remains, cobbled and concave, perhaps more greatly subsided but otherwise little changed. A sign on one of the yard doors depicts a cross looking Alsatian dog and the message: "Want to know if there's life after death? Jump this gate and you'll find out." It probably wouldn't have deterred us from bunking over to get the ball back; you know what they say about bark and bite, don't you.

Apropos of little, a little terraced house in Mill Street – next to the once-steaming sidings which linked wagon works to main line – these days has a sign in the window warning "Beware of Charlie". Though whether Charlie be a dog, a budgie or something altogether more narcotic is unclear.

There'd been railway works since early Victorian times, Timothy Hackworth's ingeniously innovative tenure, but before proceeding a word of editorial explanation. In Shildon the wagon works, which they became in the 1860s after 40 years of locomotive building, were generally known as the Shops – a corruption of workshops. To avoid confusion with places which sold bread and cheese and things, or penny ducks and ha'penny lollies, references in the book to the railway Shops are capitalised while the wagon works, knowing their place, remain lower case. Mind, we were probably about 15 before realising that there wasn't a secret retail centre, hidden like the mythical Great Steam Engine Reserve, at the other end of town.

Perhaps it should also before proceeding be explained that Main Street wasn't the main street at all. That was Church Street, where most of the shops were. St John's, the parish church, has stood since 1834 at the junction of the two, a foot in both camps. Good old Church of England.

We attended Timothy Hackworth Junior Mixed and Infants school without knowing much, or being taught anything at all, about the great railway pioneer after whom it was named but became train spotters, greater spotted train spotters, nonetheless. When we weren't train spotting we were playing football, seldom able to combine both. It was a happy childhood, never materially affluent but blessed in many other ways – not least the richness of language.

Where else might we have heard phrases like "Jump up and give your leg a dother" (Aunty Betty), like "Neither watter bewitched nor tea begrudged" (our mam, often with justification), like "As pleasant as a cow's husband" or, a favourite, "He/she talks like a ha'penny book." You know what they say about inflation.

Where else but in the back streets of Shildon might we have learned – and fought over – the arcane rules of shine-a-moggy, kicky-ock-chock and tiggy-on-high? Where else but Shildon might we have roamed, careless and care free; where else might we have kicked a tin can around when the final fickle five-bob Frido football flattened, where else risked a twopenny late-return fine on *William* books, much thumbed, from Hall-garth library?

The town after the war had a population of getting on 15,000, most of the men and many of the women – in factories, collieries or at the works – in fairly gainful employment. There were getting on 200 shops, "New" Shildon still with its own retail centre based around Alma Road but these days wholly disappeared. At the end of the war, around the time of our birth, there were seven Methodist churches, four cinemas, as many banks, several government offices – including the labour exchange - two Church of England parishes and at least three other churches, some of which offered little incentives, rewards on earth, for steadfast Sunday School attendance.

No such perks at St John's where by the age of 23 I'd simultaneously become churchwarden, church council secretary and parish newspaper editor under the wing of Canon Hugh Corden, the cricket loving, pipe smoking vicar. For some reason it's impossible to remember those times without calling to mind the Jake Thackeray song about Sister Josephine – "what a funny nun you are" – not least the rather profane business of playing knocky nine doors down a snowy Church Street at the end of a *very* merry Christmas midnight mass.

Should it really have been laid at the churchwarden's door that the Red Lion and St John's were barely 100 yards apart, or that one kicked out as the other welcomed in or that in 1970 you might still reasonably expect a white Christmas?

Canon Corden also liked to tell the story of how, when the lock on the church safe became jammed, he'd persuaded celebrity safecracker George Reynolds – one of Shildon's more colourful if controversial characters, a man who liked to suppose himself a sort of latter day Robin Hood though not a latter day saint – to effect access. Not normally publicity shy, George tended to distance himself from that tale, perhaps lest it give him a good name.

There's also a de luxe version of the story, ecclesiastical if not urban legend, which has the vicar switching on the light as he enters the vestry. "Put it off, please, vicar" says George. "I'm more used to working in the dark."

As well as ecclesiastical office, I was also from 1970-73 the youngest member of Shildon Urban District Council, a second tier local authority with responsibility for things like public health, housing, planning, minor roads and recreation. Fifteen councillors represented the Labour Party, five of us were Independents – not always a synonym for "Tory", as cynics supposed, but definitely not Labour, either. There was good reason for that.

Cyril Mitchinson, the old school council clerk, was a Quaker who assumed high office – if high office be acknowledged among the Friends - and was the first person I knew always to shake hands upon every meeting. It was an unsatisfactory time, however, the workings of the controlling group not always democratic – or so it seemed to me – my frequently fruitless protests faithfully recorded for the *Auckland Chronicle*, price fourpence, by Dennis Robinson, the Shildon-based reporter on the table in the corner.

By 1973 I was gone, never residentially to return but seldom – as they say – off the doorstep. You know what they say about taking the lad out of Shildon, or wherever, but never taking Shildon out of the lad.

Though the A-level results hadn't been bad – English, history, German – university never appealed, the absence of attraction doubtless mutual. I presented myself to the labour exchange, a big wooden hut in Main Street now a Hackett and Baines warehouse, and announced that I wanted to be a journalist. The bloke in the shiny suit and the woolly cardigan couldn't have been more taken aback had he been a panellist on *What's my line* and the contestant a sagger maker's bottom knocker. Had he asked "What's wrong with the Shops like everyone else?" it wouldn't in the least have been surprising.

No thanks to the dole bloke, things – as always they have – worked out. A kindly editor took pity. Countless millions of words later I'm still writing, still spinning stories but with the cold sobering realisation that many of those names recalled in the book should be prefaced with "the late" and that I'm nearly half as old as is the dear old Stockton and Darlington and (very likely) soon will be history, too.

I'm also massively conflicted, resolutely reluctant to run the old place down and yet not blind, however myopic, to reality. These days the population's barely 10,000, the town never recovered from the wagon works closure, the per capita crime rate said to be the highest in Co Durham. The main shopping street, Church Street, isn't just dying, it's dead and buried – despite the excellence of Godfrey Card's sausages – the town has serious issues of drug abuse and poverty and by no means alone in either,

Among the biggest hurdles is the repeated claim, however spuriously based, that Shildon is the cheapest place in Britain in which to buy a house, apparently attracting landlords from elsewhere who buy run-down properties on the cheap and rent them to incomers – "refugees", it's said – looking desperately for somewhere they can afford to live or decanted by London borough councils who don't much care where the poor beggars pitch up so long as it's not in their back yard.

Yet there are still so many positives, not least reflected in the almost simultaneous Ofsted reports in March 2023 on the town's three primary schools. Both Timothy Hackworth and St John's were rated good with outstanding features while Thornhill – known in former times simply as the Council school – was assessed "outstanding" in every respect, not so much a report as an encomium, a jewelled hymn of praise.

The report talks of a "highly ambitious" curriculum, of pupils who are hugely enthusiastic – "particularly when learning about Shildon's industrial heritage" – and, perhaps with a nod to Shildon winters in former times, of learning about how polar bears keep warm. Isn't there a joke about that? "Pupils blossom at this inspirational school, enjoy learning and make excellent progress…. Leaders have very high expectations of all pupils, both academically and socially no matter what their background. Behaviour is exemplary, pupils feel safe and happy at school."

What else? Locomotion, the National Railway Museum, is a truly world-class attraction and – like all the best things in life – is free. The Shildon Alive charity performs admirably in addressing the many social issues facing the town, the town council works effectively and imaginatively to foster community, Hackworth Park's a gem, the nature reserve at Brusselton's a wondrous surprise, the Salvation Army as always is where the muck and bullets are, the football and cricket clubs both have wider visions.

Though licensed premises generally struggle, another national trend, it's good to see Dave Reynolds and friends striving so hard to place the Railway Institute at the centre of the town's social and adult educational life as it, too, approaches its bicentenary. Shildon folk, most of them, are lovely.

In so many ways the town remains home, and in so many ways there's still no place like it.

Chapter one

Age of innocence

We were innocents in those formative years of the 1950s and since the known world extended no further than a ten-mile radius of Shildon, not even innocents abroad.

Unlike the heroes of Edith Nesbit's tearful story, we *were* always railway children, and little wonder. The line ran barely 100 yards beyond that rented terraced house, albeit silent and subterranean, out of sight but seldom out of mind. The wagon works toiled 24 hours – most of them, anyway – providing work for more than 2,500 men. The steam age still breathed fire and, forever, fascination.

It was the world's first railway town, dubbed subsequently the Cradle of the Railways. To very many it was (and is) history, to us it was just home.

Chiefly, almost daily, we were train spotters, more recently mocked as anoraks but a term unheard of back then and to call a kid a windcheater or a jerkin (as opposed, perhaps, to a jerk) just wouldn't have been the same. Besides, the caller would have been scragged.

Shildon tunnel's southern portal was just half a mile from home. Between there and the station lay what we called the Water Bridge, though George Turner Smith in his *A railway history of New Shildon* (2019) supposed it an aqueduct and not just an aqueduct but an anomalous aqueduct. What was anomalous about it was that there was usually insufficient water to provide a decent bird bath for a spuggie, though things may have been different in the winter of 2023-24 and the sodden summer which followed.

The station was an unhandsome and unimposing edifice – how greatly we envied Bishop Auckland its triumvirate – so roundly and routinely rubbished down the years that it must have a subsequent chapter of its own.

Beyond the station was the marshalling yard, said before World War II to be the world's biggest – 32 adjacent tracks, more points than an adjournment debate – and now the site of Loco-motion, the darling and precocious love child of the National Railway Museum (and there'll be more of that, subsequently, too.)

The town was on the branch line between Crook and Bishop Auckland in one direction and Darlington and the rest of the world in the other. Passenger services in the fledgling fifties were usually hauled by Class A5 or A8 tank engines, mucky little freight trains by a Q6 or J27. Equally and indiscriminately abused, they were the locomotive epitome of the adage about familiarity breeding contempt, chiming even then with *Cargoes*, the John Masefield poem we were taught at Timothy Hackworth Junior Mixed:

Dirty British coaster with a salt-caked smoke stack

Butting through the Channel in the mad March days,

With a cargo of Tyne coal

Road rails, pig-iron

Firewood, iron-war and cheap tin trays.

Spotters' spot: "water bridge" and tunnel beyond

If only we'd known that British Railways and the government would soon replace the lot with what Thomas the Tank Engine so contemptuously and so perceptively termed diseasels, we might have been a little more gracious.

There were two, perhaps two-and-a-half, exceptions to the greater-spotted diet. The first was what we knew as the mail train, around 6 15pm five or six nights a week, usually hauled by a powerful class V2 or, who knew, by something with a name which meant little or nothing – not then, not to nine-year-olds – but promised exotica, and excitement, nonetheless.

The second, less frequent but by no means uncommon, was the Sunday diversion. When engineering work closed the main line between Darlington and Durham, the Sabbath high flyers would be routed (though not necessarily fast tracked) through Shildon and Bishop Auckland, then onward on the now-gone branch to Willington and Brandon before rejoining the real rail world.

Often there'd be class A4s, Sir Nigel Gresley's legendary "streaks", imminence announced if southbound by the klaxon whistle from the depths of the Prince of Wales tunnel, the biggest thrill since Coronation day and a free feed out the back. More frequently yet there'd be named A1s or A3s, many dubbed "blinkers" because of the almost-equine smoke deflectors at the front.

Diversionary tactics, many a Sunday dinner – 11 30 in our house, washed up by 12, what's-for-tea by two – went cold in that cause. Many a Sunday School class was sinfully skived, and with shameless disregard for the celestial kiddie catcher.

The third – two-and-a-half – left Shildon station at 12.30pm on Saturdays, a weekly direct service to Newcastle (change at

Durham for Sunderland) popular with football followers and often hauled by a class B1 with names like Hirola, Wildebeeste and Addax, which for years we myopically misread as Ajax and wondered – we really did - why a steam engine would be named after a scouring powder.

It was only when Messrs Flanders and Swann sang of the Gnu and its up-country cousins – "and nor am I in the least like that dreadful hartebeest" - that things became a little clearer. The first forty B1s, with one curious exception, were all named after antelopes.

I said we were innocents. I said we'd return to the mysterious matter of steam engine nomenclature (and, honest, we will.)

Usually we'd cycle no further than the Water Bridge, regularly reminded of the doggerel "Ride a Raleigh, ride a wreck; ride a Humber and break your neck."

I rode a Raleigh, others a BSA, all survived. One of the posh kids – posh for Shildon, anyway, they lived in a bungalow – even had a Triumph Palm Beach, with straight handlebars and 3-speed Sturmey Archer gears, the childhood equivalent of go-faster stripes.

These days access to the Water Bridge and the lines below is guarded by the sort of gate that might have come second hand from Frankland Prison. Back then there was a convenient stile, allowing access to trackside and particularly convenient for me and my twin – every bit as short-sighted – who similarly struggled to read a number plate from five yards but might easily have shaken hands with the driver in the attempt to do so.

Heard but not seen, approaching trains – particularly on diversion days – would be greeted with the anxious enquiry "Streak, blinker, misery?", the last of them reserved for a querulous Q6 or a slam-door stopping train for Saltburn. In a generally very happy childhood, it was perhaps paradoxical that miseries were inevitably in the majority.

A diversion of a different sort would arise each evening as we awaited the southbound mail. A train from Darlington had usually arrived a few minutes earlier, its returning commuters heading up the unlit path past the Water Bridge to hearth and Horlicks. Regularly among them was a fair haired and possibly attractive young lady greeted by youthful cries of "Blondie". Her surname was Whitehead, a possible play on words that never once occurred to us.

It represented not the slightest of stirrings. Had Blondie's appearance coincided exactly with that of the mail train, the lass would never have had a second glance.

Sometimes we'd have enough money for a cheap day return to Darlington Bank Top station, where for a penny platform ticket mainlining might be assured. Sometimes we'd bike five miles through the nascent Newton Aycliffe new town to a spot we called Barrel Arch, where the goods line from Simpasture Junction near Shildon to the Tees at Stockton and Hartlepool – electrified between the two world wars - crossed above the main line north of Darlington.

Nearby was a little pub called the Blacksmiths Arms, known as the Hammer and Pincers, which through a hatch in the back door would sell us crisps and pop for about sixpence the lot. We'd no interest in anything stronger.

Recklessly, ridiculously, we could also get down to the tracks at Barrel Arch in order to lay pennies on the line, the egregious expectation that it would be the penny and not the damn fool child placing it there which would be flattened by an irresistible force travelling at 100mph.

Such absurd escapades were expressly forbidden to members of the Ian Allan Locospotters Club to which almost all of us belonged, the code of conduct insisting that "members of the club will not in any way interfere with railway running". It was a bit like the Wolf Cubs but without specific allegiance to God and the Queen and with the two-finger salute reprehensibly reversed.

Ian Allan lost a leg when just 15 and nowhere near rail lines, became in 1939 a 15-shillings-a-week junior clerk on British Railways' Southern region, dreamed of becoming station master at Waterloo but instead created a huge business empire embracing everything from publishing to travel agency, hotels, car sales and organic food made from seaweed.

He also had a global business selling Masonic regalia and was himself a Past Assistant Grand Master of Ceremonies (no less). My uncles Tom and Jim, one a school caretaker and the other a bus mechanic, were fairly senior in the Shildon lodge, though probably not as Grand.

Had he not left school so early, or indeed had he spent time in Geoff Hill's class at Bishop Auckland Grammar in the early 1960s, Ian Allan might effortlessly have concluded that the word "locospotters" should attract a possessive apostrophe after the s. Solecism did nothing to impede success.

Published in 1942, his first little book listed the locomotives of the Southern region, a pocket-sized number which ran to 16 pages, cost him £42 for 2,000 copies plus 5/6d for a small classified ad in *Railway World*. It sold for a shilling, postal orders so swiftly cascading that he'd to order a reprint. Soon there were ABC Locospotters Annuals for all four regions and, in 1945 Ian Allan left railway employment, real opportunities having been spotted elsewhere.

By 1959, club membership was 1/3d, plus a threepenny stamped addressed envelope, benefits to include an Ian Allan Locospotters Club pencil and "reference book", club card and a tin badge (though the posh chrome version might have cost a few pence more). At its peak, at much the same time that we gathered by the Water Bridge in the daily expression of hope over experience, the club had more than 300,000 members, not quite all of them from Shildon.

The books, by then half-a-crown apiece, contained much technical information about which the average Shildon lad understood little and cared less. We knew nothing of valve gears, tractive effort or blast pipes, cared only about underlining the numbers of steam engines seen for the first time. We called them cops which, come to think, is also what we, ever respectfully, called policemen. Club and hobby burgeoned – "the trains craze has seized boys of six and men of 90" the *News Chronicle* reported.

Allan ran enthusiasts' specials across the land, often to railway workshops though never to Shildon which by that time only made and mended trucks. Thomas the Tank Engine, come to think, was pretty dismissive about trucks, too.

Allan, it's said, always eyed value for money. *Driven by steam*, his autobiography published in 1992, recalled that on a special to Swindon he'd thought the 3/8d charge for a pot of tea, a sandwich and a toasted teacake to be exorbitant.

"I remonstrated hard. To please me, a chocolate biscuit was included in the deal," he said.

The slightly curious thing was that the hobby appeared to be lads only, and not just on dark nights and dank mornings in Shildon. Look at any photograph of Locospotters Club gatherings, try to spot a girl. Whatever their alternative amusement, they weren't at the time much missed.

Appointed OBE in 1995, Ian Allan died in 2015 on the day before his 93rd birthday. "The world's best known and probably its most successful railway publisher" said *The Guardian's* obituary. "Train spotting became a classless, cheap, adventurous and innocent national craze". It never mentioned Shildon, either.

As dieasels spread contagiously, fewer were crazy. Nicholas Whittaker in his 1995 book *Platform souls* – sub-titled "The train spotter as 20th century hero" and described on Amazon as "A hymn to 20th century eccentricity" – lamented the hobby's latter-day bad press. "No one used to take the piss, train spotting was a more relaxed hobby, as English as morris dancing and looked at with indulgence."

He himself had also given up collecting train numbers – "but" said the potted biography on the dust jacket, "still displays Pavlovan impulses by reaching for a Biro whenever he gets a whiff of diesel fuel."

Whittaker blamed supposed comedians. "These comics have a

lot to answer for" he wrote. "They make a mockery of a harmless exercise and have totally destroyed the market for anoraks"

They still sell them at Hackett and Baines in Shildon, though -

Missing link: 60004 William Whitelaw

top class trading since 1898 – and furniture that's made to last, an' all.

There were 34 class A4s – at various times blue streaks, apple green streaks, hacky black streaks – with names that were mostly self-explanatory. The first few were mainly knights of the realm – celebrated railway engineers, it transpired – followed by a few Commonwealth countries and then a small flock of birds, most famously Mallard, though we did wonder what Miles Beevor, a London solicitor, was doing in such sleek and streamlined company.

Of the 34, only William Whitelaw – 60004 – remained ever elusive, its rarity emphasised because its 33 fellows were themselves underlined, probably in blue Bic. Many other spotters were similarly frustrated. Word was that 60004 strayed seldom south of the Scottish border, perhaps lest it turn into a pumpkin. For years we hoped for a lucky streak, never once rewarded.

Numerically the A4s were followed by the A3s, all 98 named and mostly enigmatically. Why would 60039 be Sandwich or 60100 Spearmint or 60061 Pretty Polly, unless the engine driver had a parrot? What of 60078 Night Hawk, greatly familiar on diversion days and thus slightly, scatalogically, renamed – little imagination may be needed - by the disappointed denizens of the Water Bridge.

Why was 60038 Firdaussi, or 60075 St Frusquin or 60110 Robert the Devil? Somewhere in that great compendium there was even a locomotive named Shovel, though in Shildon we called a spade a spade.

Almost all, it much later transpired, had been Classic-winning racehorses. Firdaussi, owned by the Aga Khan and described as "big and lusty" – the horse, not the Aga Khan – took the St Leger in 1932; Robert the Devil, rather curiously said to be "slashing", won both St Leger and Cesarewitch in 1884, St Frusquin landed nine of his 11 races including the 2000 Guineas in 1896.

Spearmint? Derby 1905. Sandwich? Another St Leger winner, owned by the Earl of Rosebery, 1931. Gay Crusader? Times change.

The A1s and A2s seemed similarly to be themed – racehorses and Scotsmen, by and large - the frequent appearance of 60511 Airborne, Derby and St Leger winner in 1946, suggesting to the Water Bridge wastrels that it went like the wind, though not so forcefully through Shildon.

We knew nothing of horses, save for the last remaining dobbin which rheumatically pulled the Co-op covered wagon from its stable in Church Street. Betting shops became legal in the UK on May 1 1961, though such scandalous activity remained pretty much hugger-mugger around our house in Albert Street.

A gentleman called Percy Allan, doubtless honest but probably no relation to Ian of that illustrious ilk, had a betting shop at the top of the street, between Kitching's shop and the King Willie pub, the latter strictly out of bounds. Clutching her sixpenny bet, almost always because she liked the name of the horse, Aunty Betty – she who'd suggest that dissidents might jump up and give their leg a dother - would sneak out of sight out of the back door and up the battered back alley to seek her fortune. Though my old mum, her sister, would essay a certain *froideur* (as we'd say in Shildon) at the way in which the back street was becoming a primrose path, she'd frequently, anonymously, invest a tanner of her own.

Percy Allan's bookie's long since closed its account. Whether he retired to the Caribbean to live on a mountain of accumulated sixpenny pieces is, sadly, not recorded.

Chapter two

Local hero

Timothy Hackworth was the brains behind it all. Said to have been modest and unassuming, he was the man who rode the world's first steam hauled passenger train from Shildon – albeit as a sort of guard-cum-bouncer – an occasion on which it was reported that "the welkin rang with loud hurrahs" as doubtless it will again on September 27 2025.

He designed and constructed numerous innovative locomotives, pioneered Shildon Works, built houses and chapels for workers and their families, travelled the area preaching Methodism but still, it's said, might enjoy a little of what he fancied or a little jig, but only behind closed doors.

Shildon still salutes him faithfully, though the statue toppled when we were kids might have suggested otherwise.

These days a care home, a school, a Masonic lodge, at least three streets, a business estate and the town park all bear his name, though back in the 1950s the park was known simply as the recreation ground or, more familiarly, the Rec. We were unsure of the spelling. There was a Timothy Hackworth pub, too, across the road from Daniel Adamson's coach house – one of the world's first railway ticket offices. Though it closed in 2024, yet another victim of a declining national thirst, a little story must nonetheless be permitted.

Always a non-driver, habitually late-nighting around the North-East in ceaseless and oft-serendipitous search of column inches, I was accustomed to summoning taxis on company expenses. Save for one winter night around 1990, they were always pretty reliable.

On that occasion I'd ordered a taxi from the Timothy Hackworth in Shildon. An hour later, the landlord anxious to get to his bed, I phoned them and was told the taxi was outside. "No it's not" I said, "I'm outside myself and half frozen to death."

At nearly midnight, it transpired, the driver was waiting the best part of a mile away outside the darkened Timothy Hackworth museum, housed at the time in the great pioneer's former home before Locomotion properly got up steam. Advised of the error of his ways, the driver didn't get a tip.

The school opened in 1910, built on a 9,000 square yard site to accommodate up to 1,100 pupils and costing £21,467 to include all fixtures and fittings. Originally, breathlessly, it was called the Shildon and East Thickley New Shildon Council Schools, changed to mark the Stockton and Darlington Railway centenary in 1925 to the New Shildon and East Thickley Timothy Hackworth Council School.

Where "Old" Shildon ends and "New" Shildon begins is a specialist subject I've never mastered but one to which, with little hope of enlightenment, we shall reluctantly return. Don't even start on East and West Thickley and what might have lain between.

In 1976, when senior girls moved elsewhere, the school simply became Timothy Hackworth Primary. In 2010 the Duke of Gloucester paid a visit, joined in an assembly, unveiled a plaque and is said particularly to have been interested in the architecture. The school was re-dedicated by Jane Hackworth Young, Timothy's great great granddaughter, from whom we also hope to hear more. There was also a beautifully produced brochure, *A Century of Learning*, and there'll be more of that, too.

Externally it seems foursquare and sturdy well over a century after it opened. In the 1950s it was one of four primary schools in the town – two of them Church of England controlled - and manifestly both the most popular and the most successful. Brazzened-fond bairns from the other schools knew it as Tin Tacks, allegedly something to do with seats made of tin and sitting on nails, a soubriquet which eventually was adopted at Timothy Hackworth itself (though never, of course, in the staff room.)

The Amos twins joined the infants' department, presided over by the rotund and fearsome Miss Vint, in 1951. Each day began with assembly and with handkerchief parade, the we'ans required to hold the thing outstretched in front of them and whacked soundly around the back of the bare legs should it have been left at home or, no less culpably, in the poss tub.

It said much for the imagination – and indeed the optimism - of Shildon's infants that daily they'd hold out a tiny fist in the hope that the gimlet Vint would fail to notice that it held nothing whatsoever. Age not being a concern – ours or hers - she also had a cane (and used it.)

The juniors, officially junior mixed, were housed upstairs and across the playground, assembly inevitably followed by recitation of tables from one to 12 then by further research into the mysteries of the 3 Rs, necessary for the ineluctable 11+. Our year, bulging, had getting on 150 kids. The "top" class, our group of 50, was taught for three of our four years by Tom Coates, a superb, inspiring and dedicated teacher who lived about 200 yards away with his parents and who also possessed a cane which would never have atrophied through lack of application. Perhaps it was seen as an incentive for good behaviour - carrot and stick, as it were - but there seemed wholly disproportionate evidence of the latter.

Genius: Timothy Hackworth

We'd be caned for whispering, caned for talking, caned for singing – whacking lyrical? – and if not for dancing then for jumping up and down on the dinner table which in Shildon in the 1950s was probably the nearest equivalent. We were caned for poor spelling, illegible handwriting, sums that didn't add up, for "chalking on the railways" and for reading a comic beneath the desk lid, a trick probably learned from Roger the Dodger in *The Beano*.

We were also caned, invariably and incorrigibly, for being late. There were trees to climb and footballs to kick, sweets to buy and becks in which to plodge. Whatever its validity, the authorities at Timothy Hackworth Junior Mixed seemed never to have encountered the adage about better late than never – and if the mile walk to school had been anywhere near the railway line, or at least the bit after leaving the Prince of Wales tunnel, we might never have got there at all.

Peter Sixsmith, who himself became a senior teacher elsewhere, recalled at Tin Tacks in the early 1960s being caned on both hands for chewing a straw and, similarly, for a sword fight with rulers. "I really couldn't have done without a drinking straw to increase my concentration levels" he pleaded. "God knows what would have happened if I'd succumbed to some really bad stuff, like giving someone a Chinese burn or using blotting paper in a wasteful manner."

These days, if not necessarily at the time, he blames the Tory government of Harold MacMillan.

Tom Coates would provide, probably out of his own pocket, a 7/6d book token for the child who came top of the class. Usually it was Margaret Wanless, whose father was something senior at the wagon works and who spent her prize in on books by the likes of Charlotte Bronte or Anna Sewell, volumes of what formerly were called an "improving" nature.

One year, to much surprise, I beat Margaret into second place. By adding three shillings to Tom Coates's 7/6 it was possible to buy the Ian Allan "combined" Locospotters annual, covering every region, in clouds of steam and peer envy. Tom's approach clearly paid: 47 of the 50 passed the 11+, or scholarship as it was known, and in September 1958 transferred, the boys still in short trousers, the three miles to King James I Grammar School (and apostrophe academy) in Bishop Auckland.

Tom died in December 2022, aged 93. Though our paths had crossed no more than two or three times since Timothy Hackworth days, I was honoured to be asked to give a eulogy at his funeral and no matter that I nearly came to blows with the minister. Getting on 70 years later, the story of the boy with the ten-and-a-tanner prize was given yet another airing.

One curious thing, though: memory murmurs that we were never taught a thing about the early history of the railways – probably not on the Durham County Council syllabus – or even about the luminescent Hackworth himself. So what was the great man like?

There can be no doubt, never could have been, that Timothy Hackworth was a genius. Various biographies, potted and plotted, talk of indomitable courage and of a naturally fervent nature, of Herculean labours and of "inspired and prodigious work". His appearance was compared to that of a poet saint, his care for family, friends and workforce constant and unchanging.

The brochure produced in 1950 to mark the centenary of his death was almost mellifluous in its adulation: "His duties were of the most arduous and fatiguing character such as scarcely can be conceived at the present time, considering the then raw state of everything connected with railways….The entire guidance and directive devolved upon himself….The Herculean labours marked the force of mind which could gather mere fragments of ideas and unite their disjoined parts, working out of them a beautiful and effectual system of public conveyance."

The 44-page brochure was written by Fred Jewell and Charlie Browne, both local journalists based in Bishop Auckland. I knew Charles Verdun Browne a bit in the late 1960s and he never wrote like that, not when reporting from the monthly meetings of Crook and Willington Urban District Council, anyway.

Mike Norman in his deftly named *It wasn't Rocket science* (2022) wrote that Hackworth was "truly the Father of the Locomotive." George Stephenson, he added, was "emphatically" the Father of the Railway – a qualification paternally extended by Stuart Hylton in *The Grand Experiment*, published in 2007 and sub-titled "The birth of the railway age". Locomotion, says Hylton rather quaintly, was the daddy of them all.

The brakes are applied, however – not on Locomotion 1, it was one of George Stephenson's and didn't have any brakes – by the Oxford Companion to *British Railway History*, published in the year 2000, which acknowledged Hackworth as "one of that group of enterprising North-East colliery owners and engineers which saw the steam locomotive through its formative years" but adds mordantly, monstrously, that "he remained essentially a builder of slow, heavy freight locomotives and was left behind by more progressive designers."

Robert Young's momentous biography of Hackworth, his grandfather – published in 1923 and reprinted for both the 150th and 175th anniversaries of the Stockton and Darlington is, perhaps unsurprisingly, kinder to both man and mechanic but sorrowing of his lack of recognition.

There was nothing, said Young, to indicate that New Shildon had been the nursery of the locomotive, nothing to suggest that some of the most famous engines of early days had been built there or that Hackworth, their designer and builder, had lived in the town for 25 years. The old Soho works had been allowed to go to ruin and were "little more than a heap of rubbish", his house – divided into cottages – had nothing to remind a visitor of its distinguished former occupant.

"The old Stockton and Darlington Railway" lamented Young, "had a short memory for the man whom they delighted not to honour. It beatified George Stephenson, canonised Edward Pease but ignored the man who contributed so much to the success of both."

As recently as 2024, *Bradley's Railway Guide* – a comprehensive 400-page compendium of two centuries of railway history – failed to mention Hackworth at all.

Though brought up in the Church of England, his own father said to be "zealous", Hackworth became a Wesleyan Methodist, refusing to work on Sundays. Initially he held services and daily 5am prayer meetings at Soho House – his still-surviving railway home in Shildon – before building churches in both Old and New Shildon and walking up to 20 miles most Sundays to fulfil appointments as a local preacher, his presence described as "stately" – he stood six feet tall - and his powers of expression "felicitous". When he came to Shildon, paid £150 annually plus his house and coal, there were but three professing Methodists; ten years later there were 34 local preachers.

Annual income notwithstanding, he also gave £320 to Methodism's centenary appeal, the total from the entire Bishop Auckland circuit amounting to just £481.

Inclined towards abstinence though once fond of a pinch of snuff, his puritanism – says another biographer – was not of the joyless sort, perhaps unlike his friends in the Pease family, S&D owners and directors, who were Quakers. *The Peases and the S&D Railway* by Bernard McCormick (2008) records that dancing was forbidden because it led to "vain amusement and frivolity" and that music was similarly off limits because it sparked "self-gratification."

Nor did Hackworth approve of swearing. In his short biography, first published by the Wesley Historical Society in 1975 to mark the S&D's sesquicentennial, Geoffrey Milburn records that James Stephenson – known as Jemmy, George's brother and a regular driver – was much given to what football today calls offensive language. A persistent fault on one of the locomotives "drove his tendencies in this direction".

Hackworth, says Milburn, was so "distressed" by such repeated profanity that he produced a mechanical solution to the engine's problem. "Piety as well as necessity" Milburn adds, "can be the mother of invention."

Recounting the same story, Robert Young described Jemmy Stephenson's vocabulary as rich and lurid – "which must have been an object of no small anxiety to his chief."

Hackworth also liked to dance, though in later life more privately so as not to upset others. He played the grand piano – an instrument of much fascination in Shildon – and greatly enjoyed Tyneside folk songs, particularly *The Keel Row*. He even found time for a little gardening around Soho Cottage but, though the Mechanics Institute was established late in his lifetime, was never known to enter the leek show.

He had two sons and six daughters, a third son having died in infancy. John Wesley Hackworth, his elder boy, was entrusted when just 16 with overseeing delivery of a crated locomotive to the Tsar of Russia, a story of storm and shipwreck – and ice and wolf packs and bivvying in sub-zero temperatures – that might have enthralled the boys of Timothy Hackworth school more than a century later. When finally it reached Moscow, the engine's wheels were liberally sprinkled with holy water according to the rites of the Orthodox (if not the Methodist) church.

Himself to become a noted engineer, young Hackworth is said by George Turner Smith to have worn an "unfashionable" Russian-stye beard for the rest of his life as a memory of the adventure.

Further evidence that Hackworth may not have been a typical non-Conformist parent, he not only allowed his daughters to ride to hounds but sent one to a Roman Catholic finishing school in Belgium – a move, it's said, which attracted some criticism.

"As Hackworth's dedication to Methodism was evinced in so many other ways, these eccentricities were no doubt forgiven" Milburn supposed.

Timothy Hackworth was born at Wylam, in the Tyne Valley, three days before Christmas 1786. John, his father, was foreman blacksmith at Wylam Colliery, Timothy apprenticed to him after leaving school at 14. John died when Timothy was barely 17. "From that moment onwards the care of his mother, brother and five sisters became the chief concern of the youth" wrote Robert Young. "This calamity, severe and tragic as it was, served to bring out all that was best in his character.

The discharge of that trust won the admiration of the whole community."

Apprenticeship served, he succeeded to his father's position, moving in a similar role to Walbottle Colliery before effectively being head hunted by George and Robert Stephenson to become superintendent of the permanent (winding) and locomotive engines on the Stockton and Darlington at Shildon early in 1825. His locomotive Royal George, steamed in 1827, is said by Young to have "saved" the S&D which because of the unreliability of early George Stephenson locomotives had contemplated reverting from the horseless carriage to the original.

In 1833 he founded the Soho Works and for the next seven years worked alongside the S&D, designing 17 of the 19 locomotives built during that period, before complete and innovative independence in 1840. McCormick supposes the relationship between Hackworth and the S&D to have been "strange".

Like the LNER a century later, he liked to give his engines names. There was Victoria but also Albert, Whig but also Tory, Samson to labour alongside Hercules, Shildon but also Eldon, Evenwood, Coxhoe and Kelloe, properly pronounced Keller. Goodness knows where Dart came from.

George Stephenson, it might almost in passing be added, had named one of his early locomotives Chittaprat, said to be an onomatopoeic reference to the stuttering noise it made when exhausting steam. It was scrapped, some of the parts employed in the construction of the Royal George.

Hackworth died in Shildon, after a short illness, on July 7 1850. His estate was less than £5,000. "As honest a man as ever walked" said Henry Pease, "a shining example to others, a benefactor of mankind, who earned the love of the poor, who did his duty and whose end was peace."

In a notice of his death, the *Wesleyan Methodist Magazine* mentioned nothing of his railway engineering achievements but still acknowledged a great human being. "He was a man of ingenious and active mind, kind and liberal in his disposition, plain and unassuming in his manners, cheerful and edifying in his conversation, of deep and fervent piety and untiring in his endeavours to promote the wellbeing of his fellow creatures."

Benjamin Gregory, President of the Methodist Conference, was yet more effusive, talking of "a man of mechanical genius" and the engineer and manager of the first railway ever laid in the world – "a man who ought to take his place in the history of England, the history of science and the history of civilisation." The whole race, added the President, was "indebted to the Father of the Locomotive Steam Engine."

He was buried in St John's churchyard, the headstone one of few still upright. The whole town turned out to pay his tribute, it was reported. Probably they still should. George Stephenson's memorial is in Westminster Abbey.

Save for the regrettably evident necessity for greater security and more padlocked gates, the old school seems externally little to have changed. Do they still play marbles, or chucks, in the yard? Do they still race dinky Dinky cars down the slope, know the basic principles (never mind the arcane and endlessly flexible rules) of tiggy-on-high or overlap about six football matches simultaneously?

For reasons suggested in the previous paragraph, it seems

imprudent to stand staring through the railings at playtime, but in any case the school website offers an altogether more fascinating portal into how massively, and how impressively, things have changed at Tin Tacks.

Just look at the assemblies, in former times little variation on the old Light Programme "story, hymn and a prayer" God slot – five to ten, was it not? – and pretty much repeated at home time when the kids would routinely sing about day being over and night drawing nigh and no matter that the sun might still have another six or seven hours of day shift to put in.

These days assemblies are themed – Black History Month, International Day of Democracy. LGBT Tolerance, Anti-Bullying Week or (happily) Save the Children Christmas Jumper Day.

Look at the school meals menu, all chicken tikka masala, vegetarian options and fresh salad every day though there's still a choice of fish fingers and chips on Fridays. Friday was ever Fish Friday in Shildon, queues half way down the street, scraps optional, fights rare. These days the school also something called a Magic Breakfast – boiled cabbage neither to be seen, or more crucially, pervasively to be smelt.

The home page is topped with the information that they've achieved a Rights Respecting School gold award, with the school mantra – "Respectful and resilient, being the best that we can be" – and with a little drawing of the Royal George, lest we forget.

It also notes, or noted in January 2024, that the school built in 1910 for 1,100 pupils had 346, a target of 97 per cent attendance and, that week, 93.1 per cent who'd turned up. Doubtless most had good reason for absence. In the 1950s we'd sometimes spot Mr Morgan, the Vespa-patrolling kiddie catcher – even then he probably had a grand title like education welfare officer – who seemed both over-genial and under-employed. We were seldom absent, just (as we were saying) better late than never.

The website also includes a letter to parents from Lynn Boulton, the head. It talks of a nurturing and inclusive environment, of encouraging their children to be unique and of helping them make a positive difference to the world in which they live. It says nothing of what might befall the unfortunate child who arrives at school without a handkerchief.

"We believe it is important to celebrate and share British values within our whole school community" it adds.

Even hard-to-please Ofsted rated Timothy Hackworth primary "good", the last inspection in March 2023 confirming the previous findings six years earlier. Pupils, says the 2023 report, showed a high level of respect towards one another and towards the staff who try to help them.

Leaders had changed the curriculum so that it was more ambitious, lessons were "calm and purposeful", behaviour was a strength across the school, pupils said that bullying was rare, support for their wellbeing was "exceptional". So, effusively, it went on. Timothy Hackworth primary was so "good", so jolly good, that it begs the question (as it might of the head, or of the soon to be encountered chair of governors and her colleagues) of what on earth a school has to do for Ofsted to rate it "outstanding".

There's also a page about Hackworth – "a huge impact on Shildon, its growth and development".

It should also again be noted that the town's two other primaries were similarly and almost simultaneously extolled – Thornhill primary "outstanding" in every respect, St John's Church of England praised among much else for its collection point for both children's and adults' coats – "the idea is simply to leave what you can and take what you need" – aided by "Gordon, our goat of generosity."

It would be lovely to imagine Gordon to be a real goat, a sort of bearded wonder, which spends school holidays out to grass in the head's garden. Probably, though, it's an acronym.

I email Mrs Boulton asking if the old, old boy might pay a return visit. Her reply is timed at a minute to midnight on the Sunday evening of Storm Isha, one of many which blasted the UK in the discontented winter of 2023-24. You'd be most welcome, she says. Clearly there's much to learn yet.

Chapter three

Back to school

It's 8am on what these days they try to pass off as the first day of meteorological Spring and which in Wales they call St David's Day when I retrace the once-familiar route from Albert Street to Timothy Hackworth school. The rec's thick with frost, thin with dog walkers and, so far as may be seen, for recreational or other purposes hosts no children whatsoever. They can't all be late, can they? It hasn't become a tradition? Maybe they're all early.

Perhaps it's because there are no bairns to shout at that a chap in ten bob tracksuit bottoms bellows early morning obscenities – Jemmy Stephenson's "rich and lurid vocabulary" of two centuries earlier – at his poor dog, instead. Tail between its legs, the dog wanders off in search of more congenial company.

For some reason the walk seems altogether shorter, and to occupy much less time, than it did in the far-gone, filibustering fifties. Back then, unaccompanied from the age of five or six, we'd also walk home for lunch - "dinner" – on Monday's collecting piping pies, tanner a time, from genial Jack Robinson, the butcher.

The appointment with Pauline Crook, the warmly welcoming chair of governors, is for 8 30am. I'm there, checked through security and briefly baffled by it, at 8 25. It may be the first time in history that I've been early for school.

Signage incorporates the school motto, dreamed up by a year three boy in a competition: "On the track to success,"

We head across the yard to the former infants department, where a group of 15 or so, smart in school uniform, is tackling the Magic Breakfast (aforesaid). Chiefly it appears to comprise jam and toast but doubtless there are other tricks up their sleeves and by mid-morning there'll be a delivery of freshly baked bagels. "Helps keep them going until lunchtime" says Pauline.

I tell the little ones that I attended the school about a million years ago, quite likely sat on the self-same square yard of Durham County Council real estate – Miss Dowson's class – but never for breakfast, enchanted or otherwise. None questions the recollection or, more worryingly, its million-year estimate.

Pauline asks a girl of eight or nine what she'll be doing that day. "A podcast in sign language" says the girl and in five words speaks a thousand.

The tour leads past Miss Vint's old office, where the late Mike Armitage and I were once caned – when six or seven years old – not only for something we manifestly hadn't done but for something which there wasn't a shred of evidence that we had. It concerned the school field and some malcontent, appropriately, had mendaciously grassed,

A Century of Learning recalls that during World War II a tramp had taken up residence in one of the school air raid shelters at the bottom of the yard, Miss Vint sent (as the book puts it) to sort him out. She went armed with a pistol. At least Mike and I only got the stick and, if not quite blood brothers then friends thereafter for life. He died, much too young, in 2007.

Externally little's different, though the roof of the single story infants building – now reception and year one – is ringed with

Old school: L to R Lynn Boulton, Pauline Crook and Shirley Quinn outside Timothy Hackworth Primary

razor wire, and not what you'd call a safety razor.. It wasn't that way back in the day: how else might the more agile have shinned the drainpipes to rescue misdirected balls from the roof? Come to think, there are no longer netties at the bottom of the yard, either. They could be a bit cold around the extremities, goodness knows, and in that respect a reminder of home.

Internally it's all changed. It doesn't much look like the old school, doesn't much sound like the old school and certainly doesn't smell like the old school. What was it that old schools smelled of? Cabbage? Carbolic? Cheap polish? Damp? Dettol? Dumb insolence?

At once it's apparent that this place is wholly pupil-centred. Colourful notices enquire how they're feeling, encourage evaluation, assure that it's all right not to be all right. Others outline the UNICEF convention on children's rights, of which there are 54 and which relate to that gold award atop the website. "You can't explain enough about children's rights" says Pauline. "It's a very important part of the school."

There's also a so-called red room, a little fairy-lit haven to which youngsters can escape if feeling a bit off. "It's a place of calm, where they can chill if they need to" says Pauline. "Some children find it a very long day. We have to remember that."

The accepted term's safeguarding, and it's in safe hands here. The following week's papers carry the story that a London primary school head teacher had won damages after being wrongfully dismissed for "tapping" her own three-year-old daughter on the back of the hand as a disincentive to misusing hand sanitizer, a case also reported to the police who, not unimaginably, supposed it "reasonable chastisement". Miss Dowson, whom we liked, had a piece of wood the length and thickness of a Durham Constabulary truncheon – might once have been one - though her touch, memory suggests, was light.

The red room is also the spot, or very near the spot, where in Miss Dowson's class at times of transgression, we'd to stand in the corner, backs to the rest of the class and in extreme cases balancing a beanbag as lugubriously as Lord Chief Justice Goddard might in former times have worn a black cap. A possible difference, however, was that his Lordship didn't simultaneously have to stand on one leg.

In a reception class a group of children is playing – doubtless learning – happily together. One, shy and smiling, is black. "They don't notice" says Carolyn Mulley, a vice-chair who's joined the tour. "It's just another child, another friend."

We're back in an office in the main building – the parent pod, it says on the door - further joined by Shirley Quinn, the other governors' vice-chair, who's also enjoying an energetic year as town mayor. A little gallery of children's paintings covers a wall, identifying their "special person". Most portray mum or dad, one depicts Mrs Boulton in a no doubt flattering light. "It brings a tear to me eyes, that" says Pauline.

She'd been a pupil at the girls' senior school, became school secretary and then business manager before taking the chair in 2018. Shirley also attended Timothy Hackworth, Carolyn at school in Newton Aycliffe, a few miles distant, "Shirley put my name down for the governors" she says.

The old place wears its years very well, they insist, though they're a bit anxious about the roof. "It's high maintenance, you have to have a plan but they'd knock this school down over my dead body" says Pauline (she really does) though insisting that she's not worried. "We've got better things to do at Timothy Hackworth."

Somewhat ironically, the school – described at its 1910 opening as "one of the best ,if not the best elementary schools in the county" – had almost immediately developed structural problems. Two years later, original faults still not repaired, further cracks developed. Some pupils were sent to the Mission Hall in New Shildon or to the old Soho Street school.

"Everything here's in pretty good shape now. If the council has any spare money they can build us a secondary school" says Shirley, touching upon the recent, much resented, loss of Sunnydale Comprehensive, Shildon's only senior school. It would break her heart, adds Pauline, if anything happened to Timothy Hackworth.

"It's a piece of history, everyone loves this place" says Carolyn. "It's at the heart of the community."

Do folk still call the school Tin Tacks, if not derogatorily then not wholly affectionately, either? "It's mainly the older generation now and we're not offended" says Shirley. "It's part of school history, no one worries about it."

The conversation also returns to punishment, Pauline recalling that in her time the secondary school head teacher retained a slipper for purposes other than keeping one or other of her feet warm. "I never got the slipper" she quickly adds.

A Century of Learning recalled that corporal punishment – "no he wasn't a soldier" – was routine in all schools, "involving the infliction of pain in order to steer the person in the right direction." In other words, the book added, it was supposed to teach the recipient not to do it again. Canes, it said, had nicknames

like Mr Percy or The Black Rat. Though greatly familiar with Tom Coates's, we didn't call it anything at all, or nothing that might be entrusted to print. We were recidivists, the Norman Stanley Fletchers of post-war education.

It's slightly ironic that an otherwise learned biography of Hackworth should record that he also built "stationery" engines, as if constructing them from old envelopes. No child left Tom Coates's class without knowing the difference between "stationary" and "stationery" or without over several years having thumbed *First aid in English* by Angus McIver, a grammarian's gospel of adjective and adverb, conjunction and colloquialism, pronoun, preposition and present participle and, of course, of homonyms.

Stationary and stationery? There'd have been one on each hand for that.

The second part of the tour begins in the former girls' secondary school, the ground floor of the main building, to which boys in the junior mixed upstairs were strictly denied unauthorised access and still being unworldly, had no wish – and certainly no desire – for it to be otherwise.

Back then we thought the facts of life might be something to do with working the radiogram, not even on intimate terms with the amoeba until reaching Bishop Auckland Grammar School. These days, says Pauline, it's all carefully and sensitively explored – "changes in the body, that sort of thing".

They also ensure that the children know their railway history, particularly in so far as it concerns Timothy Hackworth, and work closely with Locomotion. "They're very proud of the connection with Timothy Hackworth" says Shirley. For the school centenary, year five pupils even wrote the Timothy Hackworth Rap, the last verse of which read:

He wouldn't work on Sundays

And in 1850 he died

An ingenious engine builder

We remember him with pride.

Other children have joined a road safety group – "junior police officers" – to address the perennial problem of parking outside the school, going out with a police community support officer to issue advice and "pretend" tickets to offenders.

The school's calm, ordered, no running, no shouting, no bells and no whistles. A teacher's hand gesture is enough to tell children what to do, says Pauline; they don't believe in teachers shouting. Each class has at least one teaching assistant, further hands needed because of a high number of pupils with special educational needs.

"Children regard this as a very safe place, safe and warm" says Carolyn. "There are always pupils crying at the end of term because they don't want to go home. They aren't little robots, but they're very well behaved. You rarely hear a raised voice, they're not out of control and not discourteous. They look out for one another here."

Attendance remains at around 93 per cent, the target 97 per cent. Not good enough, they admit and without Joe Morgan on his Vespa to catch them young. It's hard to get a child to school, says Shirley, if the parents themselves won't get out of bed to point them in the right direction.

Forty years after Shildon Shops were shuttered, there's still real hardship in the town. Carolyn, who volunteers at the award winning, church-backed and roundly extolled Shildon Alive charity, talks of local supermarkets donating food close to its sell-by date. "The worst stuff is thrown into a box for disposal but there are still people who'll sift around in it, basically pig swill, because their need is so great. We have a lot of children from poor settings, often not with both parents at home."

The mayor talks of a town council initiative to provide the needy with good quality second-hand coats. "Sometimes you have families with just one coat between them and they have to take turns to wear it." Mind, adds Shirley there are those who "make the wrong choices" as well.

Then we're upstairs, back where juniors mixed it, back past the basins where it was deemed an end of term honour to wash out the ink wells or to be a milk monitor, frozen liquid frequently three or four inches high atop the bottle. A mural records children's ambitions: one wants to be a top American footballer, another a ballet dancer, a third an astronaut – "the first woman on Mars". One just wants to be happy; none fancies writing a book.

The former Class 1 room, where for three years 50 of us sat as near to the pipes as possible – and in the case of the hopelessly myopic, as near as possible to the blackboard - is temporarily unoccupied. Coming out to the front, an almost daily injunction, can't have taken very long, not even when allowing for dragged feet. Somehow, sometimes, they'd squeeze a piano in, too. We kenned John Peel all right, though probably not Cushy Butterfield.

The centenary history records that the school's first BBC

computers arrived on February 29 1984, each costing £399. Now everything's smart, some might say smart as a carrot, not even a bit of chalk for a hard-day teacher to direct at the recalcitrant. Not that there are recalcitrants, of course.

All three governors talk of their pride in the school. What else must they do to edge the inspectorate towards outstanding? Is there resentment at Ofsted's perceived imperfectionism? Pauline sidesteps the question, says they constantly seek improvement, lauds the head, lauds the staff, lauds the children. Shirley's not arguing. "I really can't think of anything that would make it better" she adds. "One day we'll get outstanding, I'm sure of it."

A few weeks later I'm back at Tin Tacks, on this occasion for one of those themed assemblies and among the obvious differences that it doesn't start the day but – Friday 2 10pm – ends the week. Among the other differences, of course, is that no one gets whacked round the back of the legs for flagrantly forgetting a handkerchief.

Back in the 1950s there were also all sorts of unaddressed issues with myopia, recalled now by the difficulty in reading the signing-in instructions on the computer screen in the foyer and with no five-year-olds immediately available to advise. Right buttons finally pressed, a photographic identity tag on an orange lanyard is produced moments later.

Mrs Simpson-May, the newish deputy head, is reminded that the visitor is an old, old boy. "Nonsense, you don't look a day over…." she says, and prudently surrenders a suspended sentence.

The reception area has mug shots of staff and governors – usually smiley, almost all female – a large and lachrymose tray of onions, a couple of boxes of tinned food and a scattering of children's books, in which Roald Dahl predominates. Security satisfied, Mrs Boulton appears – friendly, welcoming. While we're catching up, a few feet apart, a little lad of six or so walks silently between us and is asked – gently, quietly, kindly - what they've been taught about not coming between folk when they're talking.

Though it's never the intention, the bairn appears abashed. That the head at once knows his name is revealing. Lynn Boulton reckons to know by name every one of the 350 children in her charge – "its something I work on" – and has now set herself the challenge of remembering all the parents, or at least those who show up.

What's yet more impressive is that, back in the1950s, she'd have had a 50 per cant chance of being right just by calling the child Michael (and the other 50 per cent were girls). Now they boast a vast millennium miscellany of monikers, from Rocco to Romeo, Aurora to Abigail, Ela-Star, Ebony-Grace, Dollie-Beau and Kienna-Faith.

Assembly is for years 1-6, reception classes deemed a bit young for so disciplined an exercise, the day's theme the right to information – article 17 of the Children's Convention. There's an assembly charter - "Silent, straight and still" - the whole thing's a bit reminiscent of Trooping the Colour, not least when everyone parades in practised silence to their places, sits on the floor and then, on their backsides, shuffles almost sequentially backwards. The RSM would be impressed.

One little soldier has his hands in his pockets, Gently, almost genially, he is reminded of the error of his ways. Neither the head nor any of her colleagues once raises their voice, much less their hand, Mrs Boulton clearly keen to accentuate the positive. One pupil's described as a fabulous ambassador, another as a shining star, a third as a cultural leader. "I can see many, many, many examples of people setting a good example" she adds. "I've told Mr Amos that this is the best school in the land and that we have the best children in the land."

Mr Amos agrees.

There's also a school song, the words a bit hard to discern but (inevitably) about being the best that they can be and about making a positive difference to the community of Shildon. I'm not sure how that one scanned

It's over in 20 minutes, school headed homewards soon afterwards. Two little lads are asked to stay behind, not because they've done anything wrong but for the opposite reason. A chap appears pushing a line of trolleys bearing the bairns' bags. "It's just like Tesco's" he says.

The biggest difference of all, however, has been that on this occasion there's been no story, no hymn and no prayer – not even the rumour of God, as a former Bishop of Durham (and Archbishop of Canterbury) once whispered. Though there's a school prayer, assemblies with a religious flavour and though local Methodist minister David Payne is a frequent visitor, this one's about the right to information, article 17 bang to rights.

I'm introduced, reduce the earlier million-year age gap to a thousand but still appear not one whit to surprise them.

The school's Easter newsletter underlines the right to know and to be informed, the previous term's activities embracing everything from Red Nose Day to Children's Mental Health Week, from Holocaust Memorial Week to Anti-Bullying Week.

By no means for the first time, the newsletter also raises road safety issues outside the school. "I know you will be aware of the danger that is caused by traffic and parking at the beginning and end of each day" Pauline Crook writes. "We are absolutely staggered by people who refuse to move their cars when asked."

Those dangers are very evident as I leave, the onions and tinned food and stuff now on a stall outside in return for small donations. The safety situation's exacerbated by chattering parents – many with pushchairs – blocking the narrow pavement with the proverbial mothers' meeting, forcing others into the road. Don't they realise? Truly it has been an education.

The third visit's for a chat with Mrs Boulton. On the fence outside the main entrance a large banner proclaims that "children's rights are learned, understood and lived in this school." Though the message is familiar, the banner seems new.

It's lunchtime. Behind the now-essential security fence the bairns are enjoying a vigorous game of football. None invites me to join in, not even in goal, much less to make a seriously belated debut for the school team. In the reception area they're playing Smooth Radio – possibly soothe radio – but unless any of the youngsters is a particular fan of Billy J Kramer and the Dakotas then possibly aimed more at their grandparents.

The head's running a few minutes late. Passed over for the school team, I spend the time dipping into well-thumbed copies of Roald Dahl, reacquainting with words like frobscuttle, lickswishy, swashboggling and snozzwanger (which, of course, was a three-footed creature which preyed on oompa-loompas.)

The head arrives cheerfully, apologetically, serves coffee and biscuits. She bears no resemblance to Miss Vint. Her mantra is that children should be safe and content.

Lynn Boulton was born in Sunderland, taught all over the country, says she's passionate about the North-East – "I think it's underrepresented nationally" – became deputy head at Timothy Hackworth in 2010 and head five years later.

"I didn't know Shildon but knew of Shildon and knew I wanted to be here" she says. "I wanted to work in this school, to make a positive difference to lots of children and the Shildon community. It's important that we work not just with the children but with families. We're their school family.

"Staff and children here make a positive contribution to society. I want them to have as good a chance as anybody else. Equity is really important, children should always have the same chances.

"There are targets, scores which are important, but children being happy and content is what I value most. It's important that we set standards, have a moral compass. It's our job to get them ready for society. What I really want is for them to be good citizens, to make a difference in the world. I try very hard to give them that experience."

Times, she says inarguably, have changed. "We work alongside many organisations and agencies. Our school may open at 8 40am and close at 4 30,pm when the clubs finish, but a lot goes on beyond that. School care doesn't end when the school closes."

Mrs Boulton's own day, as previously has been observed, may go on longest of all. She's reluctant to discuss it but estimates her weekly working hours as 70-plus. "I enjoy working at 2am" she says. "It's often when you can best get things done. I work hard because I enjoy my job. You can't do this job if you don't love it."

She's also reluctant to talk about issues of poverty and of parental responsibility but admits there are "challenges", among them mental health and safeguarding. "Mental health was already significant and it got worse because of Covid. Pupils weren't able to come to school, in some cases for almost two years. They missed a lot of learning and a lot of social skills and that's still having an impact.

"Safeguarding is a big part of what we do. Children have the right to be safe no matter what else is going on."

She praises a "fantastic" female attendance officer but confirms that sometimes she visits pupils' homes in person to discuss absenteeism and other issues. "Children have the right to be in school every day. It's a conversation I have quite often." Things aren't helped, someone had earlier observed, if the parents themselves are too idle to get out of bed.

It all goes back to being the best that they can be and not to what again the head calls scores on the doors. "We want children to get the grades but the bar is higher than that. You can't always measure success that way.

"The children are on a journey. We are there to remove obstacles and to protect them. We don't think that the end of the school day is the end of school care."

So how has the 115-year-old building withstood the demands of 21st century life and learning? The leaky roof can be quite challenging, she says – "the rain gets in some very strange places" – but externally the two sites are otherwise sound and internally they positively gleam. "Our cleaning staff and site manager are brilliant, just look at the floors."

Any whisper along the wire to County Hall of a replacement school? The head and chair of governors are on the same page, employ the same phrase. "Absolutely not. I wouldn't say no a new roof but generally it's in good repair. They don't make schools like this any more, it's special and there's a real love for it. They'd demolish it over my dead body."

I'm invited back any time – possibly, the head suggests, to learn something of – from? - the newspaper club. There's no mention, alas, of a belated debut for the Timothy Hackworth school football team.

Chapter four

Doing the round

The Jubilee Fields housing estate was conceived at much the same time as our kidder and I were and grew pretty much alongside us. Still it was growing in the summer of 1961 when we started a pre-school milk round for Jim Percival, a gentle Methodist who lived, appropriately, at the top of Wesley Crescent.

Starting at 6 15am, the round chiefly embraced the council estate, seven mornings a week and an extra 2/6d apiece - £1 in total – for collecting the money on Friday evenings. Never once did it seem risky to have kids walking round the town with pockets stuffed with cash, albeit in two shilling pieces.

Bogey boys if not yet bogey men, we pushed a little wooden cartie, precariously balanced between two bicycle wheels and stacked with up to nine crates, 20 pints apiece, either silver or red top. Never much call for gold top on the estate, not golden Jubilee. A little red light, powered by an enfeebled Ever Ready battery, served to warn other road users of our darkest-hour doings.

Dave was something of a sleeping partner, often turned 7am before he caught up. Sometimes we'd abandon the cartie to carry a couple of hand crates to the estate's further reaches, and once more with little fear of larcenous lads on their way to work. Sometimes, however – let it now be confessed – a half pint of milk might be swapped with one of the paper boys for a copy of the *Daily Mirror*, the *Sun* not then having risen above the horizon. It was considered fair exchange, if only for the Andy Capp cartoon.

Back in the early 60s there were at least four dairymen vying for the bottle line. These days there appears just one, rattling down *Coronation Street* almost every other episode, and that on the feeble pretext of letting viewers know that it's morning.

The estate and the customer list grew; remuneration didn't. Nor was there any bonus for surviving the winter of 1963 when for long weeks frozen milk would stand proud three or four inches above the bottle and we'd be clad in two or three woolly balaclavas, like poor bloody infantry on the Crimea. Whenever those bitter mornings are recalled I'm reminded of lines drummed into us at Tin Tacks alongside *The Highwayman, Abou ben Adhem* and all that tribe:

When icicles hang by the wall

And Dick the shepherd blows his nail,

And Tom bears logs into the hall

And milk comes frozen home in pail....

There was something after that about greasy Joan keeling the pot, but we never properly understood that bit.

Sixty years on I can still pretty much remember the round, recall who was TT and who pasteurised, who'd faithfully pay up every Friday evening and who – particularly an unkempt woman at the bottom of Coronation Avenue – had periodically to be threatened with having her tap stopped unless she found some funds. A pint of milk, memory suggests, was eightpence.

Charlie Raine at 75 Albert Street got a daily pint of silver top, Bert Trussler 400 yards away at 3 Birch Avenue, two pints of TT. Together Bert and Charlie for many years formed a concert party, much loved around local pubs and clubs, always signing off with the Gracie Fields number *Good night, good luck, God bless you.*

When Bert died after a battle with cancer, friends thronging St John's church were told that it was to be a cheerful funeral. We did our best until near the end, when the vicar announced that, when Bert knew he'd not long left, he and Charlie visited their valediction one last time. Charlie tinkling away on the piano, a tape recorder behind the coffin played Goodnight, Good Luck. God Bless You, and as Bert bowed out, at the cheerful funeral there wasn't a dry eye in the house.

Often the early shift might be completed bleary eyed. All these years later, I could still almost do it blindfold. On an August afternoon in 2024, I make the round trip again.

From Jubilee Road at the bottom, the estate rises eastwards. The impression now – oh crumbs, how might this be put? – is that some of the streets at the bottom have seen better days and that homes and gardens are more carefully tended the more upwardly mobile their owners become.

At the bottom many gardens are paved over, or overgrown or parked upon (with or without wheels). Several gardens have trampolines which may benefit health but do nothing for beauty, nor do great garrisons of wheelie bins add aesthetic appeal. At times it's tempting to suppose that the council has invited householders to collect four different colours and get a fifth bin free but if some of these guys have green fingers it's probably from wacky baccy.

If the question's "Where have all the flowers gone", the refrain's probably "Where are all the kids?" It's the school holiday's and

Poachers' pocket? Cedar Grove

almost eerily child-free. Some homes and gardens, of course, might have come from the middle class magazine of that name.

At the back of Cedar Grove, however, where the path runs above what's still called Tunnel Top, the Friends of the Jubilee Estate have made a very good fist of rewilding (as they put it) the area. There's even a little piece of public art, perhaps not quite up there with the Angel of the North, which may be mystifying to some but to others represents the Minions, heroes of an American animated comedy film, released in 2015, in which they take on Scarlet Overkill who wants to rule the world. Some of us would be happy just to rule the roost.

In Sycamore Square there's an Amazon van. Perhaps they deliver milk because it's doubtful if anyone else does these

Visionary: Charlie Raine

days, or newspapers, either. In Birch Avenue there's a front garden with so many gnomes that the Gnome Office might issue an overcrowding order, while from an upstairs window over the road flies the flag of St George, these days open to appropriation.

A notice at the entrance to Cedar Grove, purportedly placed by Durham police but possibly the work of the Minions, warns that quad biking, off-road biking and poaching are all forbidden. Save for tomorrow's breakfast, what on earth's to poach in Cedar Grove? A little plaque on a nearby fence proclaims "This is Anfield" and that's open to speculation, too.

Several houses have boards in the garden announcing that they're to be sold by auction. The estate agent, interestingly, isn't in Bishop Auckland or somewhere nearby but in London.

At the bottom of Jubilee Road, I'm hailed by Peter Quinn – the mayor's husband – himself a town councillor out in the garden for a fag. "It doesn't matter what the government" says Peter, "since the wagon works closed no one's ever done anything like enough for Shildon."

The nearby Spar shop opens 6am-10pm except on Sundays when it doesn't serve until seven. Sunday always was the day of rest round here.

A bit like a refrain from *Ernie*, who drove the fastest milk cart in the west, the ghost round continues past the house in Pine Tree Crescent – Jubilee Fields was nothing if not the arboreal thing – where Colin Bainbridge, a greatly talented Northern League footballer and a lovely chap, lived with his wife Esther until he died in a road accident. At the top of Coronation Avenue live memories of Mr and Mrs Wilson, who tipped an almost unheard five shillings every Christmas, at the bottom memories of that poor woman – small and fat, best nameless – who paid so infrequently and so reluctantly that that eventually even the saintly Jim Percival gave up on her.

Willow Walk's where St John's housed its bachelor curates, some more comfortable with single living than others, and where dwelt Bill Whitaker, a wonderful character who by day stood up to his oxters shovelling sewage and at other times painted or wrote poetry, alternately sensitive and scatological. It was amazing how often Bill found words to rhyme with shite.

Karen's Plaice fries gently at the end of Maple Avenue, offering chip butty and kebab meat for a fiver – you could get three months milk for that – sauce another quid. A bit further along, though not from milk round days, stir memories of Frankie Smith, who had an upstairs flat. Great character, nice guy, Frank produced *Far from a madding crowd*, a gloriously nuts Shildon FC fanzine which supporters loved and some of the lampooned players loathed

Generally skint, Frank used kitchen foil as curtains until, dazzled by the glare on their front parlours and the reflection on their neighbourhood, the neighbours launched a petition and the council drew a line – though not, of course, the curtains.

Back near the bottom of Coronation Avenue, close to where the short, fat and financially straitened woman lived, a similarly shaped female is engaged in a virulent slanging match with a neighbour, the language best described as unladylike. "She's a divvy, that one" says another neighbour and while it's possible to ponder the term's derivation there's little doubt about the intent or accuracy of its meaning. Notices elsewhere prohibit organised ball games. We'd have been OK on that one because

our football matches weren't even organised chaos, just chaos.

Bogey returned to base, back home in Albert Street, we'd join the school blazer brigade as swiftly as Superman in his phone box. Whatever the weather, however great the privations, we got there in the end.

It's school holidays, much happening at the Jubilee Fields community centre, next to the Spar shop. There are family fun days, the Jube Kids Club – £2 including a burger, a drink and a "treat" – and something that's Willy Wonka-themed after a character in *Charlie and the Chocolate Factory*. But Thursday night's bingo night.

About a dozen have eyes down, all elderly women save for Harry March, the caller (who's an elderly man.) All are greatly welcoming, friendly, community conscious folk.

It's not possible to compare bingo at the Jubilee Fields Community Centre with the unlucky-for-some version much visited by my mam and my Aunty Betty back in the 1960s at the Hippodrome, not least because I never went or ever wanted to. Suffice that they can no longer shout "Shake 'em up" because the gadgetry's digital and that most of bingo's endlessly arcane terminology seems redundant, though they still talk of Downing Street – No 10 – and of "those legs", which is 11.

In former times there'd be wolf whistling at that point; now there's probably a law against it, unnecessary offence to wolves.

Harry, coincidentally, also had a 1960s milk round, starting soon after 4am and followed by a couple of hours later by a paper round for Peter Dowson, at the bottom of Main Street. At first, he recalls, the milk was delivered by horse and cart. – "I'd to follow behind with a bucket" says Harry. "They don't do that nowadays."

Perhaps because of the very early mornings, he failed to make much of an impression (shall we say) at the Council school, now formally Thornhill. "Jimmy Wynn, the headmaster, said it was no good trying to teach me fractions so gave me a spade and told me to dig the school garden. Lovely feller, Jimmy Wynn."

Refused parental permission to join the Army, he worked instead down New Shildon drift mine. "Lying on my back in an 18-inch seam, couldn't even swing a coal shovel, water pouring down my neck. I began to wish I'd worked a bit harder at school."

Though never employed there, he particularly regrets the Shops closure. "The town had a heart of gold and Thatcher killed it. When I was young you didn't have to leave Shildon – five banks, plenty of big shops, everything you wanted. Now it doesn't have anything, even Costa Coffee closed on us."

They insist that I join the game, sharing a table with Mary Wilson and Sadie Devlin, £12 all told and no longer possible to claim it back on expenses. How the accounts department would have loved that one. Old hands deploy something called a dabber – as in yabber-dabber-do, perhaps – bingo beginners stick with black felt-tip. Sadie's one of those who thinks the old town's changed for the worse. "There's a lot of bloody idiots around and a lot of people from down south. I've never seen so many strangers up the street."

Harry has a theory that many druggies (as he terms them) were shifted to Shildon when the short-lived Bessemer Park council estate in Spennymoor, six miles north, was knocked down in the 1980s. Mary's just moved into a new bungalow on Fir Tree – "beautiful, really beautiful" – supposes there to be drug takers on every street (except, of course, in the old folks' bungalows on Fir Tree) and that they only arrest the users, not the dealers.

All that's forgotten when the first number's called, the slowly acquired art of marking six cards further frustrated by the simultaneous need to write notes and to think of the next question. It feels a bit like one of those challenges when folk are invited to pat head and rub stomach at the same time, or an A-level for orang-utangs.

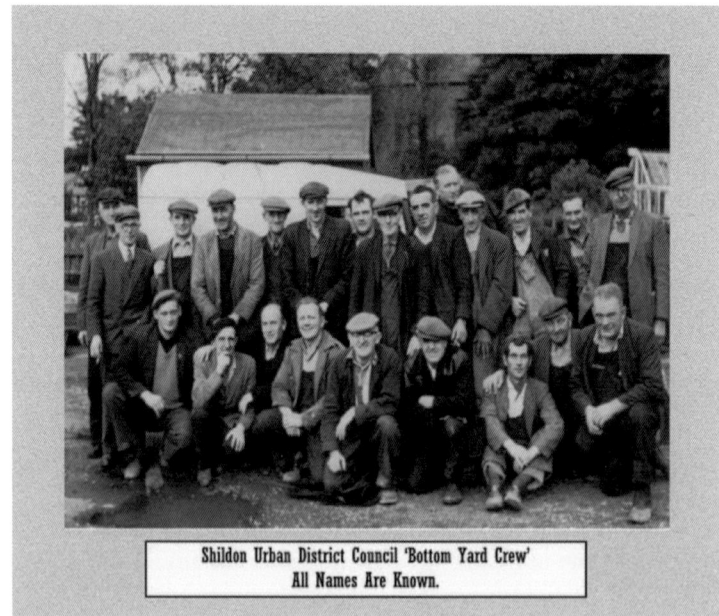

Shildon Urban District Council 'Bottom Yard Crew'
All Names Are Known.

Up to the oxters: Bill Whittaker (third right, front) and the bottom yard boys at Shildon Urban District Council

Problems are further increased by myopia – Kathy March offers her specs, "lucky glasses" she insists – and by the advice to rest the cards on an old copy of *Woman's Own*, so as not to scratch against the table top. On the magazine cover are tasters like "Loose Women confessions: sex, lust and pubic hair" and "Three years without sex: how our marriage survived." It does nothing to aid concentration.

Whatever happened to the days when *Woman's Own* was all brown bread and Babs Beverley?

The atmosphere's lovely, community spirit deftly distilled, unaffected by the fact that the lucky beginner wins first a line and then a house, £21 in total. I tell them I might be back for more. "You won't" says Sadie, cheerfully, "you're barred."

They head homeward about 8pm, leaving time for a quick Brown Ale in the King Willie – these days the nearest licensed premises to the estate since both pub and club were demolished – before the last bus, 8 45, to Darlington. The King Willie clientele's very different, the televisions showing racing, the music machine raucous and the quizmaster further amplified in order to hear himself think.

Between it all there's another game of bingo, the invitation to join in declined. What was that Kenny Rogers song about *The Gambler?* You gotta know when to walk away, know when to run….

Chapter five

Alive issues

The most vivid evidence of how greatly the old town has changed may be obtained by spending a morning at the Shildon Alive headquarters – or hub, as folk now prefer – in Church Street.

Changed for the worse? Paula Nelson, the project manager, talks of Shildon and the immediately surrounding areas being statistically the most impoverished of Durham County's 63 local government wards, of 41 per cent of children living in "absolute poverty", of "deplorable" housing conditions in parts of the town and neighbouring villages, of "rampant" drug abuse, excessive alcohol consumption and disturbing examples of racism.

Change for the better? Paula and her team – nine full and part-time staff, more than 40 cheery volunteers – seem to be doing a truly remarkable job in trying to make the town a safer, healthier, happier and more communally cohesive place in which to live.

Might not some of their clients – how might this discreetly be put? – at least be contributors to their own misfortune? "We never ever judge" says Paula. "No one walks in here and is judged, we're only here to help. People feel safe in here."

In December 2023, ten years after its formation, the organisation was given the King's Award for Voluntary Service, charitable equivalent of the MBE. Emotionally, Paula recalls the presentation: "Almost all of the volunteers were there. I held up the award and told them it was for every one of them. Unfortunately, we don't have a magic wand as well."

A client called Sophie posted on social media after the award had been announced "The town" she wrote, "would be lost without Shildon Alive".

The charity was the inspiration of the Rev David Tomlinson, then Vicar of St John's parish church. Still it's identified as a St John's church project, Carol Harris – the present vicar – is chair of trustees. "I don't go to church myself but I can see people living out their faith and it's exciting" says Paula.

Addressing the statement "What the charity does" on the Charity Commissioners website, they're unequivocal: "The advancement of health or saving of lives, the prevention or relief of poverty, economic and community development."

Stated objectives breathlessly include "To further or benefit the residents of Shildon and neighbourhood without distinction of sex, sexual orientation, race or of political, religious or other opinions by associating together the said residents with local authorities, voluntary and other organisations in a common effort to advance education and to provide facilities in the interest of social welfare for recreation and leisure time occupation with the object of improving conditions of life for residents."

There's more: support services to those in need, free meals to all school age children, food bank, community garden, housing support, credit union, advocacy – everything from crafting to cooking from caring and, perhaps crucially, to coping.

Who does the charity help, the questionnaire asks, to which the stated answer is "The general public and mankind."

At once, however inappropriately, it recalls Jacob Marley's ghost in *A Christmas Carol*. "Business? Mankind was my business…."

The headquarters, memory suggests, had in post-war times been Gardner and Taylor's painting and decorating business, fronted by a genial and white overalled chap called Cecil Gardner and by Celia his sister (or possibly his wife.) Nice lady anyway. All these years later, Paula Nelson's not going to gloss things over. "A lot of this is about crisis and crisis management, there's no other word for it" she says. "We're filling a lot of gaps that the public sector should be filling. I'm seeing people who haven't eaten for days."

The Charity Commission website also reveals that in 2022 Shildon Alive had a total income of £247,470, expenditure of £217,429, just £12,370 from a single government grant and that no trustees received payments or benefits – to which might be added the extraordinary statistic that in 2023 they "rescued" 102 tons of perfectly good food, collected by a team of 12 volunteer drivers from supermarkets, branches of Greggs and from other outlets that otherwise would have sent them to landfill.

In 2022 they gave 1,207 food parcels to families and individuals in crisis, handed out 2,160 baskets of bread, fruit and vegetables, held 1,108 advice and support sessions, gave 928 hot meals to vulnerable adults over the winter and distributed 3,890 free children's meals during school holidays. In September 2024 they took 150 people in four coaches for a day by the sea at South Shields, for some the closest to a holiday they'd get.

Numbers – and demand – will undoubtedly have increased. "There's an awful lot going on" says Paula, welly boots ready for action in a corner of her little office at the back. "I like it down the community garden" she says.

The garden, where hundreds of children and adults have learned about the food journey and benefitted along its way, is on the Furnace Pit Industrial Estate, near the former Wagon Works site, little to suggest its provenance save for a "Lottery funded" sign on the garden gate. At first they called it guerilla gardening, finding little plots to tittivate the town – "legally, of course" says Paula – before digging a little deeper. Educational, too: one chap swore he'd never before seen a cabbage.

The Furnace Pit site looks carefully tended, complete with bug hotel. Even the bugs get the VIP treatment at Shildon Alive. It's because of its charitable status, nonetheless, that my wife is dissuaded from raiding the plumptious goosegog bush (and that's our story, anyway.)

Paula Nelson was born in Gateshead, blackboarded around the North-East with her father's teaching career, moved to Shildon with her then-husband and sent her children to Thornhill Gardens school, still known locally as the Council School. Impressed by the "amazing" school life, she trained as a teaching assistant. Now 52, she has a marketing degree, loves her job, lauds Shildon and its people.

"It's the friendliness" she says. "You can go to Darlington and hardly anyone speaks to you. In Shildon everyone talks to you, especially down the gardens. Despite all the challenges, all the social issues, there's still a sense of togetherness."

David Tomlinson, a bright burning fireball later made an honorary Canon of Durham Cathedral, had started the Mustard Seed project – there's a biblical allusion – soon after he came to St John's. Paula joined after working as a volunteer on a similar project on the Woodhouse Close estate in Bishop Aukland. "I realised David was passionate about the town, he inspired me" she says. "I also realised that a lot of people from

Full Nelson- Paula Nelson at Shildon Alive

the Eldon Lane area were walking to Woodhouse Close to seek help because there was nothing around here.

"Some terrible things were happening in Shildon. People were falling off the edge. One thing leads to another – poverty, mental illness, breakdown, drugs. Poor housing's a really serious issue, mainly with landlords in the south who never come up here. Once a house gets damp it's very hard to dry it out again. We're truly a lifeline.

"We began with one small shop front, started rescuing food. I don't think we realised the scale of the problem; I don't think anyone did, except maybe David Tomlinson."

Posters in the window promote everything from "Let's talk menopause" to chair yoga, many of them linked to health and fitness. Another promotes a "Pop-up baby event", and in the town council chamber of all places, which comes as a bit of a surprise because we were always taught that babies were brought by the stork.

It's 10 30am and already they're queuing in the food shop and takeaway. "Saved from landfill, served to you" says a sign on the fast-emptying shelves. Another little notice suggests a "donation", though nothing's obligatory and there's a discreet route for those for whom next-to-nothing translates as nothing whatsoever. Pizzas predominate, flying out; if pizzas had wings, these would be 747s.

Among the volunteers in the kitchen out the back, a smiling Asian chap is cooking a curry, suggests trying it a little later. Almost certainly the busiest shop in Shildon this Tuesday morning in June, it may also be the most cheerful. Everyone smiles, chats. An elderly woman suggests she's feeling a bit fed up.

"Fed up, you should try working in here" says the immaculately aproned assistant behind the counter, and both at once fall about laughing.

Every bit as jolly, assistant Tracey Chappell introduces a sobering note, nonetheless. "Poverty has definitely worsened in the last five years in Shildon" she says. "Some of the housing conditions are absolutely dreadful."

In the next room men await their smoking cessation session, some expect advocacy, some to be part of the credit union. Some are just in for a cup of something hot, a chat and (this being June in Shildon) a warm. When BBC Look North filmed after the King's Award a man in a meagerly furnished house told them that he could only afford to switch the heating on when the temperature fell to three or four degrees – "and then only for an hour."

Paula's back in her office, has found a tube of Love Hearts – barely tasted since platonic encounters at Tin Tacks but to be encountered again in the first magic moments of Christmas Day – talks to a helper who wants to know if she should charge £1 for packets of wet wipes, suggests she makes it 50p.

"Prices have just shot up. Hells bells, a basic tin of beans was 18p two years ago and now it's 60p. An ordinary can of Heinz soup is £1 50. Shildon doesn't have a supermarket any more, just B&M. What we do is entrepreneurial, we're not just offering food, we're rescuing it."

She talks openly about social issues unheard of back in the simple 60s when the only debt issue was that that fat little woman and her milk bill. It must have got up to nearly £1.

"The amount of racism is quite frightening at times. I hear it, I see it, I challenge it. A few years ago the only overseas people in Shildon were the man who ran the Chinese restaurant or the chap who had the little corner shop. Now there are arrivals, often refugees, from Ukraine, Africa, south Asia. There are quite a few Muslim lads and lasses" – everyone's "lads and lasses" to Paula – "and they're lovely."

Drugs? "I don't think you can do anything about drugs without more police. There are lads in Shildon who'll get drunk then ring a dealer, pay £50 for cocaine and it'll be delivered to the pub. There are people who even know how to bypass collapsed veins. There are some really nasty drugs out there at the moment. It's terrifying."

Housing? "There are some lovely people living in terrible conditions, especially in New Shildon and the Dene Valley (the Eldon Lane area, a mile or so north). You can't wonder why sometimes they get depressed."

"Absolute poverty" is a term differently defined and probably depends upon who draws the poverty line – "but there's real poverty" says Paula. "Just walk up the street and look round."

Has she ever been threatened? "Not really. I've been called a few things, quite a lot of things, but I wouldn't say threatened. I just don't want people taking the piss."

All manner of food – clothing, too – keeps on arriving out the front. Cassie, a single mum with a child in a pushchair and another on the way, sums Shildon Alive simply. "It helps when you have no money. You get a lot of support, housing advice, food, everything really. No one looks down on us here. They're lovely."

The charity was moving – may have moved by the time that the book appears – to larger premises in Main Street which, as probably has previously been explained, isn't really the main street at all. They've also bought a five-bedroomed house next door to accommodate vulnerable people and families.

After two unplanned years away, Paula was also moving back to Shildon. "My heart is in Shildon, I love Shildon" she says. "There are problems, of course there are, but I'm not going anywhere else now."

Chapter six

Policeman's lot

As a wet-eared reporter in the leaky-creaky Bishop Auckland office of the *Northern Despatch*, an evening paper long since vanished into the inky trade's sad old sunset, the day's first job was to ring the local police stations – Bishop, Crook, Spennymoor, Shildon – in an attempt to glean overnight information, or indeed any information at all.

You can tell it was many moons ago because at first the Shildon call had to be routed via the local exchange in Main Street – just over the road from the police station – and the operator asked for Shildon 6. Though many parts of the country had had Subscriber Trunk Dialling for decades, it's possible that, in Shildon at any rate, STD was still a sexually transmitted disease.

The daily exercise was at best optimistic and almost invariably futile. The music hall song about if you want to know the time ask a policeman came to mind, but this lot wouldn't even have told you that without recourse to the Official Secrets Act. Even the friendly pollisses, the majority, kept it beneath their plant pot hats. Once, so the story goes, a national newspaper had rung a section office amid a particularly bleak midwinter to ask what the snow was like and been given a half-decent description by a young officer subsequently bollocked. "It's white and it's falling from the sky" said the inspector. "That's all you ever tell those buggers."

Memory murmured, however, that the Shildon lads had once volunteered the information that the Midland Bank – not 100 yards from their four-square base – had overnight been daubed

with three-foot graffiti of a distinctly sixties sort. Make love not war, that flowery-powery kind of thing.

Memory erred. "It was you who said you'd been told by someone else" recalls PC 1346 Alec McCoy, now 80 and in good fettle. "We told you we hadn't seen a thing."

Alec was one of seven or eight officers stationed permanently at Shildon in the late 1960s, the figure recalling an *Auckland Chronicle* report in 1976 that seven of the town's eight telephone boxes were out of action due to vandalism. They were days when "in Bishop" never meant "doing the shopping" but lying in the General Hospital and "in Durham" meant languishing at Her Majesty's pleasure. The section, as the constabulary termed it, was led by Sgt 158 Ernie Coates, an old fashioned, teak-tough polliss much the better for knowing. Tommy Trebilcock, the best remembered, was a ruddy faced west countryman and wartime RAF veteran who achieved almost legendary status. They declaimed doggerel about Tommy, invented heroic promotions for Tommy – chief inspector at the very least, though he never so much as wore stripes – claimed almost as a badge of honour to have been clipped round the ear by Tommy, though it's doubtful if he clouted anyone around the ear in all his service.

Alec McCoy recalls the occasion that he and PC Trebilcock were part of the ceremonial line-up to greet judges at the opening of Durham Assizes (as then they were). "All of a sudden a wigged judge broke the line, came over to Tommy and shook him warmly by the hand. Tommy had the DFC and the judge had spotted the ribbon. He could be a cantankerous old bugger but he really knew the job, I had a lot of respect for him."

PC Trebilcock also made a point of telling younger colleagues

Constabulary duty: Ivan Cliff (left) and Alec McCoy

that he didn't mind when he took annual leave, so long as it was the last week of July and first in August. Both he and Ernie Coates are long dead. "Bit of a character, Tommy" says Ivan Cliff, from 1969-72 Shildon's resident detective constable, by way of a bit of an understatement.

Other uniformed officers stationed at Shildon ("your worships") included Norman Woods, John Wilkes, Ray Bradley and Andy Wilson, known as Stamper for reasons unexplained and perhaps best left that way. Ivan Cliff had not just succeeded Det Con Dennis Stanley but moved into his predecessor's police house.

"Dennis was still in bed asleep on the day we arrived with our furniture" recalls Ivan, now 88. "He took a bit of shifting."

Whatever went on behind the heavy duty door of that stone built station was more *Dixon of Dock Green* – perhaps with a slight strain of *Z Cars* – than it was *Happy Valley*.

Ivan moved up to become detective chief inspector at Consett, his former Shildon colleague Alec McCoy joining him as a detective constable. It's in Consett that we reunite for a chat, to recall the days when drugs were something you bought in little glass bottles from Timothy White and Taylor's – "there was a county drugs squad but there weren't any drugs, not in Shildon, anyway" – and when constabulary duty was done very much differently from today.

According to the *Crime Rate Pro* website, Shildon in 2023 was the second most dangerous small town in Co Durham with 177 crimes per 1,000 people against a county average of 115. Churchill Support Services, a security firm, claimed in June 2024 that the town the previous year had recorded 182 offences

per thousand people – 1,758 crimes over the year – making it the worst in Co Durham and the fourth "most dangerous" in North-East England.

In February 2025, Durham constabulary reported raids on homes in Birch Avenue, Byerley Road and Queen Street as part of an "organised crime" investigation into the supply of Class A drugs across the north. Several arrests were made.

While recalling Mark Twain's famed aphorism about lies, damned lies and statistics it's clear that things were pretty worrying, nonetheless. Former mining communities like Horden, Easington and Stanley – the usual suspects, it might be supposed – were high on the not-wanted list, too.

Things ever change, of course. A booklet produced in 2023 to mark the 125th anniversary of the Dean Street football ground recalled an incident in 1893 when seven youths, all named, were summoned to Bishop Auckland police court for playing football in that very town centre street, PC Smith telling the court that he had "serious complaints from the Local Board about this sort of thing." The poor lads were fined half-a-crown apiece and sent to kick about elsewhere.

It forms part of the Consett conversation. I learn more over those three pints in Wetherspoons than I did in three years of nine o'clock calls while seeking snippets for the Northern Despatch.

Alec was one of the Horden McCoys, the real McCoys as doubtless they would suppose, at Shildon from 1967-73 – a time when local police officers drove round in little mini-vans which cramped their style and stunted their ambitions. He supposes himself lucky – "I was just five-foot-ten-and-a-bit, only

Cracked it: George Reynolds

just met the minimum requirement back then" – but equally supposes that these days police officers are too short. "You're meant to look up to them" he says.

They talk about Nat Card the butcher and about his dog – "queer dog, Nat's" – about Stan and Mary Marshall who ran the fish shop in Church Street ("lovely people, great fish and chips"), about little George Wookerjee who served a good pint of Cameron's at the Cross Keys in Cheapside.

They talk, too, of the policeman's ball – old jokes about dance or raffle may be exhumed here – one April evening in the 1970s when the snow was so sudden and so savage that most of the guests had to spend the night on the Civic Hall floor.

They also admit that what might be supposed pursuing enquiries would sometimes take them onto licensed premises and not always within permitted hours, much to the frustration of a particularly puritanical chief inspector in Bishop Auckland who longed – better late – to nab them. "We usually knew when he was around" says Alec, mysteriously.

"We were much closer to the community in those days, we were encouraged to be" says Ivan. "If that meant having a couple of pints late on then so be it. It worked. The big difference came in 1984 when Maggie set the communities against the police in the miners' strike, at least around here. That changed a lot."

For a time each officer was allocated a named beat – "me on one side of Church Street, Norman Woods on the other" – a "discretionary" system meaning that they could be called upon at any time, day or night, to an incident on their patch. "We attended every incident, every burglary, every assault, every theft" says Alec. "These days it all seems to be done on the

phone. We used to walk around the town talking to people, that's the difference."

Another difference, of course, was that there wasn't so much serious crime and that, if there were, they generally had a pretty good idea – unless he were already in Durham – of the identity of the gentleman who'd done it. Suffice to say that he lived in New Shildon and wasn't so much known to the police as on their friends and family list. "Not of the brightest" says Ivan, perhaps euphemistically.

Alec recalls asking for five minutes of the recidivist's time, a chat which resulted in charges and another custodial sentence. The defendant turned to the policeman as he was led down. "You asked me for five minutes and I got three bloody years" he said.

These days an officer's kit is a testament to technology and to the impetus for self-preservation. In the 1960s they went equipped with a truncheon – neither Ivan nor Alec ever drew it in anger – a pocket book, a whistle, a 3ft tape measure for road accidents and a stick of chalk for marking out the relevant measurements. Personal radios were in audio infancy; usually they'd just phone divisional headquarters in Bishop Auckland. An occurrence book, necessarily completed at the end of every shift, recorded the minutiae of the day.

Still there were fights, drink not drug-fuelled, and unlike their Victorian predecessors without particular emphasis on rebellious railwaymen. Alec recalls intervening in a mass brawl outside the King Willie, losing his helmet (and probably his dignity) in the process. "The last I saw of it, it was being kicked down the street" he recalls, an insolence which enraged Sgt 158 Coates.

"Ernie knew who'd be responsible" Alec recalls. "He found one of them, told them if the helmet wasn't back at the police station by half past three that afternoon, all hell would be let loose. It was duly returned but the badge had almost been kicked off. We had to take it to Bird's garage to get it welded back on. When I first went I was terrified of Ernie but I'd a lot of respect for him as well.

"We got a bike allowance, just a few bob each month but it helped. The only problem was that I didn't have a bike. Ernie said he had an old one in the shed and he gave me it. That's the sort of man he was."

Dull moments? Very few, he insists. "Some of it might have been twopence ha'penny stuff but there was always something going on."

So what of the late George Reynolds, high profile safecracker who if not quite felonious in plain sight left little doubt that he wasn't always tucked up by ten o'clock? "I suppose you could say we tolerated one another, he was all right with us" says Ivan guardedly. "He exaggerated his criminal activity, liked to tell stories, but we got on all right."

And the occasion, ecclesiastically avowed, when GR was called in by the Vicar of St John's to open a stubborn safe in the vestry. "Rubbish" says Ivan, though his former colleague is blunter yet. "George couldn't crack my arse" says Alec.

On the day that we swap stories in Spoons, the paper has carried a report about a 2.30am incident near Shildon railway station in which a car had been driven across someone's front garden, and left a hole in the wall before the house was ransacked and set alight. Many years after they handed in their warrant cards, the former officers are pretty sure that drugs will have been at the heart of the matter.

"We never had that sort of thing in Shildon in my time" says Alec, who later became markets manager for Wear Valley district council. "Those six years in Shildon were the happiest of my life."

Chapter seven

Black economy

Every town has a Black Path, as if following Henry Ford's famed advice to prospective Model T purchasers that they could have any colour they wished so long as it were that one. No matter that the Black Path which habitually we Shildon spirits haunted has now formally become the Black Boy Rail Trail, it will not be allowed to divert reminiscence's ramblings.

Effectively, probably coincidentally, the Black Path and the Black Boy Line were one and the same. Opened in 1827, worked by horses and by a stationary engine near Rose Cottages at the top end of town, the Black Boy diverted from the Stockton and Darlington main line near the Soho Works and ran past what is now the King William area to collieries around Eldon Lane. That more than one pit was called Black Boy – named after a local pub, apparently - should not have been allowed to confuse folk, but probably did, nonetheless.

Though a great deal of coal went that way, chiefly headed towards the Tees at Stockton, the line proved unsatisfactory – not least to travellers on horse-drawn rail carriages obliged to wait their turn at the foot of the 1-in-20 southbound incline. Two hundreds years later, passengers waiting interminably for the No 1 Arriva bus service to Darlington would know the feeling.

So they decided to burrow Shildon Tunnel, a mighty and a momentous enterprise 120ft beneath the town. Work began in the Spring of 1839, cost put at between £100,000-£120,000, the intention both to undermine (as it were) the Black Boy and to extend the railway to the booming collieries of the Crook and West Auckland areas. They might even carry a few passengers.

The effort was immense, the ingenuity unimaginable, the water ingress torrential. Frank Lawson records that little shanty towns grew up to accommodate the navvies – 236 workers on the tunnel and associated works, about a quarter Irish, with 115 women and children beneath their wing. In the crowded shanties it was fourpence for a bed, a penny for a table (on which, presumably, to sleep) and a ha'penny for the floor.

The tunnel was 1,225t long, 21ft high and 23ft wide, lined with more than seven million bricks. Amid much pomp, it was formally opened on January 10 1842, the first train – albeit horse drawn – completing the gloomy rite of passage three months later. Occasionally there were accidents in the pitch blackness, as on August 27 1880 when the 7 30pm from Bishop Auckland with about 50 passengers came off the rails and travelled for another 200 yards, though happily without hitting the tunnel walls.

"Women could be heard shrieking and crying and two or three created a condition of affairs almost bordering on panic by sillily shouting that there was another train coming the other way" reported *The Northern Echo* the following morning. "The steam of the locomotive clearing away, it was soon perceived that there was no element of danger."

The 7 25 from Darlington had a problem, nonetheless and – headed by a pilot engine – was diverted down the old Black Boy line, these days long lifted. Subterranean and silent, the tunnel serves still.

When finally the first train from Shildon reached Stockton on September 27 1825, a great banquet awaited the mighty (and what the French call *paysan* food, undescribed if not indescribable, for the workers). The banquet was held in Stockton Town

Hall, encompassing eight hours and 23 toasts, finishing after midnight. Though none (alas) can source the menu, toasts – many accompanied by an appropriate song – ranged from the King first to George Stephenson in 23rd place and from the Tees Navigation Company to the Lord Lieutenant of Durham, inexplicably to the tune of Old Towler.

The toast to the Coal Trade was followed by *Weel may the keel row*, a choice of which T Hackworth, raised in the Tyne Valley and a bit of a jigger, would doubtless privately have approved.

The dignitaries on January 10 1842 were wined and dined in the Cross Keys, alongside the Black Boy Line in Cheapside, a long-vanished pub which in post-war years had seemed small and unprepossessing (but which served a very good pint of Strongarm), The workers were fed and watered at six other pubs in the town.

Thousands, many flag waving, had come to Shildon from all parts. Accompanied by Lord Prudhoe's brass band, a procession headed by Luke Wandless, the chief engineer, made its way to the tunnel's southern portal – the band said in one of Gerald Slack's books to have been playing *Merrily danced the Quaker's wife*, a curious choice since Bernard McCormick's volume on the Pease family records the prevailing view that dancing was frivolous, unacceptable and quite likely the work of Satan himself. Was someone having a little joke? Would they have dared?

A platform had been erected inside the tunnel, the last brick baptised with wine. Playing goodness knows what but probably playing hell, the band was then obliged to undertake a musical march to the far end of the candlelit cavern.

It's coincidental that on the Saturday in February when I set off to retrace the Black Path, starting from Shildon station, there's a piece in the paper about the launch of something called the Gem Trail, a series of art installations running the mile or so from the nearby Locomotion railway museum to the town centre, each mounted on an "authentic" railway sleeper and celebrating (it was said) the "often overlooked stories of North-Eastern women".

The laudable aim's to entice folk from the museum to the town centre, the route different from the Black Path. "We wanted to showcase some of the amazing female stories in our part of the world" said Jo Howell, one of the artists. "The contribution of men in the North-East has long been celebrated, we wanted to help restore the pioneering female figures to their rightful place."

That's for another walk, another day, another dolour.

Sporadically gas-lit in childhood, effectively barely lit at all, the Black Path led from near the station, up past the Water Bridge, around what we used to call White's Corner – a house with apple trees and forbidden fruit, frequently filched – past the Tunnel Top, on to the King Willie and Cheapside then past Rose Cottages and down the other side to Eldon Lane, where still stand more S&D cottages.

In one of Rose Cottages, the one where the S&D's G12 property plate remains on the wall, lived in later life a wonderful character called Charlie Raine and his wife Connie, recalled while earlier on the milk round, he a retired Shildon Shops man and former LNER champion boxer who in 1976 had appeared on the BBC's affectionately remembered *Down your way* radio programme – presented by *Test Match Special* man

STATION PATH SHILDON

The Line Towards The Prince Of Wales Tunnel
Aquaduct On The Right & Allotments On The Left

Straight and narrow: the black path in former times

Song bird: Jenny Wren

Brian Johnston – when it visited Shildon. Though the effect may have been lost on radio listeners, Charlie talked – as he had fought – with his hands. "If I lost a finger I'd have a speech impediment" he said.

Other *Down your way* guests were wagon works manager Jeff Breckell, Cecil Attwood who founded the Dufay Paints company at the All Saints end of town and was made OBE for services to industry, school teacher Ethel Malcolm, Bill Giles, Frank Thompson and Dave Kell, who led the Methodist singing group Geordie's Penker which to mark the S&D's 150th anniversary the year previously had made a record called *Iron Road* containing the lines:

And who needs Presley when you've got Nigel Gresley

He'll convert you quicker than old John Wesley

There should have been medals for that, too.

Charlie also formed a concert party due with Bert Trussler, great old entertainers in the music hall tradition. At 80 he'd had a heart attack – "all they told me was that I had to give up sex for a month" he insisted – a few years later he underwent a cataract procedure, after which I visited and found him ecstatically reading *The Northern Echo* again. Was it my stuff, I wondered?

"Bugger your stuff, it's the race cards" said Charlie before tottering off with his two bob each way to Percy Allan's – a route which, happily, led past, or into, the King Willie.

In the pub and elsewhere, he'd also accompany on the piano a lovely lady called Jenny Wren, who did a boisterous *Laughing policeman* and was once on Tyne Tees Television singing *Jake the Peg* "I cadged a leg from one of the dummies at Doggarts' store in Bishop Auckland" she recalled. "I had terrible trouble with the driver of the OK bus to Newcastle, trying to get on with a leg under my arm."

Still fighting against the proposed closure of the Timothy Hackworth care home in which she lived, Jenny was four months past her 100th birthday and in a wheelchair when she successfully led a protest outside Durham County Hall. By way of unsolicited testimonial ascribed her relatively youthful appearance to regular calls from the Avon lady. She died aged 101.

Charlie's brother Norman, known to Shildon folk as Knobser and himself an amateur boxing champion, had served as an RAF bomb armourer during World Wat II, suffered a fractured skull which left him epileptic, became a pub landlord and what these days might be termed a masseur, plenty happy to vouch for his magic touch.

He and his wife Olive lived in a "bookless" prefab where their son, Craig, was born in December 1944. Craig won a scholarship to Barnard Castle public school where he became a boarder, went on to Oxford, married one of the Pasternaks and became one of the country's best known poets. His background worried him, though. "Everyone else's parents used to be accountants or surgeons or something" he once said of his time at Barnard Castle. "For a while I said that my dad was a football manager, but by the time I was inviting them back, they thought he was terrific as I did."

Described by fellow poet Philip Larkin as a "bearded looney", Craig also appeared to think little of his home town. On one occasion he described it as "typically ugly and small" and the

locals' pride as "faintly ridiculous". He'd also written that Stephenson built *Rocket* in Shildon and of enduring family holidays in Saltburn and where the end-of-the-pier show was "terrible."

Saltburn never had end-of-the-pier shows. Craig was nothing at all like his Uncle Charlie.

Once the lineside embankment from the station and along the Black Path was protected by nothing more than a two-rail wooden fence, still visible to the mind's eye. Now the fence is steel, 6ft high and with the sort of topping upon which it would be perhaps crucially painful to be impaled. The steps down to the Water Bridge are yet more fiercely protected, a notice advising that the fine for trespassing on the railway is £1,000. In the 1950s, memory suggests, it was not to exceed forty shillings and a clout round the ear from PC Trebilcock.

The problem thereabouts, on both sides of the path, is that the fencing would have to be a great deal higher to stop rubbish being thrown over the top and in truly startling quantities. The most clearly visible, at least to these enfeebled eyes, are hundreds of beer cans. There are also a couple of traffic cones and – how on earth did that get there? – a supermarket trolley. It would be a terrible advert for the old town were the garbage not shifted before the world starts to wander, and to wonder, in the summer of 2025.

On the bank above the tunnel's southern entrance is a memorial bench to several folk. Among those remembered is Des Elliott, a contemporary who was just 18 when killed in a fall from the steep embankment wall in 1966. The fence guarding that bit is yet higher. A stone nearby also has a plaque affixed, its mud covering and closeness to the ground again presenting a problem for the myopic.

The tunnel ventilation shafts, chimneys perhaps 12ft above the ground, are long demolished – they're smokeless, pretty much, these days. Across the road from the King Willie are a few new houses, for some reason called Brancepeth Place – what's Brancepeth to do with anything? In the end garden a union flag sulks motionless from atop a pole, as if waiting for something to celebrate.

Opposite the King Willie is a chaldron waggon, said on a plaque to be of the type that hauled coals along the Black Boy line. Engraved on a wheel is the information that it was manufactured in Motherwell in 1894. In Shildon of all places, couldn't they have found something home made?

Much more concerning is that, at this end of the town, there are hardly any information boards to explain what all the fuss is about. Like Jemmy Stephenson, who cussed and swore because he couldn't get the footplate fire going, Shildon is in danger of hiding its light under a bushel.

Time for a swift one in the King William, said to have been built in 1831 but with a chequered recent past. Closed, re-opened and closed again, it became a curious kind of candy store before returning to square one and starting again as a pub. At one end of the bar the television's showing football, at the other some long-gone gig by the Everley Brothers. There's no piano.

A chap insists that he once saw the Everleys at Shildon Civic Hall. Whether he did or he didn't, it's pretty certain that they never sang *Jake the Peg*.

A few yards away was Coulson's newsagent's, from which on Saturday evenings I'd earn an extra 2/6d by delivering the Pink, that weekly miracle of hot metal, and still be home in time for the *Billy Cotton Band Show*. Formally the Sports Despatch, a sister paper of *The Northern Echo*, the Pink was produced ten miles away in Darlington, unable further to report until the final whistle shortly before 5pm and then locked up, printed, bundled, tied up with string and tossed blithely into the back of a great queue of waiting vans. Dozens of men awaited at every paper shop, anxious for the Late Final word, the boys hoofed off round the streets.

Most big towns had their Pinks, a few dressed their Saturday sports editions in green, one in blue. None has survived the technological revolution that literally has decimated the provincial newspaper industry, in the Pinks no longer.

Next door to Coulson's was Fred Lockwood's, a butcher who still sold penny ducks for a penny and object of much local indignation after a 50 per cent increase to three ha'pence. A few doors further stood Bedda's fish shop, next to that the Cross Keys where a great banquet had once been held and (who knows) the Quaker's wife had danced, as mischievous as she was merry.

The Phoenix Foundry, fed by a little siding from the Black Boy line, was long gone before we arrived though Phoenix Place and Temperance Avenue remain. Temperance Avenue may be Shildon's shortest street. It stirs another childhood memory, and thoughts of Guy Fawkes night when kids were said to be "on" bonfires though not, of course, in the same way as effigies of Mr Fawkes.

One bonfire was on Cheapside, opposite Rose Cottages, another barely 100 yards away behind Phoenix Place. Territory was defended, raids planned, threats issued. Sparks seldom flew.

From where the stationary engine stood, the track descends past the tunnel's northern portal to Eldon Lane and to sundry Black Boy pits. Greatly uneven at the best of times, it's tricky going on treacherous on days like this one. Again there are no information boards, no indication that it's part of world railway history. Great opportunities await in 2025; it would be greatly sad if Shildon missed the train.

Chapter eight

Action station

The first train from Darlington to Shildon leaves at 6 44am, thereafter at hourly intervals – approximately five-to – until the shut-eye service departs Shildon for Darlington at 21 33. The plan's to spend an entire June day in and around the station, to awake long-dormant memories, to get some sunshine and perhaps to listen to some music.

Might the remotely controlled music machine, said to deter the desperate, play *Morning has broken* – maybe the Cat Stevens version – or perhaps *Good morning Starshine* or maybe, appropriately, reprise the Seekers' *Morning town ride?* It's seven o'clock silent, birdsong accompanies alone.

Shildon station seems to have had a permanently bad press. Even when what's claimed the world's first ticket office opened in Daniel Adamsson's coach house – still standing – in 1825, intending passengers may have travelled with trepidation.

The Grey Horse inn, also owned by Adamson senior, was across the road. "Many stopped for refreshment only to be beaten up or robbed and in some cases were actually murdered, for the inn was a notorious haunt of smugglers" wrote Robert Corkin in *Shildon: Cradle of the Railways*, published in 1977. If Adamson were a bad lot, his horse – the eponymous grey horse – was reckoned positively nefarious.

The town's second station was opened back at the Masons Arms in 1837, said to have the world's first railway clock which faced the single platform opposite, among the site's potential advantages that the pub's ale was reputedly much safer to sup than the putrid, polluted drinking water which then was all that was to be had, though some may have struggled to taste the difference.

The disadvantage, it was said, was that the trains were often late and that an ill wind frequently blew. So when a third station opened in 1842, better to serve the newly opened line through the Prince of Wales tunnel, hopes may have been high. They were ill-founded: this from a *Northern Echo* report of 1875, intended to celebrate the fiftieth anniversary of the S&DR.

"Shildon station is a disgrace to Durham, to the Stockton and Darlington and to the railway system. The booking office is a shanty perched on the top of a high bank entirely disconnected from the low lying, draughty sheds which are supposed to shelter the passengers who have the ill luck to alight on its platforms. Perhaps this wretched apology for a station is continued in existence as a memento of the past."

Then this from Robert Young's biography of Timothy Hackworth, his grandfather, published in 1923: "Shildon railway station possesses every distinction which discomfort can produce and is the dreariest in the United Kingdom. Its single interest is the old stone blocks on which the platform is partly built, at one time used as sleepers on the old railway, and even these are merely there as an economy in using old material."

Robert Corkin – who thought Shildon a "small, rugged town" – also supposed the station to be "dreary", neither the first nor last thus to employ that greystone adjective – while George Turner Smith in *A Railway history of New Shildon* (2019) wrote that the 1842 station had been "ramshackle" but had been upgraded, after many complaints, in 1899.

"It was a typical rural station of its time, not earth shattering by national standards but at least an improvement on the wind-swept study in reinforced concrete that you see today".

So when Peter Semmens in *Exploring the Stockton and Darlington Railway* (1975) thought the station to be "fairly conventional", the gaffers in York must have supposed themselves suffused with superlatives by comparison. Semmens went further, extolling the view from the top of the coal drops, not 100 yards away. "On a clear day the distant Cleveland Hills can be made out, with the characteristic shape of Roseberry Topping some 23 miles away."

On a clear day some of us still short sightedly struggle to see the signal box, not 100 yards in the opposite direction, On a maudlin midsummer day like this one in June 2024, when the temperature peaks at 12 degrees and the station lights never switch off, it's hard enough to make out the opposite platform though still possible (when passing) to see the signalman's Rolls Royce parked out the back of his eyrie. Perhaps he is one of those railwaymen frequently out on the streets these past couple of years in search of a better deal.

Though much changed since Smith's monument to brutalism, the station – long unstaffed – remains on the same site it occupied nearly 200 years ago, when Kilroy was probably there. Other ghosts may walk, too, great gantries of them. There are porters who still carry on regardless, passengers who travel eternally, firemen who still kindle the flame. What, too, of poor John Cree, Locomotion's driver, among the railways' first fatalities in 1828 when the engine's boiler exploded at Heighington.

Though still distant from the platforms below, the booking office – presumably one of the 1899 improvements – was an evocative place, smelling of floor polish and summer Saturdays, alive with expectation until gutted by arsonists in the 1960s. One of them lived near us, canny lad, sent to a reformatory where, duly, he reformed.

The porters' room and parcels office were between booking office and platforms, usually visited after midnight when the drains and sewers committee of some loquacious local authority had incorrigibly overflowed and reports for the next evening's paper had to be written up at home. The "News intelligence" envelope was pushed through the letter box in the sure and certain hope that, intelligent or otherwise, it would be entrusted to the guard of the first train to Darlington and make it to the ever-ungrateful sub-editors. Even the Last Train to San Fernando may have gone before the drains and sewers committee had exhausted its agenda.

The waiting rooms had stoves, the sort said to throw out heat, the platforms had barrows and bogies on which "Shildon Pass" was inscribed and with which we'd play childish games until chased by peevish porters. The station buildings carried adverts for Brooke Bond Tea, for Oxydol and for Virol which (it was confidently asserted) nervous people needed.

Pursued from the platform, we'd train spot from behind – usually from behind – a two-rail wooden fence which separated the back line, as we knew it, from the passenger station. The back line was used exclusively by goods trains, from which as we watched the guard would use a pole to separate his van from the rest of the train in order that the van might freewheel down to the sidings. "Gravity marshalling" they called it – a dangerous and sometimes a lethal business.

These days the two-rail fence is replaced by 7ft wire mesh, the

Burned down: the old booking office

back line by undergrowth and greenery, the steam engines by diesel multiple units and the fun by functionality, which has a lot more syllables and isn't the same thing at all.

My dear old dad was a member of Old Shildon Workmen's Club, though his annual pint – consumed in haste every Christmas morning between eight o'clock stockings and 12 o'clock turkey – was unlikely greatly to have overbalanced the accounts. It wasn't the pint he joined for, it was the perks.

One of them was that members' children got five bob (or some such fortune) apiece by way of Christmas present, possibly a bag of nuts an' all, on condition that their fathers joined the festive queue half way to the Hippodrome in order personally to collect it. Another perk was the annual club trip, always by train, always to Redcar, always always rammed.

Some kids had a Sunday School trip, too, though St John's appeared to frown upon such material extravagance, perhaps for fear that one or other of the commandments might have a forgotten sub-clause proscribing such wanton goings-on. For us Church of England urchins, it was supposed, the reward must be in heaven.

While the bucket and spade brigade would surge towards Shildon station, the black path fair wick with folk, things were by no means as thronged as they were at what was called Redcar Special Platform, at which every outing in North-East England appeared to arrive at five-minute intervals, a remarkable exercise in shunting and signalling about which someone should write a book (but appears not to have done.)

Old Shildon club trip seemed always to be hauled by 67777, bright burnished for the occasion, a class L1 tank engine known

to young beneficiaries as the Flying Sevens and at the head of a non-corridor train which stretched the length of the platform and might ultimately overflow it.

Always, or so it seemed, we ate egg and tomato sandwiches by the boating lake; always, for this was Redcar, it appeared overcast. Always we spent part of the return journey wondering how men who'd spent much of the day bibulously might make it home on a train with no corridors and thus, of course, no netties. Doubtless they had avenues down which, then as now, it would have been imprudent further to enquire.

Redcar, to borrow a more modern phrase, was clearly the go-to place for Shildon folk, though Colin Randall – son of Ernie Randall, Old Shildon WMC's secretary in the 60s and 70s – recalled in one of his many admirable blogs that they longed for the club trip to be Whitley Bay, even Saltburn.. Whitley Bay had the Spanish City, Saltburn had a pier, Redcar seemed peerless.

Ernie was a Londoner, retained every cough and spit of his Bow Bells accent, was cutting room manager at Northern Clothing on the industrial estate. "How could a Cockney, let alone one who'd never clocked on for a single shift at Shildon Shops, occupy such a position?" his son had wondered out loud.

As at Christmas, club members' children received a few bob to spend at the seaside. The only problem, Colin wrote, was a minority of bairns saw neither the pocket money nor the sea – until Ernie and his committee hit on the idea of paying out the 2/6d (or whatever) at journey's end. "That way the children still got to see the seaside even if their pocket money was swiped from them when the train reached its destination."

Right lines: the station in former times

Colin started, alongside me, in the Bishop Auckland office of the Northern Despatch, rising to become a senior executive of the *Daily Telegraph* and of publications abroad. A lifelong folk music enthusiast, he also wrote a song called *Shildon club looks grim today (the fruit machine it wouldn't pay)*, though he gainsays memory's assertion that it was to the tune of the Red Flag. His dad's funeral was held at a thronged All Saints in Shildon, fellow club officials forming a guard of honour.

The brochure produced in 1950 to mark the centenary of Timothy Hackworth's death noted in wonderful detail that the first Mechanics Institute outing, September 2 1848, had also left for Redcar's sandy shore, no fewer than 1,016 club trippers taking advantage – though whether hauled by the Flying Sevens is, sadly, not recorded. Everything passed off in a comfortable and pleasant manner, said the brochure, save for "one or two" exceptions.

One or two? The institute committee had felt obliged to write to the S&DR. "We would direct your attention to the subject of being obliged to put up with trucks unseated and unswept and think that Mr George Stephenson, passenger agent, ought to be spoken to and in future the trucks done away with – they are neither comfortable nor convenient. We also think there should be some reduction in the price of trucks."

The day's takings were £39 3s, of which £19 10s was paid to George Stephenson, £1 3s to Mr Braithwaite for services unknown – perhaps he had charge of the tea trolley – and the remainder given to the Institute treasurer.

By 1850 the S&D must have addressed the Institute's cattle class concerns because no fewer than 2,200 passengers joined the Redcar outing – 180 travelling first class at 1/6d apiece,

maybe having heard about the trucks – but proceeds slightly affected when a "bad half crown" was discovered. The event made a profit of £50 17s 10d. Even if only for a day trip, Redcar was here to stay.

Of all the images in all the (very many) books which chronicle railway history in these parts, none is more compelling than that of a detachment of Enniskillen Fusiliers on guard at Shildon station. That many of them are on their bikes suggests that it may have been the mounted division. Other pictures show grim-faced troops protecting railway property at other locations in the vicinity from anarchy and insurrection.

It was August 1911, part of what left-wing publications like to call The Great Unrest – the capitals curious for such fervent anti-capitalists – a national transport strike that began among Liverpool seamen and which became so serious that two warships were anchored on the Mersey in what might be supposed a shot across the bows.

It spread chiefly to the railways, where the basic wage was just 18 shillings a week, the action in Shildon said "locally" to be known as Knox's strike, though firing even the most streamlined search engine offers little of supposed relevance save for a couple of attempts on goal by little-known footballers of that Presbyterian surname and a bit of blackboard bother at Knox Academy, in Scotland.

Whoever Knox was, the unfortunate chap who found himself at the centre of the Shildon hoo-hah was Christopher Churchman, the station master. Not were matters helped that the strike's second day, August 19, was also the day of Shildon Show, hundreds of visitors and exhibitors prevented from attending. By no means for the first time, or indeed the last, Durham's miners hadn't been very happy, either.

As elsewhere throughout the country, "scab" trains were still being operated by "blackleg" labour. Poor Churchman had had the temerity to wave his fist at a group of the picketing strikers at the station entrance, though it's possible that strong words were also exchanged and that Churchman's language was itself pretty irreligious. Robert Corkin takes up the story in *Cradle of the Railways:*

"There is no doubt that alcohol played a major part in the troubles that plagued Shildon. Engine drivers and firemen seemed to spend every penny they possessed on ale and then after a belly full plan a full scale battle with the police or with anyone who trod their path. The drivers, stinking with ale, ran after Churchman, pelting him with stones. He reached his home where he lay on the floor in terror, for dozens of stones came hurtling through his windows, sending broken glass flying in all directions."

George Turner Smith tells the tale slightly differently and rather more graphically, albeit with the familiar preface that the Shildon workforce was "not famous for tolerance or sobriety" or for tugging feudally at forelocks, either. It was thus unfortunate he adds, that in Churchman they should have encountered the most unsympathetic railway official in England, a man who went out of his way to antagonise the strikers.

The militants, says Smith, pursued him to end of the platform where he sought sanctuary in the signal box. Once there, he stood by the window "slowly and deliberately eating his substantial lunch with exaggerated enthusiasm." The object of this award-winning performance, Smith adds, was to demonstrate that, unlike the starving men outside, he remained a wage earner and could therefore afford to eat well.

The strikers bombarded the signal box with ballast from the track, threw the footplate crew off a locomotive in the nearby marshalling yard, released the mechanism to empty loaded trains. Churchman, who in photographs appears almost benevolently affable, ran for the somewhat optimistically perceived safety of his home in Soho Cottages – the little row where Timothy Hackworth had lived – only to find that it, too, came under attack. Thereafter he was given a police escort and the troops summoned (though presumably from Catterick and not on the first boat from Enniskillen.)

Smith supposes 200 fusiliers to have been deployed to Shildon. A latter day left wing website, with much reference to blacklegs and to bourgeoisie, puts the figure at 540, a deployment with which David Reynolds in his superb history of the Railway Institute, pretty much concurs. Another 1,000 military were sent to Darlington where there was "local unrest". In Liverpool two men were shot dead by soldiers in a protest that left 165 in hospital and 96 arrested; two more died at Llanelli. Outflanked by the Fusiliers, the strike lasted just four days, though bitterness and repercussion endured much longer, not least in Shildon.

Reynolds quotes the *Jarrow Express* – perhaps not much happening on South Tyneside – of August 25 1911: "With the exception of Darlington and Shildon the North Eastern men have been a pattern to others. No unseemly conduct has placed a black mark against them. Throughout all the week they have acted in an honourable and gentlemanly manner."

A "special edition" of *Railway review*, dated August 1911, reported events beneath a perhaps contentious four-deck headline: The Great Strike/magnificent response/railways blocked/

Unmanned: the station today

We won!"

Unearthed by George Turner Smith, the November 1911 issue of *Railway Gazette* carried a poem entitled "Eighteen bob a week."

To them, of course, it is quite just to draw a princely ration

While we must get our grub on trust and slave at some dull station.

Be bullied here and bullied there and take it all quite meek

To drive away all earthly care on eighteen bob a week.

Hartley Appleby, a later and more uniformly esteemed station master, would do the rounds of signal boxes on his patch. If they knew he was coming, which very likely they didn't, the signalmen would hide their sandwiches. The station master, it's recalled, didn't mind whose bait he ate. Suitably well fed, he lived to be 100.

Save for a couple of mutterings about the cancellation of the 13 13 – unlucky for some, if ever – all is peace and light, peace and half-light, today. I could do with a sandwich, though.

These days it's only passengers, a few men and a dog, who may use Shildon station. It wasn't always so. Prolific author Ken Hoole's *Railway stations of the North-East*, published in 1985, not only included 1911 ticket statistics for every station on the patch but goods traffic returns from two years later.

Shildon was on the list between Shield Row and Shincliffe, serving a population (it said) of 14,916. In 1911 the station had issued 136,879 tickets – perhaps including concessionary fares for the Shops folk – and handled 15,777 tons of "creosote/tar/pitch", 5,911 tons of scrap, 4,559 tons of manure (a hefty odure) and 3,664 tons of "oils". There'd also been 48 trucks of "livestock", though whether a throwback to the Institute outing is unclear.

Bishop Auckland, by comparison, was said to serve a population of 27,998 and to have issued 447,315 tickets – more than the 420,5119 recorded at Darlington. Bishop handled 3,460 tons of scrap iron and steel, 3,239 tons of flour and bran – presumably a self-raising nod to Messrs Lingford, the baking powder barons – and 1,562 tons of timber, perhaps chiefly to make matchbox holders at the grammar school. Darlington also handled 2,472 wagons of livestock, 34,042 tons of "bars, joints and girders", 25,314 tons of scrap iron and steel and 22,570 tons of creosote, tar and pitch.

The 2023-24 figures recorded that Shildon station had 54,624 "entries and exits", 13,886 of those journeys starting or ending at Darlington. 11,094 journeys were with full-price tickets, 37,778 with "reduced price tickets" – presumably children, senior citizens and those fortunates still entitled to the once-ubiquitous privy tickets – and 5,042 with season tickets, making Shildon 1,963rd nationally – not bad for a station, and a line, which Dr Beeching had earmarked for closure, appropriately in 1973. There was no mention of creosote/tar/pitch.

The passenger service was far less regular, and perhaps less reliable, than today's. The national timetable for the summer of 1922 indexed Shildon between Shifnal and Shillelagh – a station unsurprisingly in Ireland, end of the branch line from Woodenbridge – helpfully also noting that Shildon's market day was Friday. The line was listed as Darlington to Bishop Auckland and Blackhill, the first train to Bishop at three minutes past six and the last to Darlington at 11 33pm, though even approaching the witching hour old timetables insisted on the term "afternoon". Nearly 12 hours apart, only two trains ran on Sundays, neither beyond Bishop.

By the time that the LNER timetable (price 6d) appeared for the period October 1946 to May 1947, table 137 was headed "Darlington to Bishop Auckland, Tow Law and Wearhead", Tow Law and Wearhead being on different extensions but with through trains to both. The day's first train was the 5 54 to Crook (6 28) and Tow Law (6 40), the last at 11 22 (in the afternoon), tunnelled and tucked up in Bishop seven minutes later.

That the North Eastern Railway timetable for 1862 had failed to include any mention of Shildon was because the NER didn't take over the Stockton and Darlington until the following year. Even then, says a footnote in the facsimile edition, the S&D men remained pretty much a law until themselves.

So back to Shildon station on this June day in 2024, and it's clear that they've been making an effort. Both platforms are decorated with artwork – there's even a lengthy poem – reflecting the town's railway heritage. Using a light bulb image is clever. Slogans promote the town as "a place of possibility" offering "the perfect conditions for ingenuity". Perhaps they'd heard of those news intelligence packets, shoved in the small hours through the parcels office door.

The effect's marred by a potted guide to the Black Boy Trail, promoting sites like the Cross Keys pub – demolished at least 25 years previously – and the Timothy Hackworth Museum in Soho House, replaced by Locomotion in 2004.

At 8am on this meteorologically mournful morning the temperature's eight degrees. "Shildon, cloudy" says the smart phone screen, self-evidently. By 10am it's up to 11 degrees and by noon a plus-one. Still it's Shildon, still cloudy. It would be good to buy a paper but where to find a newsagent's? Once I could have named eight or nine, most with delivery boys on half-a-dollar a day. Now, paper thin, there may not be any.

Save for a school party headed for Locomotion, few alight or join. A chap's singing "Happy birthday" to his dog, which seems unmoved by the offering. Occasionally it seems possible to hear the approach of a steam train, a ghost train, before concluding that that must be blowing in the wind as well.

The 12 33 departed for the coast, the next train in either direction cancelled – "train crew member unavailable", a familiar Northern Rail lament – thoughts turn to lunch. Shildon never was the sort of station that had refreshment rooms, not even a little tea hut, nor even one of the those sixpence-in-the-slot machines which sold soup that tasted of sump oil.

On the nearby Jubilee Fields housing estate there's a fish shop called Frydayz but this is Wednesday and appears not to be one of Frydayz days at all. There's a little café at the top of Church Street, though, everything about it themed Sunderland red and white. Regardless of football fealty, they do a very good corned beef pie and chips.

The station buildings now comprise a prefabricated shelter on either platform, bravely decorated with S&D imagery and with a single metal ledge – it may hardly be called a seat – about the width of a paperback novel upon which the weary must rest disproportionately formed backsides. Near them on each platform is a single backless bench, about six inches from the ground, akin to something designed for the punishment block

Flying machine: 67777

at one of His Majesty's more mean-spirited prisons. Shildon may indeed be the cradle of the railways, but on benches such as this sleep would be utterly impossible

As in former times, it may be the least comfortable station on the network and little solace that the title may be shared with several hundred others. Probably also like several hundred others, the automated information service is excellent.

Save for the melancholy weather, however, the worst thing about this midsummer day on Shildon station is that it's not steam powered and thus neither unpredictable nor adventurous. A cop must nowadays be assumed a British Transport Police officer and not a first sighting, joyfully underlined in a dog-eared Ian Allan annual. A train is a class 158 diesel, two-tone monotone, take it or leave it because that's all there's ever going to be.

In childhood's grimy age there was anticipation on every occasion that one of many signals jerked noisily to attention and no matter that optimism so often succumbed to realism. There were high-tolling B1s, querulous Q6s, even occasional visitors disoriented from the LMS, manly mail trains and, of course, there were diversionary tactics on Sundays. Now the single signal slides silently. Whoever would have supposed that I'd think wistfully of 68696?

On the stroke of five o'clock, as if governed by Greenwich Mean Time – which quite likely it is, though not followed by the news headlines – the music machine switches itself on. It's not even Eine Kleine Nachtmusik. It's all the dolorous day needs, the unwanted accompaniment so lugubrious you could weep for it and likely to have the exact opposite effect of what apparently is intended. From a distant street, Mr Whippy

intones *Popeye the Sailor Man*, positively life-affirming compared to the unchained threnodies on Platform 1.

A little lineside reading, I fall between rumination and reminiscence to perusing the compendious *Bradshaw's Descriptive Railway Hand-book of Great Britain and Ireland*, published in 1863 and so popular when appearing as a facsimile 150 years later that, in 2012 alone, it was reprinted eight times.

It's a sort of Round Britain Tour, split into four geographical sections. Shildon's at best marginalised, literally a footnote in history, or – and at first review seems entirely to have been wiped from the map despite inclusion in the index between Sherwood Forest and Shimpling, a south Suffolk village where these days they grow grapes.

Then, at the bottom of page 82 of section four and beneath the heading "Darlington to Stanhope and Carrhouse" is squeezed the following: "Passing Aycliffe, near which is Heighington church, we reach Shildon, at which place the Stockton and Darlington Company has their locomotive works. It is also the junction of the line to Haggerleazes."

That's it; strangled at the birthplace of the railways. Other places, of course, attract a much more generous press. Darlington ("omnibuses from every train") had a population of 15,781, about a sixth of the 2025 figure, "engaged in the cotton, flax and worsted mills foundries and glass works" and where the "celebrated" bull Comus – possibly synonymous with Comet, locally famed - had been sold for £1,050 (and presumably not for quarter-pounders).

Redcar (population 1,330) was described as "a small bathing place near the Scar Reefs", its population briefly doubled whenever Shildon Mechanics Institute decided to have its club trip there.

Barnard Castle (pop 4,178) boasted the Kings Head Hotel, fairs at Easter and at Whitsuntide and, then as now, a Wednesday market. Stanhope, in Weardale, was reckoned to have a population of 9,654, possibly including sheep lost or otherwise, though more than 8,000 had work in and around the lead mines.

The line between Durham and Sunderland is described as the "Pensher branch", as locals would have pronounced it, though Bradshaw concedes that sometimes it answered to Painshaw. These days that monumental village identifies simply as Penshaw. Pensher has gone up market.

Then there was Bishop, blooming Bishop, said in 1863 to have a population of 6,480, a hotel called the Talbot and (of course) the Bishop of Durham's palatial pad with its fine this and fancy that, glorious prospects and wondrous art collection. Bradshaw also felt it right to note that "the comedian Sherwood" was a native of Bishop Auckland, though no amount of research – quite a bit of research, at least – can discover who he was or what he had to laugh about. A day on Shildon station might have knocked the smile off his face, anyway.

The 18 13 from Darlington decants a few white collar workers, though not even Blondie to whistle on her way. Shortly after 6 30pm, when in former times the Night Mail would have had Shildon lads abandoning homework in their excitement, I join two conductors, two revenue protection officers and five passengers on the 18 33 and head eagerly, prematurely, for home. Enough excitement for one day.

Chapter nine

Museum piece

Outside Locomotion, the National Railway Museum at Shildon, diesel engine 08911 – intriguingly named *Matey* – is shunting in the same apparently desultory manner as 68696 and its oft-abused and frequently filthy predecessors would all those years ago when a vast marshalling yard overflowed the site. Picture postcards proclaimed it the world's biggest.

As locomotive names go, *Matey* may not evoke the horripilant thrill of *Sir Nigel Gresley*, the canard magic of *Mallard* or even the dark continent mystique of some of those loping, anteloping B1s. but begs questions nonetheless. The museum had an operations manager, it's explained, lovely chap but so unable to remember names that everyone simply became Matey. Affectionately, amicably, it stuck (though there are those who will remember that Matey was once bubble bath, too.)

We'd roamed that way as kids, jam jars for taddies and jam sandwiches for sustenance. Shildon sidings were past their pre-war peak – marshalling yard and engine shed had closed in 1935, the shed shifted to Fylands, formally West Auckland, 50s fiefdom of the formidable Alderman James Robinson Stirling Middlewood - but seemed magnetically attractive even so.

Nearby were Elephant's Trunk, curiously named but great for sledging, and Crows' Wood. Like Black Paths, every town may have had a Crows' Wood, and cared little about where the apostrophe might nest or indeed whether the blighter nested at all. Later reading revealed the undergrowth alongside the tracks to be a habitat of the dingy skipper, an apparently rare butterfly and a "priority" species.

It seemed a bit disappointing, for all that. If your town's going to host a lepidopterists' love-in, might not the butterfly in question have been a painted lady or even a red admiral and not just a dull old dingy skipper?

A bit further along lay what long had been known as the Cattle Bridge, perhaps for obvious reasons. Across it, beyond the Wild Wood and into what the Water Rat supposed the Wide World. were Fairy Glen and a perhaps equally mythical farmer called Clarey who (it was alleged) would chase errant children while armed with a blunderbuss.

To some it stirred images of Farmer Jenks, among William's many sworn enemies in Richmal Crompton's eponymous children's books, to others it seemed redolent of Foxy, a chicken-thieving character in the *Topper* comic when such things cost threepence. Foxy's nemesis was identified merely as Farmer, though he had a blunderbuss, too. You wait hours for a blunderbuss and then two come along at once.

It's possible that Shildon parents had invented Fairy Glen in order to enchant the little ones, though one of Frank Lawson's volumes records the legend that Oberon and several hundred of his gossamer-winged associates had once appeared to a village lad from Middridge, no more than a mile away. The Middridge lad was known as Silly Willie, which could explain a lot. Remembering the Water Rat's wide-wise words, we didn't venture much cross the Cattle Bridge, anyway.

Locomotion was opened by Tony Blair, Prime Minister and MP for Sedgefield, in October 2004. "Envisaged as an accessible store shed, it quickly became a full tourist attraction" Anthony Coulls, a curator, wrote in a guide published in 2012. Anthony, who now lives in Shildon and loves it, also recalled the desperate days when wagon works closure was rumoured.

"The whole raison d'etre of the town was under threat, but a combination of political pressure and lack of orders resulted in its eventual closure with the loss of 2,900 (sic) jobs" he wrote. "For 20 years Shildon became a place that very few had heard of and even fewer visited."

Anthony's in-laws are from Ilkley, the well-heeled West Riding town which in the depression days of the 1930s had effectively "adopted" struggling families in Shildon in much the same way and at exactly the same time as the top hatted sons of gentlefolk at Eton College had put a tailcoated arm around the young unemployed in St Helens Auckland, a couple of miles along the road.

I've arrived at Locomotion to see Andrew McLean, assistant director and head curator, at 11 30am. The day has begun with breakfast – a very good breakfast – at the former wagon works canteen, now the George Samuel Brewery and Canteen and still decked with enlarged photographs of the Shops workers anticipating a good spread. It won't be the last visit.

Along the trackbed between breakfast and briefing, or just off it, lie Timothy Hackworth's Soho home – once absurdly threatened by a relief road, later itself a well-furnished little museum, now being repurposed, possibly as a holiday cottage – and also several 19th century railway buildings, already restored.

Number one: Locomotion

Though scaffolding surrounds the impressive coal drops, where locomotives would be refuelled until Shildon shed shut, it's expected that their glories will again be revealed – and a steam shuttle service run – when the bicentenary celebrations begin.

"Fantastic assets" said the Locomotion website a decade ago, though regretting the joint predations of neglect and vandalism among that group of seven buildings. Now much work is complete. Already it's verdantly green and greatly pleasant around there.

Nearby is a poignant little development, identified as Dyllon and Quinn's Garden, a memorial to tragic Shildon siblings and with a great flight – there may be a better collective noun – of bird boxes.

A sign on the path to the museum advises that the verges are being managed for biodiversity, perhaps even to woo the elusive dingy skipper. Managing the local litter louts may prove trickier. Near where Matey agreeably potters, another sign proclaims that the birth of the railways did more to shape the modern world than any other invention. "We are on a journey to become a reinvented 21st century attraction" it adds.

Chiefly they're excited about the 2,000 square metre New Hall, nearing completion at the time of the visit, to be home to an additional 46 railway vehicles and locomotives. The biggest collection under one roof in Europe – and looking to tell "coherently" the story of Shildon and the railway – it will be laid out across three pairs of tracks in a building said to have "the aesthetics of an engine shed". The website talks of a "wider transformational masterplan" and of "a multi-million pound programme of investment, improvement and change". Durham County Council, says Andrew, have been greatly supportive.

"New buildings, new galleries, visitor attractions, outdoor spaces and vital conservation work. A safe environment for our collection" the website promises. "By doing this we will use our collections and buildings to inspire the next generation of engineers and scientists." A sign near the entrance simply announces "Transformation in progress."

Another poster details the back-of-a-lorry arrival of the Gaunless Bridge, recently in the museum car park at York, built by George Stephenson in Newcastle in 1823 to span that unprepossessing little river at West Auckland – said to have much the same etymology as "gormless". Just two coaches sit in Locomotion's car park, though clearly with much the same qualities as the magic porridge pot which (it will be remembered) just kept on disgorging. The museum's alive with excited children – "a fun family day out in the birthplace of the railways" it promises - and though it's a charity and donations are welcomed, like the best things in life it's free.

Ahead of them as they enter is the huge and immaculately preserved locomotive *Winston Churchill*, its headboard proclaiming the London to Paris Pullman though used yet more memorably to haul the train carrying the great war leader's coffin. Behind it, dwarfed, is *Sans Pareil*, if not quite unequalled then certainly one of Hackworth's finest.

"It could go at up to 15 miles an hour" a teacher tells her young charges. "To many people that would have been terrifying." The bairns gather round for a team picture. "Don't say cheese" they're told, "say Locomotion."

There's much to fascinate, from opulent royal trains to the Percy Main snowplough and from the Advanced Passenger Train to a City of Sheffield sewage department truck (which, admittedly, may not enthral in quite the same way.) Recalling the phrase about getting in where draughts can't, Thomas the Tank Engines makes an ineluctable appearance, too.

A personal favourite remains the big old departure board from that enviably fascinating station at Bishop Auckland, trains every half an hour to Shildon and sundry lesser places in one direction and to Etherley, Beechburn and Crook in the other.

A living museum they like to call it and on a Friday morning in March it's positively animated, wick with people. pregnant with possibilities and a huge, huge magnet for Shildon.

Andrew McLean's father was a senior figure in the British Rail public affairs department in York at the time of the glamorous, glorious Cavalcade which marked the S&D's 150th anniversary in 1975. Then but a bairn, he still recalls the thrill of it all. "It was the first time I'd seen Mallard and I was absolutely in awe" says Andrew, who has a history degree and a curatorial background in stately homes. The cavalcade of steam from Shildon was fantastic, he says, made him really excited about railways. "I still am. I have very strong memories of the day, though bits of it were bedlam it was a magical occasion."

Though such an event could never be repeated – not least because the wagon works had acted as a giant marshalling yard for a happy heritage of steam engines – a strong first impression is that the folk from the Science Museum, who control Locomotion, still really want to affirm Shildon's place on the map. The old town will still have ample opportunity to inhale a whiff of steam in the summer of 2025. We chat in the museum's café – Café No 1 - seats and tables second hand from Eurostar, champagne and *croque monsieur* replaced by Brooke Bond and bacon butties.

"We've exhibits of world importance here, like the Rocket and the Advanced Passenger Train" says Andrew. "They're not in London, they're not in York they're in Shildon. Hackworth and the S&DR were in Shildon not Stockton or Darlington. Shildon was the birthplace, the world's first railway town, there's no doubt about it. There's a feeling that this is a community asset as well as a national and international museum."

What of the claim, historically long held but recently questioned, that that happy shunting ground – 27 miles of track, had it been laid out end-to-end - really was the world's biggest? Andrew says it's hard to be sure. "Maybe Chicago became bigger by about 1927 but Chicago was a huge city not a small town. Shildon was certainly in the world's top five."

Anthony Coulls had noted that in its first year the museum hoped to attract 60,000 visitors and in fact drew 210,000. Attendance peaked when, uniquely, six A4 Pacific locomotives – blue streaks once more – were gathered together in 2014, dipped inevitably during the Covid crisis, is likely stratospherically to soar again in 2025. The aim's an annual 200,000 visitors.

Though the website also talks of "embedding the museum at the heart of the community", and of creating new jobs, how might its own success radiate to and cheer the rest of the town, particularly the centre, barely a mile but sometimes a world away and still in evident need of resuscitation? "We try very hard to promote it" says Andrew. "We have strong links with the Railway Institute and with the schools and want to push it in any way we can. Unfortunately, we don't have a Jonathan Ruffer in Shildon."

Jonathan Ruffer, born at Stokesley in North Yorkshire, is the philanthropist who seeks through huge and culturally inspired investment to transform the fortunes of Bishop Auckland. Everyone would like a Jonathan Ruffer – though as things will turn out, there are those in Shildon not at all pleased with the gentleman.

Might it be possible to have regular steam services on the line from Darlington, at least during the summer of 2025? Andrew's uncharacteristically cautious, like the brakeman on the Percy Main snowplough. "Lots of people are looking at what's possible" he says. "Our legacy will be that everything is better – better exhibits, better presentation, better interpretation. This is our moment to get it right and whatever happens, there'll be plenty going on at Shildon."

Even if it still snowed, which it hasn't since about 1963 when milk came frozen home in pail, it would no longer be possible to sledge down Elephant's Trunk. No caws for alarm, Crows Wood's gone a bit quiet, too, and as for the dodgy, dingy skipper….

The area around Elephant's Trunk is now a Persimmon Homes development called Middridge Vale, rooflines making the most of the elevation in an attractively higgledy-piggledy sort of way and with road names like Wordsell Way, Sturrock Court, Ivatt Walk and (of course) Gresley Drive. Peppercorn Close, as potential residents may or may not be aware, has nothing to do with cheap rent but is a salute to Arthur Peppercorn, the last chief mechanical engineer of the old London and North Eastern Railway.

All were railway engineers, most previously honoured in the names of Class A1 steam engines. Archibald Sturrock was 60118, H A Ivatt 60123, Wilson Worsdell 60127. Sir Nigel Gresley was 60007, as any son of Shildon could have averred.

Elusive: the dingy skipper

Brilliantly and beautifully blue, 60007 steams yet. What, though, of Sterling Way? Could this be Sir Patrick Stirling (60119)? A nineteenth century Scot, he became superintendent of the Great Northern Railway and is now remembered by Persimmon Homes in a spelling mistake.

The company researcher might also care to note that Shildon wasn't the home of the No 1 Locomotive, as nonsensically they claim, but – as with some hindsight it became – of Locomotion No 1.

Slightly surprisingly promoted alongside an image of Durham Cathedral, the development is said on the Persimmon website to be sold out. An estate agency offers a smart looking four bedroom detached for £209,950, which seems pretty good value. In November 2024 Rightmove was describing Shildon as "charming" and properties, perhaps inevitably, as "stunning". That some of them "nestled" may these days go without saying.

A detached house in Clarendon Court, five bedrooms and four bath or shower rooms, was available for £340,000, On Wordsell Way a house with five bedrooms and three bath or shower rooms was £265,000 and on Ivatt Walk a "town house" with three bedrooms and as many bath or shower rooms was £140,000. Half of Byerley Road seemed to be for sale, too, and for very much less, pretty much everything a "unique" or "fantastic" opportunity.

As might have been said of Elephant's Trunk, downhill all the way.

It's a few weeks after the Locomotion visit, a moisty March morning, when Sharon and I use Middridge Vale as the starting point for a dander down Memory Lane – my memories, anyway, she's what Yorkshire folk would call an oftcumden. Across the tracks, Matey still potters almost amicably about Locomotion. Much stirs.

There's now a surfaced path, popular with dog walkers, between Shildon and Newton Aycliffe. It's hoped that the entire S&D route may similarly be signalled by the time of the bi-centennial. Blithely ignoring the Water Rat's injunction to the Mole, and armed with nothing more than a two-and-a-half inches to the mile Ordnance Survey map with which to deflect blunderbusses and frustrate fairies, we leave the path, cross the Cattle Bridge and strike out for the Wide World.

Remember Ratty's warning to his new friend? "That's somewhere that doesn't matter, either to you or to me. I've never been there and I'm never going, nor you either if you've got any sense at all. Don't ever refer to it again, please."

The map's sufficiently big to accentuate the insignificant. There's "Tip (dis)" and "pit (dis)", football grounds and cricket grounds, even a prominent direction to Busty Terrace, but there's no mention of Fairy Glen.

The day's as drear as most of the 180 which have preceded it, the dingy skipper doubtless able happily to merge into its melancholy surroundings. About half a mile above the railway line, Matey still making friends, there's a remarkable surprise, however. Land around Eden Grange has been transformed into a 12-acre development – "a little piece of paradise" says the website – for glamping, fishing and wedding parties for up to 150.

The glamping pods have names like Snowdrop, Honeypod and Bilynda Rose. Each has a private firepit and outdoor hot tub when not so long ago, many Shildon homes didn't even have a bath and a firepit needed a bleezer. There are posh teepees, known as tipis, and shepherd huts of the sort to which Lord Cameron of Chipping Norton is said to retreat at the bottom of his garden. Inevitably, absurdly and as with new homes on the Persimmon estate, the development "nestles". There's a restaurant called the Hidden Gem and there are four lakes. Not even Timothy Hackworth, a man of fervent imagination, might have conceived all this on his doorstep – and it'll be lovely if the sun ever shines.

The only problem's the approach from Dale Road, potholed like Blackburn, Lancashire – which, it may be remembered, had four thousand - and choked every few feet by litter of every description (and probably stuff which, happily, the myopic eye may not see.) No fault of the Eden Grange folk, it's hardly a bridal path – barely even a bridle path – this.

The plan's to head across the field paths to Middridge Grange and Middridge Grange Mill before joining the main road at Redworth. The fields being impossibly, impassably, muddy – talk about "What's a little wet to a Water Rat" - we head back to the car, drive to Redworth and walk from the opposite direction.

Middridge Grange, closer to Redworth than the village from which it takes its name, was the 17th century home of the Byerley family, after whom one of Shildon's main roads – the one on which Timothy Hackworth primary school stands – is named. Colonel Anthony Byerley (1620-67) was a Royalist who led 1,000 men during the Civil War, many of them – reputedly of indomitable spirit and nicknamed Byerley's Bulldogs – garrisoned at the Grange. A memorial plaque in Heighington parish church, a mile to the south, salutes him yet.

Robert, one of the colonel's sons, was a soldier and adventurer who owned Byerley Turk, a charger said to be the earliest of the three stallions from which the entire modern thoroughbred racing stock is descended. Racing folk will doubtless understand. Frank Lawson records that in 1821 the Grange had been home to 31 males and 27 females, mostly working on the land.

Down the bank, the old Mill is dazzling with daffs alongside a bright-babbling brook. Could this be Johnny Best's Beck, another part of childhood folklore but never really located? It's not on the OS map, either – and who, better or worse, was Johnny Best?

Times change. A little sign on the Grange gate merely announces "Border collie on patrol" and even the dog seems to be on its dinner break. A man wanders over as we lean on the gate, laments the weather, wonders if we're going much further and is told that, far from it, we're going to dry out in the pub. "Can I come with you?" he asks and would have been welcome. After that, as the Rat observed, it doesn't matter.

A few weeks later still, a sparkling springtime Sunday, we're back at Locomotion to try to walk the so-called Gem Trail, inaugurated in February 2024. It proves a cussed and cross-grained exercise, tarnished to say the least of it.

The aim, laudable enough, is to link the 1.5 miles between museum and town centre with nine art installations celebrating the role of women in the area's history "and their contribution to industry, the suffragette movement, science and nature". The first installation's in the museum itself, though none has much idea of its location or significance.

"You need to ask Beryl" they say. Beryl's out to lunch.

A leaflet offers little else of usefulness, save that the Gem Trail is a Discover Brightwater project and that, overall, the Brightwater initiative has attracted £3.3m in grants, chiefly from the National Lottery. A "landscape partnership" they call it, having doubtless first beaten their community chest. These are not just ordinary installations, these are "community" installations.

"Be part of something pretty amazing" it says.

"Pretty confusing" says Sharon.

"Brightwater", it should be explained, is a marketing name for the River Skerne which rises near Trimdon in east Durham, mooches around Sedgefield and places, flows (on a good day) through the centre of Darlington and meets the more turbulent Tees a couple of miles south at Hurworth Place, The river's name, adds a Brightwater website, comes from the Viking "skirr" meaning bright or sparkling, adding with commendable honesty that "skirr" could also mean rubbish tip but that they didn't think "Rubbishwater" had the same appeal.

That Brightwater is said to have "19 different project streams" may not necessarily be a tributary factor.

The website also introduces a buzz-word character called Bounce the Bee who announces that he lives in Shildon "which lies on a very special river called the Skerne" and that he needs help to find the hidden gems. Had Bounce cross-pollinated such manifest and misleading nonsense at Timothy Hackworth Junior Mixed and Infants he'd probably have felt the sting of Tom Coates's stick – the nearest the Skerne comes to Shildon is at Aycliffe Village, about five miles east. Finally underway, the Gem Trail then heads in the opposite direction.

Unless Johnny Best's Beck, a tadpole among waterways, is included, Shildon doesn't lie on any river at all, and certainly not the bright-eyed Skerne. Then things gets worse.

Though other Brightwater material talks of "an enchanting treasure trail and adventure guide", not only does the leaflet give no clue to the identity of the women thus being celebrated, it offers no hint that further information must be obtained by smart phone scanning *en route* QR codes, mounted on redundant railway sleepers. While a reluctance to use traditional display boards may be understandable – plentiful evidence of graffiti and grimmer – none of the installations offers any suggestion to the technologically untutored of what they're doing there in the first place or how further information might be obtained.

This is up-its-arse arts. Readers must excuse the vulgarity but it's an egregious exercise in exasperation. Thus many, not least the elderly, are at once denied enlightenment.

The leaflet also urges "Find nine letters on the sculptures to make a word" and thus underlines another problem. The first installation's inside the museum, closed on Mondays and Tuesdays. The ninth and last is in the town library, closed on Wednesdays and Sundays and open for just three hours on Saturday mornings. Rather resembling the logo on the side of a fridge – Frigidaire or something – a logo on the map identifies the site of each installation.

Though withholding any information about women in history, or guidance for those bewildered on QR Street, the on-line guide also several times states that those on the trail might see birds and dogs and that the critturs might (heaven forfend) be noisy. On yet more occasions it urges caution when crossing the road. It's not so much a trail guide, more a Tufty Club flyer.

The lady of this house is technologically adept – smart, you might almost suppose. She is unable to scan the first QR code. Truth to tell, she is unable to scan any of them. Though the sun's glorious, it's a walk in the dark.

The trail leads past the coal drops, now happily restored, and along Surtees Avenue – locally another of those Black Paths – and through Timothy Hackworth Park, stirring memories of former triumphs (and many more disasters). Near the bottom entrance to the Rec is an installation amid a grassy area, the QR code about three inches from the ground.

Another is said to be at the top of the Rec – near the former site of the world's most noisome netties, the area now rather more fragrant – though we are unable to find it. Nearby also is the eight-column drinking fountain, now dehydrated but a grade-II listed building, where in former times we'd truly be little squirts.

Immediately over the fence is Windrush, home in the 1950s of kindly GP Frank Hutchinson and of his very own Windrush generation. Susan was in our infants class, always in possession of a handkerchief, before seeking private education in Darlington. A bit further along Central Parade is the former Midland Bank, dated 1899 but contentiously closed like all Shildon's

Daddy of them all: Byerley Turk

banking establishments. These changing times it's home to a "flower designer and flower school."

Timothy Hackworth's grave, that also of his wife Jane and of his second son – another Timothy – lies in St John's churchyard, next door. In front of the graveyard, in the newish Town Square and pretty much on the site of the Co-op grocery department, stands a statue of Hackworth himself, apparently holding a model of Royal George. Mounted on a wall high out of reach, another "installation" – the eighth, presumably – may be of Jane, though the lady supposes it to bear likeness to Elizabeth Fry. Half the women of Victorian England bore a resemblance to Elizabeth Fry.

Further ferreting back home reveals that No 8 is indeed Jane Hackworth, and that two of the other installations honour the Aycliffe Angels – wartime munitions workers who, goodness knows, deserve recognition – and Dr Margaret Bradshaw, a celebrated Upper Teesdale botanist whose first book was published when she was 97. It's been like an ambulant game of Guess Who and it's we who hold the wooden spoon.

Spring sunshine notwithstanding, the old town's green and pleasantness notwithstanding, we're disenchanted with the enchanting and not a whit wiser than when we left. It's querulously that we head back through the churchyard, down another Black Path and back to Locomotion, so satanically grumpy that momentarily I read a sign for Hornby Dublo model trains as "Hornby Diablo". We are no more clued than when we started. It's the smoked ham sandwich in the museum canteen – "hand crafted", "lovingly prepared", "sustainable" – which really narks Sharon, however. It's been made in Croydon, the packaging adds.

How the hell can a Shildon sandwich be sustainable if it's been made in Surrey, she wonders (and won't even have travelled by train before being deposited, nestling, thereabouts.)

At 3pm, sun blazing, just five cars are scattered around the car park. Shildon, and Locomotion, deserves better, much better, than this.

E A D Bibby, the genial woodwork master at Bishop Auckland Grammar School, once awarded me eight out of 100 for a matchbox holder, that minor monument to second form craftsmanship. The eight, he wrote in the end-of-term report, was for spelling my name correctly on the back of the bit of wood.

In the £8m New Building at Locomotion, opened in May 2024, exhibits include something identified as a "platelayers' velocipede", which on the reasonable assumption that the railways had more than one platelayer represents impeccable use of the possessive apostrophe. Like Alf Bibby, it's good to accentuate the positive.

With the best will in the world, however – and none may harbour greater good will towards Shildon than I – much of the rest is disappointing.

We turn out during half term, a week after opening, the New Hall widely publicised and the overflow car park overflowing. How many visitors, not least children, might leave with the impression that the Railway Museum has missed the train?

Basically it's little more than a glorified storage shed – six parallel railway tracks, 46 exhibits, but in every sense linear, static not just because everything's inevitably stationary but because it's not emotionally moving, it fails to stir the soul.

The website talks of "celebrating the role of Shildon as the world's first railway town" but there's little of a coherent narrative, little that's joined up – where's a shunters' pole when one's needed? – little to suggest that this is much else than a very expensive sub-shed.

Where's the human interest, the real story of the life and death of the wagon works and their community, the timeline, the cinema, the attempt to engage the young and to embrace the old? Where the narrative and not the reading between the lines?

Alongside the slogan "Built in Shildon", painted prominently on the floor, stands a class 31 diesel which could hardly have been built in Shildon because Shildon hasn't – save for a magnificent exception to which we shall come - built locomotives since 1871. The little information panel recalls more memorably that class 31s were known as "goyles" – short for gargoyles – a nickname which "disparaged their awkward appearance."

A few little audio-visual points offer information snippets, some about the wagon works, but can only be accessed singly and only by perching on a little metal cracket (may a cracket be metal?) that's difficult for the infirm and impossible for the disabled.

Most of the exhibits are what broadly might be termed trucks – tankers, cattle wagons, superfreight containers, more hoppers than the three-legged race at Timothy Hackworth Junior Mixed and Infants annual sports day. The Percy Main snowplough has cleared a way from the main building, its towering size a further reminder of changing climate, as has that waste-not wagon from the City of Sheffield sewage disposal department. Painted on the side is the instruction that it must only operate between Ickles siding and Thrybergh, on what may or may not have been the scenic route.

A Phillips Petroleum wagon carries a Teesside telephone number, perhaps akin to one of those canine identity discs lest it become lost; a huge EWS coal hopper retains its graffiti, a nod to latter-day audacity and perhaps to authenticity, too.

There's also a diesel shunter, built in Darlington in 1953, which seems a bit perfidious save that Darlington probably had no say in the matter. The information panel adds, fascinatingly, that the last shunting horse wasn't retired until 1967.

Shildon's a strand not a thread, a thought but not a theme, a hint but by no means a history. One of the audio-visual clips talks of the development of better protective clothing at the Shops – "they gave us special jackets, very warm but at least they kept out the sparks" – a wooden coal truck was one of 17,000, colossal number, built there between 1902-23.

A passing paragraph notes vaguely that Shildon folk "did what they could" to address declining orders and ultimate closure, another – inarguably – that the Works formed a community proud of what they produced. What of the battle, what of the war? There could be so much more.

The main museum building is so vivid, so vital and so vibrant; the restored coal drops and neighbouring 19th century buildings have been so impressively restored under Science Museum curacy; the areas round about are a happy tribute to those with environmental vision. It's all that excellence which makes the New Building seem old hat, an £8m opportunity knocked.

It's in the Railway Museum café, immaculate exhibits illumining a grey autumn day towards the end of 2024, that I take coffee with Alan Ellwood, a Shildon historian of extraordinary

dedication and, happily, a master of technology. "Ten thousand images on that dongle" he says, waving something the approximate size of a boy scout pen knife. Alan flies drones, too. "Great for pictures, great for all kinds of things" he says. At Tin Tacks they were workaday wasps.

Alan had followed me onto an early morning milk round for Jim Percival, delivered groceries after school for Thompson's Red Stamp stores – top of Main Street – and on Saturday nights turned up at Rufus Pedelty's paper shop to help keep the town in the Pinks. He became training manager for the globally renowned Cleveland Bridge company in Darlington, once hosted Prince Philip on a factory visit. "He was supposed to stay in our section for 12 minutes and was there for 45. You hear all that blather about him – he was brilliant."

Though there's a marked facial resemblance, he's no direct relation to Eddy Ellwood, Blackhall Colliery lad, who was five times named Mr Universe and four times won the Britain's strongest man title. "Different side of the family" says Alan who until recently ran the Shildon Recall History Society, now itself in the past. "We only had four or five members and not much money at the end" he says. "It's a shame that history only seems to interest older people."

Once he had 22,000 Shildon-related black-and-white and colour images, including Chares I's death certificate – signed, among others, by Colonel Robert Lilburne, a Cromwell man and one of an eminent family with Shildon connections. "He was at the execution" says Alan.

We also fall to talking about a plane crash, May 31 1944, in which a Short Stirling 517 crashed onto East Thickley Farm – known locally as the Store Field – between Middridge and

Shildon, killing all seven RAF crew aboard. "It was a Saturday afternoon and the weather wasn't very good" says Alan, who's raised funds for a memorial, his local knowledge unsurpassed.

He'd himself contemplated a book, getting on 25 years ago, indicates with hands a yard apart the amount of information he'd gathered. That it's never been published is regrettable, but I remain hugely grateful for his help with the images in this one.

Chapter ten

The pits

Once a year, second or third Saturday in July and certainly throughout the 1950s, we'd be awoken about 6 30am by the sound of a colliery band (or bands) on the first leg of their journey to the Durham Miners' Gala, otherwise the Big Meeting and sometimes just Durham Day. Half asleep, ever innocent, we assumed the early start to be because it was an awfully long way to walk.

Shildon was a pit town, too, atop once-rich seams like the Busty and the Brockwell, the Harvey, the Hutton and the Low Main. Easy to forget. In the 1920s around 4,000 men worked at the town's pits, more than the Shops ever employed, though most of the mines were exhausted – they and the poor miners, very likely – by the end of the 1950s.

One book reckons that in the 19th century alone, 29 pits were sunk in the Shildon area, mostly hitching a lift on S&DR chaldron wagons in the years immediately after the railway's arrival. *Shildon Coal*, a 1995 booklet produced to raise funds for the local Salvation Army, explored 15, McCormick has eight Shildon pits upon nationalisation in 1947 with a similar number still in private ownership. Some had quaint names like Coppy Crooks – still used by some for an area north of West Auckland Road – or confusing names like West Durham Wallsend. Dabble Duck, later the site of the town's first industrial estate, was said so to be named because the workings were so wretchedly, woefully, web-foot wet.

Down by what became the Hippodrome corner and served by the Surtees Railway spur to the S&D main line less than a mile away – another Black Path to many – Shildon Lodge Colliery (1830-1926) was the town's biggest, known to many as Datton Pit and the level crossing over the Darlington-Bishop Auckland road as Datton Gates. Several histories insist upon the story, however apocryphal, that the name arose when a group of Irish miners were asked which pit they worked down.

One pointed towards the pit head. "Dat un" he said.

Though Brusselton colliery toiled until 1968, that was half a mile west of the town. Middridge drift, to the east, survived until 1970. As sites were cleared, the most visible evidence of a coal black past was the concessionary half loads dumped regularly outside dependants' homes in our cobbled back street, impassably impeding our regular football games.

Sticky wicket: miners play cricket at Adelaide Colliery

We had a coal house, too, next to the outside netty and to where me dad kept his bike – his Iron Horse, he called it, appropriately enough - but our coal came in sacks from Harold Walker, emptied through the little door in the wall and never once forcing play to be abandoned. The Aged Miners Homes, a few hundred yards away at the top of Eldon Bank, doubtless had many residents back then whose cv fitted exactly what it said on the rent book.

These days it's doubtful if any would qualify, though – to the tune of *Yellow submarine* – Shildon Football Club followers still sing "We all live at the top of Eldon Bank" in moments of particular euphoria. Goodness knows why.

Doubtless there were calamities, probably fatalities, at the wagon works. Little is recorded of them. Had they occurred above ground with anything like the regularity of death down below the unions would have had the Shops workers out on the streets – historically it didn't take much to upset them. The pits were damn dangerous places.

The Durham Mining Museum's wonderfully researched though ineluctably melancholy website carries not just pit-by-pit lists of those killed while digging for coal but, very often, gruesome details of the manner in which their last shift ended. However grim, almost all are preceded by a disclaimer that the list is by no means complete and with an exclamation mark to assuage the incredulous.

Only the occasions when five or more died in the same incident are officially classed "disasters". Lady Bracknell comes incorrigibly to mind: "To lose one parent may be regarded as a misfortune…."

At Shildon Lodge, where during World War I around 900 men and boys toiled to keep the home fires burning, "at least" 82 were killed in its 100-year history, around 20 of them teenagers. They included 12-year-old Edward Brice, a wailer – "boys employed to pick out any stones or pyrites which have escaped the attention of the screen man" – when caught between a truck and an embankment wall.

Another 12-year-old, identified only as W Hollandsworth, had been killed in 1867 when caught between two wagons; John Thompson was just eight when - four years earlier – he fell from a wagon when playing and was found "crushed and quite dead.".

Dabble Duck, formally Shildon Colliery, lost at least 19 men and boys during its 40-year paddle until 1924. Usually the tragedy made no more than a paragraph in the local papers. Mordantly, miserably, it wasn't really news any more.

Dabble Duck's deaths included that of 56-year-old Matthew Henderson, "severely" crushed in 1880 when kirving his jub and George Askew, killed in 1902 when he lost control of the engine and ran the kibble hard along the bottom. Others had spragged their jub. At least the linguists might have learned a lesson.

Adelaide Colliery, sunk by the Pease family and others in the 1830s, was worked for 95 years, had 139 coke ovens, up to 500 miners and at least 48 fatalities, the youngest also just 12. Deaths included pony boys, aged 12 and 13, killed together in 1874 when tubs "jumped off the way". One was found dead, it was recorded, the other groaned and died shortly afterwards. Brothers George and Thomas Pratt died at Adelaide in 1869 after a "two ton" stone fell on them. The deceased were taken

Datton: Shildon Lodge

killed by a fall of stone and a third killed by choke damp. Only Princes Street Drift, worked from 1938-58, may have escaped without death toll.

Might the miners who lost their lives even have been remembered here, but for that 6 30 wake-up call all those years ago?

The pit long submerged, the Dabble Duck industrial estate (as it became known) was formally opened in 1949 by Bishop Auckland MP Hugh Dalton. Three years earlier he'd officially opened Shildon's first prefabs, still warmly remembered among the post-war generation.

In 1952 the North Eastern Trading Estates brochure listed six factories on the estate, between them with 626 employees, though Astraka and Alfred Morris Furs may have been one and the same, much later prompting Chris Lloyd in *The Northern Echo* to dub Shildon the "fake fur capital of the world." Others were no less impressed – "the finest faux fur items the world has ever seen" says a website, "so much so that faux fur was synonymous with Astraka and Shildon became the epicentre for faux fur in the 1960s."

to Bishop Auckland workhouse, a move unlikely to have added much dignity to the sad occasion.

Sometimes the records seemed similarly unsympathetic. Patrick Joicey, a 17-year-old trapper killed by a fall of stone at Middridge Colliery, east of Shildon – one of 15 who died there – was said to have "left his door and went where he had no business to be".

Even at Coppy Crooks, never employing more than 50 men below ground, three died – one crushed by the cage, another

Even the *Catholic Herald* joined the praise: "These furry fashions, many of them so like the real thing, are mothproof, odourless and non-inflammable. The increasing use of such fabric will no doubt have far reaching effects, especially among the gin traps of far-off lands from which many of the most beautiful fur coats were gathered at the cost of a great deal of animal pain."

Chris Lloyd echoed the sentiment: "Alfred Morris clearly felt that synthetic Astraka made in Shildon was as good as real Astrakhan from Iran – and nowhere near as unkind."

**Coal Picking at Furnace Colliery (New Shildon)
During The General Strike Of 1926**

Pick and shovel: scavenging for coal during a strike at Furnace Pit

Originally known as Alfred Morris Furs, the company had been relocated to a hall in Eldon in 1944, initially employing just three people. They moved up the hill to Dabble Duck five years later and by the 1960s employed more than 400, mainly women, making "fake" furs, clothing everyone from the Bolshoi Ballet to the British women's ski team at the 1980 Winter Olympics in Lake Placid. In 1981 they diversified into beachwear.

In 1988, however, the company went into receivership with debts put at £73,000 – chiefly unpaid rates to the council. It was a pity: so far as simulants were concerned, Astraka had seemed the real deal.

P Fangenhal were described in 1952 as "fur dressers and dyers", Migal Ltd made shoulder pads, Northern Clothing did pretty much what it said on the label and then there was John Binns, on no account to be confused with the mighty department store

chain once familiar across the North-East.

John Binns operated the Orchard Silk Mill, even built houses – Orchard Way, off the nascent Jubilee Estate – for its key workers. Shildon was taking the smooth with the rough.

The six are long gone. A stroll along the factory road in November 2024 reveals much change, not least that it's so quiet. Who'd have thought that the estate once epicentre of the world's faux fur industry might now be home to the Classy Pawz dog grooming parlour or to Hibbotts Artisan Spirits or the Happy Barista Coffee Company? Mind, who'd have thought that the town that turned out tens of thousands of railway wagons would have had a silk mill, and a place that made shoulder pads, too?

Inevitably there are units to let, others which look abandoned. "Space available" says a hoarding, with images of telescopes pointing hopefully towards the heavens. The Siberian Stove Company – "veteran owned" says the fascia – is also among the more surprising enterprises. Not yet Siberian, but Shildon may be feeling the cold.

Fur and wide: Astraka workers show off their wares

Chapter eleven

Public affairs

We were Red Lion lads mostly, two or three nights a week and always after Evensong on Sunday, if only in a sporadically successful attempt to lead the curates astray. Extraordinary what a pickled egg can do to compromise canonical self-discipline.

Though he enjoyed the occasional glass himself, Hugh Corden – St John's vicar in the late 1960s and early 1970s – declined to set foot in any pub in Shildon, regarding it as what my old dad termed *infra dig* (though my dad used the phrase in a rather different context). Nor was my dear old dad much of a beer drinker, said of him that he might down the first in five seconds and make the second last six months.

Though the King Willie was closer to home – indeed, on the way home – probably we thought that was a bit infra dig, too, and unlike the Lion, they didn't sell pickled eggs.

How many licensed premises did the old town have getting on sixty years ago? Those two, the Cross Keys where the great Shildon Tunnel Banquet had so improbably been accompanied by Lord Prudhoe's band, the Fox and Hounds, the Three Tuns, the Dun Cow which now is the Royal George, the Surtees (later the Grey Horse), the Alma (until recently the Timothy Hackworth), the Queens Head and, very near the end of their shelf lives, the Bay Horse and the Foresters.

In what may be supposed New Shildon, the Greyhound and the Commercial occupied nook-and-cranny corners within staggering distance one of the other. Close enough to the wagon works to offer hope at the end of a long shift were the Masons Arms (where all of this began) and the Locomotive, while the Black Bull became a youth club, and not the euphemistic sort which never really enquired how old its fresh faced customers might be. On the other side of the level crossing the Redworth Arms was kept for a while by former first division footballer Laurie Brown, the most engaging of men, in the days when that's what former top footballers did after hanging up their ten bob boots. Shildon born and raised, Laurie joined Arsenal around 1960 after working as a joiner at Doggarts in Bishop Auckland. "Even the baths at Highbury had marble floors with heating underneath" he once recalled. "In Shildon we didn't even have a bathroom"

Additionally there was Old Shildon Workmen's Club, (New) Shildon Workmen's Club – self-styled Palladium of the North and with ties that boasted as much – Elm Road Workmen's Club, Jubilee Fields Workmen's Club, the social club on the former British Railways sports field and the Railway Institute, set up in 1833 for the purpose of moral and intellectual improvement and not, most definitely not, for a couple of pints and a game of housey. Hackworth was the first president.

What, indeed, would the fastidious founder have made of an Institute event in 2024 when entrants were invited to consume as many jaffa cakes as possible in two minutes, during which time they were allowed sips of water. "We didn't want to make them ill" it was explained. It was won by a Ukrainian lady with 10, the nearest native challenger feebly two cakes short of a conquest.

In the early 20th century Shildon had both Liberal and Conservative clubs, the latter in Spensley Street just off Church Street – its days may long have been numbered – and for a few years in the early 70s welcomed the GR night club, initially opened in the old Snowplough Hall at the bottom of Main Street by unrepentant former safebreaker George Reynolds, earlier introduced.

One midweek night in 1972 he'd booked for £10 a duo called Peters and Lee, little known at the time of the contract but at No 1 in the hit parade – a song called *Welcome home* – by the time that their elderly Thames van pulled up, good as their word, outside the GR. Familiar in leather trilby, bought to cover his comb-over, George waited anxiously outside and was at once asked if – since they really were top of the pops – his guests might have a little something to top up their tenner.

George pulled the agreement from his jacket pocket, asked them to read the details. £10, they said. "Then that's what you're getting" said George, on the night that the nation's No 1 played Shildon and lost.

Now long demolished, New Shildon WMC attracted numerous star names, few more famous than the American singer Del Shannon, who'd had several UK number ones in the 1960s. The event swiftly sold out, club chairman Jack Stabler seated by the door to turn away the ticketless - which included Shannon himself. The singer protested his identity – "they all say that" said Jack, so adamantly that Del boy forlornly headed back down the stairs, where he was met by club secretary Peter Murphy whose knowledge of the pop music scene was perhaps a little greater than the chairman's – and thus the show went on. The occasion's immortalised in the Del Shannon museum in Coopersville, Michigan, the town of his birth, if not necessarily in Shildon.

Perhaps it might at that point be interwoven that we were children of an incorrigibly superstitious mother, crossing on the stairs a portent of certain doom. As for walking under a ladder or throwing leaves onto the household fire….

How many licensed premises survive in 2025? The Fox, the King Willie, the Queens and the Red Lion have all reopened, not necessarily permanently, perhaps with optimists behind the bar and perhaps on a more permanent basis than in recent times, The Royal George still tries for a head of steam but the Timothy Hackworth's boarded, seemingly forever off the rails. The curtain has long since fallen on the Palladium of the North, as with Jubilee Fields club. Save for the Stute, only the Loco and the admirable George Samuel Brewery tap – opened in the former wagon works canteen, making ale with names like Coal Drops and Leaves on the Line – survive in what might be supposed New Shildon.

The Masons, built around the time that the first passenger train juddered off, had briefly been reborn in the 1980s as Spanners, a putative "fun pub" which for various reasons reimagined fun and not least because it had no seats. Subsequently, briefly, it became Paddy O'Shea's, ersatz Irish – or "Irish my Erse" as someone rather rudely supposed. Yet more improbably, it then re-opened as an African-themed restaurant – African plus deals on multiple burger and chips - called Cape to Cairo and without an alcohol licence. Its survival seemed uncertain.

Shildon lads have long liked a drink, as euphemists might have it, though Bernard McCormick's claim in *The Peases and the Stockton and Darlington Railway* that the town had "over 400" pubs may have been imagined when someone had had a drop too many. Robert Corkin's excellent little *Shildon: Cradle of the Railways* has hardly whet its whistle (as those early engine drivers might have supposed) before addressing the drunkenness and debauchery with which the nascent railway town was

Dethroned? The King William

visited.

The Grey Horse was run by Daniel Adamson, who – as we've said - also had the ticket office across the road and ran horse drawn trains along the Surtees Railway to join the S&D main line near what is now Shildon station. Adamson later found lasting fame as the man who surveyed the Manchester Ship Canal – but the Surtees was conversely notorious, says Corkin, and the crime rate soared. If his tales of murderous activity are true, it gave new meaning to the phrase about dying for a drink.

The town had grown quickly after railways and railwaymen arrived. Frank Lawson found an 1834 directory which listed five pubs in New Shildon: the Bay Horse, Black Bull, Globe – a curious establishment to which shortly and with some trepidation we shall return – the Letters and, of course, the Masons Arms. In Old Shildon the Dun Cow had joined the Grey Horse, though there was no mention of the King Willie, said to have been opened in 1831. Lawson supposes the list not to have been exhaustive.

As the number of incoming railwaymen swiftly increased, so (of course) did their thirst and so the number of pubs. By 1838 there were "24 or 25" pubs to assuage a population of around 3,000. Newcomers around that time included the Traveller, the Locomotive Engineer, the Grey Mare – subject in the 1960s of a rather irreligious song at St John's youth club, though nothing to do with steam engines.

George Turner Smith gently if mischievously supposes that the 19th century residents of central Co Durham – and particularly, he says, the population of New Shildon – "liked the occasional tipple". He then details a catalogue of drunkenness and devilry by engine drivers and their similarly sozzled firemen which suggests not that they enjoyed an occasional livener but that the men of the Stockton and Darlington Railway were permanently and paralytically pickled. "Beer fuelled belligerence" he finally concedes, "became a regular occurrence".

Nor were the railwaymen's drinking habits the only problem. In 1835 it was reported that "Wm Brown and Jno Greathead", engineman and fireman on the S&D, had brought a "woman of ill fame" from Stockton to Shildon about ten o'clock at night, entertaining her in one of the lineside cabins until the next day. Each was fined ten shillings – and charged half-a-crown for the young lady's fare.

Perhaps the S&D didn't help itself, almost from the outset running two pubs in Stockton – maybe one of them where that infamous lady led the locomotive crew off the rails? – with a further interest in the New Inn at Yarm. The Railway Tavern in Darlington, built for the S&D in 1826-27 and said by some to be the world's first railway pub, is now Grade II-listed and serves yet.

In 1856 a Mr Longstaff, secretary of New Shildon Mechanics' Institute – unlicensed, yet to be renamed the Railway Institute, still promoting moral and intellectual succour – wrote in his annual report that the year had been unparalleled for crime, including battles in the street. The Institute, conversely, tried valiantly for better things. In 1848, marking its 15th anniversary, they held nothing more intoxicating than a tea party, attractions including a display of stuffed breads and another of working model steam engines, so much tea and coffee consumed that they'd to fetch more water from a cistern in the wheel wedger's shed.

The Stockton and Darlington men also seemed particularly fond of fighting one another – and, alas, the poor parish policemen. "We confidently hope" Longstaff added "that Parliament will seriously take a review of secondary punishment and introduce measures for the greater security of life and property."

In *Timothy Hackworth and the Locomotive*, however, Robert Young regards the early workforce very differently. "These men were sober, industrious and independent. Many settled in their own houses and between them and their employer was a sincere respect and affection which remained throughout Hackworth's life."

It may be what these days is supposed a minority view, though the brochure published in 1950 to mark the centenary of the great engineer's death thought Hackworth to have been a "centre of attraction for drivers and firemen, all of whom earned extremely good wages." Itself a sober little publication, the brochure said nothing about the frying pan/fire business in The Globe.

Hackworth, devout Methodist that he was, may particularly have been aware of the problem because his little place of worship in Chapel Street adjoined the small-world Globe, one of the more notorious boozers. The Globe, as the Bible might have had it, seemed not always to have loved its neighbour. "The drinkers used to bang plates during services in the chapel next door" Corkin notes.

Several histories record, often with ill-disguised mirth, an incident at the Globe which for several years had also acted as an S&D clerks' office where the men were paid out - men, as George Turner Smith more credibly puts it, with a "long-standing and formidable reputation for insobriety" - and thus not so much led into temptation as given a satanic season ticket.

On this occasion a passer-by heard what he supposed to be a riot within, looked through the window and saw in progress a curious sort of gambling game centred upon whose pocket watch would keep going longest when dipped into a hot frying pan. "What percentage of the family income got beyond the walls of the Globe is questionable" adds Smith, dryly.

In the back room of the Red Lion, or on Sunday lunchtimes in the half-hidden little snug in the Fox and Hounds, gambling was never more serious than pontoon for a shilling a corner, or whatever the maximum stake allowed by HM government at the time. Shirley Simpson, the bookie's wife, was regarded as semi-professional.

Other authors talk of the "tough, aggressive nature" of the not-so-good folk of Victorian Shildon, of a bolshy workforce "not famous for tolerance or sobriety" and of a tendency to ugly scenes. "Battles with the police made dockland streets look like a playground" says Corkin, matters not helped that the new line to Stockton ran close to several pubs – not least at Simpasture, near what is now Newton Aycliffe – where drivers would simply leave their locomotives and nip in for a perhaps protracted quick one.

On one infamous and well-chronicled occasion, a horse drawn coal train set off independently, the driver fast asleep in the dandy cart behind.

"Engine drivers and firemen seemed to spend every penny they possessed on drink, then after a bellyful plan a full scale battle with the police or with anyone else who trod their path" says Corkin. "Not only did they enjoy a battle, but they seemed to be joyously happy with their stupidity."

All that seems to have changed. It's impossible to recall pitched battles in the back room of the Red Lion, not even over whose turn it was to buy the Friday evening whelks from the bloke in the filthy white jacket, and for that we and Durham Constabulary must truly be thankful.

The George Samuel Brewery began in the former wagon works canteen in 2019, ill-timed for Covid, The premises were said to have been "in a quite dilapidated state", the project "daunting". Old pictures blown up on the walls now show the Shops workers sitting down to their bait, most of them still wearing caps. They'd never have got away with it at home; nor may many have remembered to say grace before what they were about to receive.

The brewery was started by Andrew Ferriman and his wife Laura – who rather resembles the political editor of the Spectator magazine but upon reflection probably isn't - at the back of their rural pub near Northallerton in 2013, George and Samuel the middle names of their sons. Later they moved back to Spennymoor, their home town, brewing in the garage before the move to Shildon. "We wanted a place with character, not another standard industrial unit" says Andrew.

The taproom doubles as a canteen, popular at lunchtimes and with an excellent full English breakfast. There's also a monthly acoustic music night, so full on a Friday in August – Storm Lillian notwithstanding - that we've to squeeze in next to the fermenting tanks. There are worse places to be, of course. Entertainment's by a couple of elderly acoustics called Why Not – don't ask why – from the top end of Swaledale.

Cask ales like Drop Hammer, Terminus, Leaves on the Line and Harvey – named after a three-foot seam – are described as "hand crafted", a 21st century nonsense for which (see under "nestled") they may, just, be forgiven. Framed on the bar, a certificate announces that their chocolate honeycomb milk stout – another 21st century innovation, said to taste not unlike a liquid Crunchie – was not just voted best among 250 ales at the recent Liverpool beer festival but was the quickest that Merseyside drank dry.

The atmosphere's effervescent, the band exuberantly excellent. "Feel free to join in. All we ask is that you join in the same song that we're singing" says Roger Jones, wearing the same sort of pork pie hat as did Paul Simon when he started to go bald, though whether for the same reason is, of course, not revealed. They mightn't have gone down as well when the wagon works were still night shifting, of course – how were the poor lads supposed to get some shuteye?

They do songs by the Beatles, Rod Stewart, the Monkees. They sing *The Gambler*, which makes me misty eyed, sing the Geordie anthem *Fog on the Tyne* with the claim that in 1971 it was banned by the BBC for containing the term "wee-wee". A little surprisingly, this proves more or less to be true. Forever in blue jeans, improbably lissom, some even find space to dance.

It's a great evening, perhaps one of the most memorable occasions on licensed premises in Shildon since they chucked their pocket watches into the frying pan and wagered which might most greatly withstand the test of time.

Chapter twelve

Stute observations

It's Friday evening in the Railway (nee Mechanics) Institute, the world's first of its kind and, not far behind the Stockton and Darlington, fast approaching its bicentenary. On the bar are questionnaires seeking opinions on what they do well and what should be additional future priorities – promoting physical or mental wellbeing, perhaps, learning how to get to grips with technology, a safe space and activities for teenagers.

My suggestion that they sell pork pies may be supposed neither intellectual nor inspirational – not least because it would apply equally to Church of England services, mother and toddler groups and Weight Watchers classes as well.

The plan's to have a beer with recently appointed chairman Dave Reynolds, a man of infinite enthusiasm and endless ideas, an innovator who's also a town councillor, director of the Shildon Heritage Alliance, writer, historian, gardener, film maker, musician and finds time to hold down a full time job as well, all of it particularly commendable for a boy from Bishop Auckland, where his mother still lives "She keeps wondering about how I ended up in Shildon" he says.

Dave's suggested that first we have a game of draughts, dismissing protests that I've not played since rainy lunchtimes at Bishop Grammar. "Everyone claims that" he says and, however unlikely, it would by no means be a first for the Institute. Published earlier in 2024, entitled *An Insatiable First*, its wonderfully and comprehensively researched history (author D Reynolds) records that while the committee's annual report in 1860 "bemoaned the members' apathy towards intellectual improvement" they'd painted a draughts board atop a table in one of the smaller rooms – thereafter designated the draughts room – and bought both draughts and chess sets for that purpose.

Though an improbable event in 2024, unlikely to usurp dominoes (in the bar) or bingo (concert hall) – it seems prudent not to mention speed jaffa cake guzzling – in the late 19th century draughts was sweeping the board.

The Northern Echo of March 23 1888 reported a friendly match between six members of Shildon Liberal Club and six of the Mechanics Institute – the Liberals won, in those days they tended to – while the *North Star* of November 2 that year detailed a contest between the Institute and the Bishop Auckland Cocoa Palace Club, which the mechanics, perhaps huffed, also lost pretty comprehensively.

By the following Spring, however, they'd wiped the board (aforesaid) with Darlington North Road Institute in the semi-final of the North Yorkshire and South Durham Draughts Association Challenge Trophy but bowed to West Hartlepool Liberal Club in the final.

What's perhaps even less well known is that celebrity safebreaker George Reynolds – decidedly no relation to the Institute chairman – was himself a draughts aficionado, having been taught the game by a young cell mate while at Her Majesty's displeasure. After he became owner and chairman of Darlington FC, a room at the immodestly named George Reynolds Arena was furnished with four or five inlaid draughts tables.

"I always wondered why there were so many but then he made it clear" former club director Peter Ellis once explained.

Reborn: the Railway Institute

"George being George he wanted to take on everyone at once."

As comprehensive as Dave Reynolds's book may be, however it happily omits to mention the occasion – 1970s, probably – when for some perceived journalistic misdemeanour I was barred from the premises, eventually allowed back in but only through the side door and when the then chairman wasn't looking.

On the Friday evening in June 2024, alas, draughts are excluded. For one thing we also want to get Dave onto a brass band wave and for another so many others are anxious to sit down with the chair that there's a danger of missing the last bus back to Darlington, once the 11 o'clock but these days homeward before nine. It's hoped that there'll be another chance to catch up with Mr Reynolds, but in the meantime, back to his book.

So why, it asks right from the start, write a history when the place is 190-odd years old and not wait for its own bicentenary in 2033. Dave answers his own question: "There is a very real possibility that the organisation might not survive to reach its bicentenary. Unless there is a greater understanding and appreciation of why our ancient institute is important, it may soon be gone for ever."

A Save our Stute campaign, the initials appropriate, had been launched in 2019, the building described as venerable but vulnerable. Three years later a structural survey concluded that following what Dave supposed "decades of neglect" £2.27m would be needed to make it physically sound again.

From its formation in 1833, the emphasis had been on members' intellectual improvement, though somewhat ironic that the inaugural meeting should have been in the cellar of the Globe Inn, scene of that infamous wager to see whose pocket watch might tick longest in a pan of frying fat. Whether bingo may be supposed intellectually improving should remain a debate for a different time and place.

By 1851 the reading room at the Masons Arms, where first the Institute met, was becoming cramped. The committee's end-of-year report expressed the hope that with better facilities for improvement – the Victorians were very fond of that word – "the moral, social and intellectual enjoyments of the members of the Institute, and the inhabitants of the village, may be promoted."

Since bingo probably wasn't much played in Shildon at the time – though reckoned to have been invented by the eyes-down Italians in 1530 – admonitory attention turned instead to playing cards, lest gambling be encouraged. Some still hadn't forgotten that business with the pocket watches. Card games were eventually allowed between limited hours, in small rooms between what in other circumstances might be termed consenting adults in private.

"Naturally a number of members flouted this rule" says *An*

insatiable thirst. "The committee are reported to have dealt firmly with anyone brought to their attention."

Really? You wouldn't want to bet on it.

Though early Institute officials were awfully fond of their tea parties – an event in December 1848, Timothy Hackworth in the chair, was set for 650 but 850 crowded in – the intoxicating allure of the demon drink seemed never far away. After the opening of the Station Street premises in 1860 – the New Shildon Saxhorn Band prominently in attendance – it was reported that five shillings had been spent on bread, twenty shillings on cheese and twelve on ale. "At the subsequent committee meeting" the history records, "the wisdom and moral basis for the provision of alcoholic drinks was retrospectively brought into question."

The Masons Arms had become unsatisfactory, overcrowded and with overflow activities held elsewhere. Station Street, 200 yards away, seemed for the better in every sense bar one. Though a billiards table was permitted, there was also a reading room, a Library for the Promotion of Useful Knowledge and lectures with titles like Hogarth's pictures, Sanitary science and the water cure and – honest - Icebergs and glaciers in south-west Durham. A little learning, tip of the iceberg, was clearly deemed to do no harm at all.

Every picture, the Institute was also building up a portrait gallery, many of founders and railway pioneers – "a source of inspiration, and perhaps expectation, for the promising young men of the area."

Too soon, however, the Station Street premises began to prove as socially and structurally unsatisfactory as had the Masons

Arms. Though the building was in a bad way by the turn of the century, though the North Eastern Railway had provided new premises for its other principal institutes at Gateshead, Darlington and York, the company seemed reluctant to help the Shildon lads, leaving them to fear – by no means for the first time – that they'd missed the train.

A disruptive industrial relations record may also have had something to do with the delay, perhaps explaining why the stone over the door reads 1911 but the premises weren't officially opened, by Albert Pease, until February 8 1913. The Station Street building was converted, however improbably, into one of many Essoldo cinemas across the North-East and one of four picture houses in Shildon.

Pease, one of that Darlington family of railway and social pioneers, offered the opening hope that the handsome new building would be a very great blessing to the town and so, though recent times have been more difficult, it proved.

The main hall could hold 486 people, the library had 4,500 books, there was a reading room, a magazine room which doubled as a ladies' reading room – *Woman's Own*, perhaps, certainly the *Women's Suffragette Journal* - a games room, billiards room with four tables and a bathing room with three slipper baths. Everywhere were portraits, paintings and relics of a community founded on steam.

In the 1960s, however, much of the book and painting collection was disposed of, to Dave Reynolds's considerable disappointment. "Had it been retained, or even placed out of the way in storage, it might have been a very valuable collection both monetarily and culturally." He himself offers mitigation. "The Institute had been founded and governed for many decades

by men who wanted 'good things' for the working people of Shildon – a sense of improved prospects and certainly a more responsible and educated workforce.

"The situation had now evolved to a point where members wanted a committee that would steer things in directions they preferred."

In March 2023 a new library – the MacNay Room, named after Thomas MacNay, the institute's first secretary – was opened on the first floor, largely focusing on books that were railway related or had links with Shildon and its surrounding area. Many had come from the Friends of the North Road Museum in Darlington. None was a bingo book.

Dave Reynolds writes of a "cultural treasure" and of "one of the most significant industrial cultural buildings in Britain, if not the world" but one which in 2020 was losing £1,000 a month. In June 2023 a secret ballot of members agreed by 200 votes to two that the Institute should be come a Community Benefit Society – "not in itself a magic wand" he said at the time, "but at least a ticket to meet the Fairy Godmother." In partnership with the Heritage Alliance, it was registered on January 3 2024, a ten-year plan devised for the Institute's revival.

It's November 2024, four months since last we sat down at the Stute for a semi-formal chat, and much has been happening. The Institute has formally become that Community Benefit Society, has formed TeamStute - - a bid to harness multiple talents, with not so much as a pint token by way of perquisite – and talks of creating "a refreshed legacy for the future."

Dave's meetings have included one with Fiona Hill, the miner's daughter from Bishop Auckland, who became a top defence adviser to the US government and is now Chancellor of Durham University. Though that £2.27m repairs bill remains daunting, he looks to the wondrous rebirth of Redhills, the former miners' union headquarters in Durham, and of what is now the Witham arts centre in Barnard Castle.

They're also much focused on the Stockton and Darlington bicentenary, 2025 events ranging from a tea dance on May 10 – "Timothy Hackworth himself presided over the earliest" – to a three-day exhibition called Blood, Bone and Muscle from June 26-28.

"Shildon didn't have the money or the influence to feature in the name of the Stockton and Darlington Railway but it was in exactly the right place to become the industrial operating powerhouse" says the prospectus. There'll be talks, films, a sports and games festival and on September 27 2025, 200 years to the day since Locomotion began the journey that changed the world, a Bruce Springsteen tribute act.

It has to be said that the significance, the symbolic link between the singer they call The Boss and the world's first public passenger railway is not immediately obvious, but these guys know what they're about. Springsteen is himself touring Europe in 2025, tickets starting at around £200. The Stute is likely to be a few bob cheaper.

Dave's still worried, fears that Shildon may be sidelined by bigger brethren, had the previous evening chaired a public meeting at which Shildon Town Council's relatively tiny budget was compared to that of the boroughs of Stockton and Darlington and of Durham County Council. All seek a cut of the bicentenary cake; some worry about crumbs.

Both Stockton and Darlington will have processions, if not quite a cavalcade. Though Locomotion will be a centre of attractions throughout the celebrations, though there's talk of a picnic in the park – what was that about crumbs? – Dave and colleagues propose a Shildon-centred procession of their own, dubbed a Little Street Cavalcade. Why don't they do something for themselves, they asked in a community poll.

Ninety seven per cent of those who responded to the questionnaire were in favour of a Shildon "fringe" event, a carnival procession that will now take place on Saturday August 2 – the same day, deliberately, as a big town council event in the park. "We feel that the main celebration missed an opportunity to showcase Shildon people" they say.

"Look at the history books" says Dave. "Shildon was pretty much overlooked for the golden jubilee in 1875 and again for the centenary in 1925. We were only at the centre of things in 1975 because the wagon works marshalling yard was the only place where the great cavalcade could be formed."

In January 2025, the start of the bicentenary year, LNER named a main line express train Darlington. Not even a little diesel multiple unit, pottering up and down the branch, carried the name of Shildon.

So how did a Bishop boy become so enthusiastic – so passionate – about Shildon? "*Cherchez la femme*" he says simply, or would have done had we been in Cherbourg, not Shildon. "She wanted to move here but we split up on the very day that we signed the contract on a house. I stayed, started running and walking around the town and realised that Shildon and its surroundings were beautiful, so much to admire. That's how it all started."

The Institute will return to its early Victorian roots, he hopes, not just a social centre but a base for learning and literacy. Goodness knows it's big enough. "We started out as a library for working people. We want to try to be something like that today, not just for our current membership but to give the town's younger people more cohesion and confidence, to give them more opportunities in life and to attract professional people to the town.

"Shildon also has more single elderly people, elderly and lonely, than the national average. They feel isolated, alone; we need to address that, too."

Much else may be happening, much changing for the better, but at the time that *All change* followed *An insatiable thirst* to the printer, there still weren't any pork pies.

Chapter thirteen

Shops talk

If England were a nation of shopkeepers, as old Boney is supposed to have observed, then probably he was thinking of Shildon – a town of perhaps 15,000 people said in 1921 to have 157 shops.

In post-war Shildon when we were growing up there were more shops than corners, more butchers than Smithfield Market, enough fish shops seriously to question the adage that there could be plenty more fish in the sea. It might incidentally be added that the 1921 census included a "female fisherman", though where and how widely the lady cast her net is, sadly, not recorded.

The housewives of Shildon talked not of going to the shops, incidentally, but of going up the street – presumably lest anyone think they be doing a guvvy job at the wagon works – and seemed always to up the street wearing a headscarf. It also explains why, in at attempt to avoid similar confusion and as explained in the foreword, the book has tried throughout to capitalise Shildon Shops but to leave the wagon works in lowly lower case.

One of Frank Lawson's invaluable tomes records that in 1938-39 – around the time that mains electricity came to most of the town – there were 14 grocers, 12 butchers, nine boot and shoe repairers and nine stationers, eight confectioners, eight builders, seven drapers, six hairdressers, five milliners, four painters and decorators, four fruiterers, four cycle dealers and three motor engineers.

There were two chemists, dairies, tailors, tobacconists – among other things – plus a fishmonger, a wallpaper dealer, a printer, a ladies' outfitter and (apparently) just one baker when there might have thought, unlucky for some. to have been a dozen. There's no mention of candlestick makers nor, more surprisingly, of newsagents though that's something we may read about very shortly.

Probably Frank Lawson was pretty much on the money. A brochure produced by the Urban District Council in 1937 to mark the Coronation of King George VI and Queen Elizabeth carried ads for 13 butchers, nine grocers and general dealers, six hairdressers and barbers, five fruit shops ,half a dozen outfitters and, wheels within wheels, several cycle dealers. Many others may have found other uses for their Coronation coppers.

None of the listed telephone numbers reached beyond double digits. The post office was Shildon 1, the police station Shildon 6. Lucky for some, John Adamson the funeral director was Shildon 21.

Fred Moody & Son ("house furnishers") offered "the largest display of modern furnishing in the district", Hackett & Baines' department store promised men's flannel trousers from 2/11d, worsted from 5/11d. A three-piece bedroom suite – "fully guaranteed" – cost £5 12s 6d while a pair of ladies' summer shoes might be had from 2/11d.

Bishop Auckland Co-op – "pioneers of the Co-operative movement in Durham County" – boasted 19,504 members and a share capital of £568,292. Not only were there branches in Shildon and New Shildon but everywhere from Butterknowle to Byers Green, Cockfield to Coundon and Fishburn to Ferryhill Station.

Other advertisers ranged from the Picture House ("pleasant Sunday evenings") to South Shildon Colliery ("best household coal delivered in bags and put into your coalhouse"). Shildon Male Voice Choir – "of BBC fame" – had advertised and so, twice, did the First Shildon Boy Scouts Troop, once to encourage hiring the scouts' hall – venue 13 years later of the exhibition to mark the centenary of Timothy Hackworth's death – and on the second occasion to promote their gymnastic displays.

Of the 102 commercial advertisers, only Hackett and Baines – founded on Main Street in 1898 and still headed by Philip Tarry, the founder's grandson - remains in business in the town, now specialising in furniture and in clothes for large men and still, happily, thriving. There never was a Hackett mind, or for that matter a Baines, either. "I think my grandfather just liked the names" says Philip, insistent that the secret of longevity's success is unchanging. "Service, absolute service."

Elsewhere on Coronation day, May 12 1937, the LNER and Wesleyan brass bands accompanied a procession from All Saints to every corner of the festive town and a further torchlight procession culminated at 10pm with a Recreation Ground bonfire and community singing with bands and choirs. An estimated 3,000 children received gifts, a small beaker for the under fives, large beaker and "tea" for those between five and 15. Shildon did their Majesties proud.

The "souvenir programme" – price sixpence – for Queen Elizabeth II's coronation in June 1953 had just 32 advertisements, including good old Hackett and Baines with premises in both Main Street and Redworth Road. Most of the shops were also taking part in the council's "Spot the deliberate mistake" competition for which the entry fee was 3d.

George Gittins, pharmacist in Main Street, recommended Enerjoids for those feeling run down; Allison's, a few doors away, offered a "royal display" of Coronation souvenirs. The Economic Tea Stores were next to the King Willie on Cheapside, the Bon Bon Café was doing luncheon and afternoon tea, J Crooks & Sons in Alma Road advertised Kodak Brownie 127 cameras for £1 6s 6d ("including tax") while Coxon's in Church Street was getting quite excited about "the new cami-top Trousseau slip", and for only 17/11d, about 90p today.

The Burnie (Gardens) Residents' Association advertised twice-weekly beetle drives in the Temperance Hall and in the Assembly Hall in Main Street – probably not the same as a cattle drive – and dances in the Club Hall. "A Burnie presentation is a guarantee of your entertainment" claimed E S Randall, the secretary, the same Ernie Randall who became an outstanding secretary of Old Shildon Workmen's Club.

Several businesses on the Dabble Duck industrial estate, still just two or three digits in their telephone numbers, had taken advertising space. Northern Clothing offered raincoats in "London shrunk" gaberdine and overcoats in Crombie and in Harris Tweed; John Binns – based at the Orchard Silk Mill – were said to be "weavers of repute for more than a century" while Astraka took two pages to proclaim that Shildon wasn't just the birthplace of the railways but of Furleen, "the first nylon simulation in the world to be commercially produced."

Back on the shop front, Lawson in 1958 listed 11 stationers, nine butchers, eight boot and shoe repairers and seven fruiterers. Even in 1975 the council-produced town guide was able to claim that "the (Church Street) shopping centre is extensive and bright with modern shopfronts."

Alma Road, New Shildon 1934
People Pose For The Camera On This Busy Street

Alma mater: Alma Road in 1934

No longer. Probably no different from much of the rest of the country, Shildon has put up the shutters. Church Street morphing into Memory Lane, I take a wistful tour.

It's early evening and ghosts, great grocered garrisons of them, walk this darkening street. Some still wear long white aprons, others butchers' bloodied stripes; some of the ladies have grey hair tied in tight little buns, some of the men look forward to Wednesday, because Wednesday has shades of half-day closing and they might get a kickabout in the Rec.

On the wings of time comes the aroma of Hay's wondrous plate pies, 1/6d to feed three or four, the all-pervading smell of yeast from Walter Willson's, the pong – there can be no other word – from Margot's, the ladies' hairdresser near the King Willie. There are seven butchers and three or four bakers, several clothes shops – "fashion" shops, indeed - fruit and veg shops, a pet shop that sells ants eggs to feed the goldfish, a radio and television shop with a line in Tri-ang train sets, a Caxton-esque printer – John A Stoker, it says over the door - a furniture store called Woodhouses which doubtless coincidentally is housed in wooden premises and thus more spectacularly and more readily burns to the ground, circa 1960.

At one apparitional end is Jack Whitfield's little corner shop, where even then Wagon Wheels seemed annually to diminish and next to that a little shop simply identified as Jacques – was it Bill Jacques? – a sumptuous nick-nackery where nothing may have cost more than sixpence and two-thirds of the week's receipts may be in elastic for making stocking garters – what else? - and thread for cottoning on.

At the other end is the Shildon branch of the Bishop Auckland and District Co-operative Society, a multi-departmental emporium where Stanley Matthews football boots promise great things for 19/11 but have never made me into a wizard of dribble or in truth of anything else. The overhead change machines whizz and whistle miraculously on a journey through time, the store horse clops querulously and incontinently about its business. Upstairs, Mr Sunter – typecast for Grace Brothers, himself as smart as a carrot - might even measure you for a suit.

Twice a year a big notice, "Dividend declared" – usually about two shillings in the pound – appears in the windows, prompting the closest that Shildon might see to a gold rush save for the first day of factory fortnight. These days the Co-op has a food store at All Saints, dividends different.

It's possible on this ghost walk also to recall Fred Elwell, who in the 50s and 60s sells electrical goods and model railways and who lives opposite us. The Elwells' son Paul, a contemporary, has as a consequence the sort of electric model railway about which we can only dream and which in any case we'd never have been able to get out of the station (or possibly even out of the box). We never were very technically minded, me and Dave, probably best to have stuck to going like clockwork.

Paul became locally famous, got on Tyne Tees Telly around 1963 for leading the protest against plans to turn the Hippodrome, last of Shildon's four cinemas, into an unlucky-for-some bingo hall. Deliberately similar to those waved by the Campaign for Nuclear Disarmament around the same time, placards demanded "Ban the bingo". Like our Tri-ang train set, that didn't work either.

Before the war there'd also been a branch of Doggarts, the Bishop Auckland-based department store chain remembered for its little green vans and for its clubs, legendarily sold on whenever the train fare was needed to watch a Co Durham club - though never Shildon – at Wembley. The premises became the National Insurance office, which probably didn't accept Doggarts' chitties, and later Peter Hankey's furniture store.

Perhaps chiefly, however, we Shildon kids of the post-war years are most fascinated by Walter Willson's, billed as the Smiling Service Grocer, because signage outside indicates that this was the company's first branch. Walter's – everyone seems on first name terms – was founded in Bishop Auckland in 1875 by the elegantly named Walter de Lancey Willson, whose father had been the workhouse governor in Bishops Stortford and who by the time of the 1881 census could record several shops and a staff of 65 men, 14 boys and five household servants.

Soon there were almost 200 shops across the North-East, more branches than Hamsterley Forest, old Walter had a country estate in what is now Cumbria and in 1905 sold out to Stephen Aitchison, his son-in-law, who subsequently was knighted. Walter was 61 when he died in 1907, his estate put at £200,000. Whatever that's worth in 21st century terms, it's an awful lot of yeast.

In the days when they called it "going up the street", the street would likely be thronged. Though Church Street began barely 100 yards from our front door, however, there were shops yet closer than that. Across the back alley, guarded at the rear by a rather excitable dog called Rex, was a little shop called Cook's which sold sweets in quarter pound measures, sticks in wire-wrapped bundles and apparently little else. Next to Percy Allan the bookie's, Bertha Kitching's little front room shop also sold sweets and barley sugar sticks while, 100 yards in a different direction and somehow yet smaller, Davison's majored on

lemon drops and Lowcock's lemonade.

Cook's was in the Market Place, yet closer to home, though none could recall the street being used for that ancient trading purpose. A couple of doors up was a little gent's barber's called Hunter's, where young John Hunter had worked as his father's lather boy before gloriously getting ahead. An advert in a 1948 Shildon FC programme (No 843, price 2d) found him in Main Street – "specialist in Eugene permanent waving". Other advertisers included Shildon Garage ("taxis for all occasions, cycles stored"), a fruiterer called Morris in Church Street whose civility was said to be guaranteed and dear old Charlie Raine, painter and decorator, for whom many years later optical surgery was to prove so great a boon.

Subsequently styling himself "John Hunter of the North", John – a delightful man with a goatee beard and a mischievous twinkle – opened several further hairdressing salons, journeyed into travel agency, owned several racehorses, earned a reputation as a raconteur, cropped up periodically on Tyne Tees Television and became vice-chairman of Darlington FC.

Though he and his wife Mary lived in Darlington they also had a villa in Majorca, where once the local paper came to interview them. "It's lovely here" John told the *Majorca Mirror* (or whatever), "but it's not as nice as Shildon."

How greatly things have changed. It's early evening in February 2024 and the Church Street shops not permanently shut are shushed and shuttered. There are two butchers but no bakers, no clothes shops, no proper furniture shops, no banks and definitely nowhere where bicycles might be peddled. Even the Costa monger has gone cold, the premises adding to the abandoned. At 5 30pm, however, 11 multi-national takeaways are warming up for the evening – few have customers – and seven hairdressers continue to cut it. All have occupied chairs, some have two or more staff in action. There are also three nail bars – "Thai", "Oriental" and simply "Shildon Nails." How many times, it's possible to wonder, have the lads gone in to ask for a dozen six-inch and half-a-dozen four.

Inkcantation, offering "handcrafted electric and pneumatic tattooing", is steel shuttered, too. Something intriguingly called a café and "Spanish cleaners" appears to have closed down - *Private Eye* magazine's use of the phrase "Spanish practices" saunters insidiously to mind and is swiftly, judiciously, sent upon its way. The penny-in-the-slot arcade's long closed, too, by that token allowing fly posting in the window to promote the forthcoming American wrestling at the Civic Hall.

On the only occasion that I saw wrestling at the Civic Hall, the MC had to intervene half way through a round to beg the local kids not to chuck chips into the ring. "The wrestlers might slip and get hurt" he said, apparently oblivious to the irony. This may not wholly be relevant, no more than the fact that I once saw the Irish singer Dana, a Eurovision Song Contest winner, at the Civic Hall. No one threw chips at her.

Shildon Alive, the much lauded community initiative saluted earlier and said to be outgrowing its former shop premises, offers support, food and companionship to those in need. Shildon Foundations, allied to Sunderland FC, offers social support from the building that once was Elliott's bakery. The estate agency suggests evidence for the repeated and widely publicised finding that Shildon is the cheapest place in the land in which to live but tells only part of the story.

In the window there's a property on Jubilee Road for £69,950

– "ideal investment opportunity" – and in Scott Street and Cheapside, appropriately named, are houses for £49.950. "Must be viewed" it says. Even the hospice charity shop immediately across the street has its price. £45,000. So much for charity beginning at home.

Next day on the Rightmove, website, however, there's a three bedroom house in Redworth Road for just £5,000 – possibly overpriced - another at the bottom of Main Street with the same guide price and several others offering change from £20,000.

Though not in Church Street, there are nearby chip shops called Karen's Plaice, Sarah's Plaice and Main Plaice. While all should know their plaice, it suggests a certain lack of originality. Almost empty, a No 1 bus heads back towards Darlington but passes unchecked. There are more fish to fry yet.

Three fish and chip shops fried most every night within 200 yards of 30 Albert Street. Mrs Gerard's was at the top of the street, priced for feeding the birds – you know, twopence a bag – Mrs White's at the allotment end of Foundry Street and John Beddingfield's in chirpy-chippy Cheapside. There'd be fights over scraps.

There were at least six others, including a shop in Adelaide Street run by Albert Finn who held high office in the National Association of Fish Fryers – perhaps not abbreviated to NAFF – and who, with the imagination later familiar in a town of plaice names, answered universally to Fishy Finn.

Robinson's fish and chip shop was on the corner of Byerley Road and Diamond Street, 100 yards from Tin Tacks. John Robinson was in our class, a little lad who was both the best fighter and the best marbles player, though the former may

Prosperous: Church Street in former times

have been more eagerly sanctioned by the Board of Control than by Miss Jones, the junior school headmistress.

Often we'd play marbles in the mucky little back alley behind the family fish shop, ground pockmarked like the dusty side of the moon. There were mysterious terms like "nowts" and "everies" and sometimes nowts and everies. I didn't understand. Often the visiting kids would leave empty handed, all marbles forfeit. Did John have home advantage? Too late now.

Joe, his dad, was a Burma Star holder, taught unarmed combat to the Gurkhas, owned and operated a one-man haulage business, chiefly leading bricks. John followed him behind the wheel – not an integrated transport system, not a global logistics solution, just a lorry driver and a great guy, driven by everything except ambition.

Perhaps it was appropriate that the best fighter in Timothy Hackworth Junior Mixed – though we never really knew about the girls' prowess in that regard – should become a formidable martial arts man with a particular expertise at breaking techniques. Great hods of house bricks, great streets of paving stones, would shatter beneath his bare hands or, more usually, his bare feet and always for a health-related charity. He could work his way through 42oz steaks, too, a definite red meat man.

Mind over matter, Robbo also took to walking barefoot, topping both Snowdon and Ben Nevis – "I could overhear people asking each other if they'd seen the dozy devil with no shoes on" – and aiming to complete the set on Scafell. On another occasion he planned a 20-mile barefoot walk from Chester-le-Street to Heighington, for some reason opposed by Durham Constabulary but joined by eight others more conventionally shod, seven Shildon lads and the eighth seeking naturalisation.

Geoff Wilde, the newcomer – he lived in Middridge, a mile down the bank – walked ahead with a yard brush, in order to clear the road of more injurious impedimenta. John the Baptist came to mind. Also among the support party was Michael Coyle, a Shildon wagon works man who read *Lord of the Rings* on night shift – there really will be more about the perceived nocturnal goings-on at the Shops – who left after being

confirmed diabetic and subsequently gained three degrees, including a doctorate.

A chap from the BBC rang just as we were leaving, asked John why he was walking barefoot. "I certainly couldn't do it on my hands" said John. He made it – of course – walked into the reception with his little grandson on his shoulders, demanded the first dance, supposed that he might put his feet up, if only for a day or two.

A small man of immense stature, he developed a brain tumour, fought gallantly and for once in his life lost. John died in 2008, aged 61. His dad died shortly afterwards.

The day's wanderings have begun at what the bus timetable still calls All Saints, though both church and school of that name are long closed. Among earlier vicars was Frank Hampton, also chairman of Shildon Football Club; among later incumbents was Raymond Cavagan, who also managed to run a travel agency (though only, he would suggest, for those holidays that might be perceived as pilgrimage).

The way leads down Redworth Road to the track of former railway lines into the wagon works and to the former level crossing behind the gates of which motorists and pedestrians would seethe numerous times each day as little tank engines essayed the locomotive equivalent of a slow, very slow, foxtrot. Usually they seemed to be numbers 68242 or 68696 – mucky little beggars from West Auckland shed and nameless at that lowly junction, of course, though we called them all sorts nonetheless.

Regrettably it hasn't proved possible to source a photograph of much maligned 68696, though a model can be had – "with main chuff beat" – for £195.

Some of us thought that the railway line best marked the border between Old and New. Others drew the boundary further north, maybe the old Surtees Railway track from the Hippodrome towards Soho Cottage and the existing railway station. Perhaps shrewdly, the station's just called Shildon.

Call it what you may, the area around the crossings prospered. There was a bank, several pubs, - including the Masons Arms, from which it all began back in 1825 - a thriving workmen's club, that self-styled "Palladium of the North", another Walter Willson's, Syd and Tommy Armitage trading on opposite corners of Madison Street.

Another little shopping centre, on Alma Road a few hundred yards away, had a pharmacist – which seemed also to sell an awful lot of alcohol, no doubt for medicinal purposes – two more pubs, newsagent, fruiterer, draper, butcher, wet fish shop and Calvert's – we wondered as kids if he were related to Eddie Calvert, the trumpeter – the shop where I bought my first record, a strange little number called Come outside by a one-hit wonder named Mike Sarne.

In St John's Road, an otherwise residential area a couple of hundred yards up the hill, Gus McDonald sold and mended bikes and could talk the hind legs off a cuddy. Goldsbrough's gent's outfitters next door once sold me a cheesecutter cap for the milk round and, a few doors up, the lovely Bertha Abbott sold sweets and blow-hard bubble gum to the homeward hordes from Timothy Hackworth Juniors.

As effervescent as a sherbet dip and altogether nicer, Bertha was 91 when asked to open the annual St John's church garden party – accomplished by singing *Daddy wouldn't buy me a bow-wow* which she'd first performed on the same stage at the age of 12. "It's the song that shot me to stardom" she said.

She'd written a memoir, recalled the Sunday evening Cockerel Walk in Bishop Auckland where likely lads paraded before quite-likely lasses, marked both her 90th and 95th birthdays by riding pillion on her nephew's motor bike but sadly was robbed of the ton up when she died in 2005, aged 97 – five years younger than her father, Walter Tillotson had been, a century marked with a party in the recreation ground rest house.

There was a butcher's, at least two other sweet shops, a dentist – chicken and egg job, if ever – and goodness knows what else, Just one thing unites those myriad businesses: without exception they're no longer.

Arnold and Peggy Scott ran a little bakery shop, what these days might be called an artisan bakery, straight across the road from the railway lines that shuffled and shunted to and from the wagon works, though a 1960s town guide put it more historically: "overlooking the first passenger railway in the world."

Other still-remembered businesses in those early guides included Haines Bakery ("we are the breadwinners"), the Central Garage – better known as Freddie's – Fred Simpson ("the progressive bookmaker"), Charles W Hancock who had pharmacies in Redworth Road and Main Street and a daughter in our class at school, Coxon's ("for the main line to fashion") and the amiable Chris Hunter, confectioner and tobacconist in Church Street, said to be a member of the Pipe Club and to stock English and Dutch cigars (for which there was doubtless much demand.)

The Scotts had two sons. John became an RAF squadron leader and Wilf, to whom more refulgently we must return, for if ever there were a railway child it was Wilf Scott.

"It was the biggest train set in the world" he said of the view from above the shop on the corner of Mill Street. "You could look inside the cabs from our front window. I knew all the drivers and got half a crown from Herbert Dobson for looking after his engine on Saturday mornings while he came in the shop for a coffee."

The mind stalls a bit at that one. Was looking after Herbert Dobson's engine the equivalent of the street kids who these days demand a couple of quid to "look after" your parked car, and with the likelihood of a couple of flat tyres or a phial of lighter fuel if the offer is declined?

On Saturday mornings, Wilf and John would also light the bakery's coke-fired oven. "We'd pretend it was an A4 Gresley Pacific" – remember those streaks? – "and that we were lighting boilers in Darlington shed" he said. His own train set was magnificent, even better than Paul Elwell's.

He'd attended St John's Church of England school, failed the feared 11+. "The headmaster told my parents just to send me down the pit or to the wagon works like everyone else" Wilf recalled. "I suppose what I really wanted to do was be an engine cleaner at Darlington and then work my way up."

His parents found the money to send him to the fee-paying Scorton Grammar School, near Richmond, 6 20am departure every morning, change trains at Darlington. "I didn't mind" said Wilf, "it was trains." Thereafter he gained two degrees at Reading University, worked variously as an artist and inventor,

Firecracker: Wilf Scott

antiques dealer and bargee before – "barely enough money for ten cigarettes and a half of beer, certainly not both at once" – turning to fireworks and lighting up the sky.

"I wouldn't care but I hated fireworks and Bonfire Night" said Wilf, "though I'd go round next day to collect all the scrap metal and sell it to Taffy Rowland."

He formed a company called Pyrovision, became a fizzing, coruscating, sky's-the-limit star in fireworks fantastical firmament. In the pyrotechnical panoply, in the great celestial scheme of things, Wilf Scott was a local lad made god.

They won top prize at the Monaco International Festival, lit up the Edinburgh Festival, iridescently illumined the Lord Mayor's Show. They worked for everyone from the Russian government to the World Wrestling Federation (the two of which should on no account be confused) and from Tina Turner to the Rolling Stones. A personal letter from President George W Bush, thanking him for his work at the G7 Summer in London in 2004, hung framed in his hall.

It was at Queen Elizabeth II's golden jubilee celebrations in 2002, however, that the Shildon lad most memorably saw his name up in lights. Wilf had charge of the 14-minute firework display, a job which involved several days clambering around the roofs of Buckingham Palace with umpteen tons of explosives and just weeks after a fire at the royal home. "The royal household was very brave to let it go ahead" he recalled.

The spectacle was started by the monarch pressing a button which propelled rockets over the palace. "The one thing you learn in this industry" said Wilf, "is never to stand a reigning monarch on a pile of explosives and ask her to press the button.

Next time I want to be in charge of the concession toilets, because the stress really was too much for me."

When Shildon Works closed in 1984 he'd sought funding for a display – "I very nearly got it" – featuring a pyrotechnic steam engine and a representation of Margaret Thatcher, and with few guesses about who'd have come off second best.

Smut smeared contemporaries, we met for the first time in 50 years close to his home near Cambridge – OK, a pub near his home in Cambridge – a couple of months after the Golden Jubilee celebration. "She's probably got me off the Christmas card list already" said the man who made the Queen's eyes water, but when the New Year honours chimed, the monarch had personally invested him a Member of the Victorian Order.

Having many times lit that blue touchpaper, the rocket man retired to Richmond, North Yorkshire, at 60. "I'd had enough of standing around fields in the freezing cold and the mud" he said. There was an autobiography, *From the pits to the Palace* – sub-titled "The explosive adventures of Wilf Scott" – and an ultimately unfulfilled wish to meet reformed safebreaker and worktops millionaire George Reynolds. "He's a proud Shildon lad like I am" he said.

If not quite a shrine, the house was a museum, full of his quirky-clever artwork and of a wonderful model locomotive collection that included 68292, one of those everyday engines whose driver would stop to get his pipe, or the caffeine equivalent, outside Scott's café. "Sometimes it takes me half an hour just to get to bed" said Wilf. "I'll stand in front of a cabinet and wonder where I got them all from."

Wilf died in 2019, aged 72, the death notice in the paper talking of "a supernova of the fireworks industry" and of "a peaceful death among his collection of trains".

We'd had another pint or two the previous year, a month or so before Bonfire Night. Perhaps because Taffy Rowland was no longer around to salvage the scrap, Wilf insisted that he wouldn't be turning out. "I don't want to miss The Archers" he said.

*A little further on from the former bakery shop, not far from Hackworth's former headquarters, the Salvation Army citadel stirs memories of Ken Smith, another former classmate at Timothy Hackworth Juniors and, like the rest of his family, a devout and committed Salvationist "You don't have to be musical to join the Salvation Army but I suppose it helps" he once said.

Ken married Kathy, planned a honeymoon on the Scottish island of Lewis, stayed overnight on the mainland before taking a Sunday morning plane to Stornoway – hitherto unknown to them, the first-ever Sabbath flight to those strictly six-day shores where still they tied up the playground swings lest the we'ans become sacrilegious. Thus it was that bride and groom were greeted at Stornoway airport by a maul of media men and about 50 placard waving protestors forecasting eternal damnation and citing the fourth commandment, the one about never-on-Sunday.

Not only would Ken and Kathy have been able to quote the fourth commandment word for word – and the other nine, an' all – but had it been set to music he could have played it on his cornet.

Numerous activities at the Citadel include a twice-weekly food bank, a "warm space" for those feeling the financial heat, dance sessions for tots and free soup on Tuesdays. Hackworth would surely have been proud of them, an Army marching with the times, yet Vera Chapman's book of photographs of Shildon in former times includes several of aproned soup kitchen staff during the General Strike of 1926, the minister usually seated, unsmiling, in the middle. A century later, it's possible to wonder how much has changed.

Two hundred yards away, a hand-written notice outside the Spiritualist Church – one of its four foundation stones laid in 1909 by the Shildon Lyceum Children - announces that it's closed until further notice. Lol Brown's funeral was held there, mourners greeted by a music machine playing Jim Reeves singing *Welcome to my World*.

Immediately over the road, the Masonic Hall's steel shuttered but appears still to be about its hugger-mugger business. A chalk board outside announces that "you" raised £420 but not how or for what. Fear not, brethren, your secret's safe with me.

The walk leads past Timothy Hackworth Park, formerly the Rec, and onto the Jubilee Fields housing estate where for those four years as kids we'd delivered milk seven mornings a week, half-a-crown a day and another 2/6d for collecting the money – from most of them, anyway – after school on Friday evenings. Ever enthusiastic town mayor Shirley Quinn, a wonderful worker for Shildon, leaps from the Jubilee Fields Community Centre to offer a look at all that's new and all that's possible with creative funding.

It includes a striking mural of the Water Bridge. Shirley says that everyone used to gather by the Water Bridge. "I know" I tell her, "I know."

Twilight retrospection over, I head to the annual meeting of Shildon Football Club, where my 800 shares are worth 800 x nothing whatsoever but they're a tremendous, sociable and forward thinking bunch. Also there is George Thompson, who had the paper shop opposite the Wagon Works – "officially took it over on the day in May 1973 that we won the Cup" he says and means Sunderland, of course, not Shildon.

Back then, he says, the town had 19 butcher's shops, four of them in New Shildon – "Tubby Ireland, Dunns the Salvation Army family, Borrowdale's and him outside the Furnace Pit" – and Byerley Road had a shop on every corner. Back then, adds George, he'd sell hundreds of copies of *The Northern Echo* every morning, perhaps not so many of *Lord of the Rings* but an awful lot of Woodbines and mint imperials as well.

It all changed on that dark day in July 1984 that the works buzzer blew its last. "When Shildon Shops closed" says George, "it finished this town for ever."

Chapter fourteen

Card school

It's the Glorious Twelfth of August, coincidentally but entirely appropriately, when I ring Godfrey Card seeking a chat and it's the 13th when I pitch up at the butcher's shop in Church Street – simply Godfrey's – that he's run for 54 years.

The Flying Scotsman is enjoying a summer residency at Locomotion, her periodic whistle a birdsong reminder of happy days. Immediately outside Godfrey's shop a helmetless imbecile – the word is over-generous – is riding his motor bike at speed along the pavement, periodically essaying wheelies.

Sometimes it may seem almost a blessing that the main thoroughfare is these days almost deserted.

Godfrey's 74, grey bearded and genial, reckons that when he opened these premises in 1970 Church Street alone had seven other butchers. "There was Eric Anderson, there was Jimmy Smith, Percival's, Flower's, Studham's….down Main Street there was Jeff Morland, Alan Morton over the road and Charlie Taylor on the corner,"

That shilling booklet marking George VI's coronation carried adverts from Smith's ("can't be beat, best quality meat"), Studham's ("for quality and value"), Robinson's and Taylor's alongside rival butchers S R Hodgson in St John's Road, S Kitching in Strand Street, Smith's in Redworth Road, Davison's in Cheapside, Archie White's in Scott Street ("pressed and potted meats and polonies"), Claxton's in Byerley Road and George Wright and P B Hobbs, both in Church Street, the latter promising food fit for their Majesties to eat.

Several other grocers and general dealers promised "home cured" cooked meat, another professed itself the best shop for bacon.

Among those who hadn't advertised was Fred Borrowdale – Adelaide Street, memory suggests – whose secret pork sausage recipe was passed on closure to Jeff Morland who later worked for Godfrey's and shared it with Alex, the Cards' daughter. Still they sell Borrowdale's sausages, £3 50 a pound, though it was possible to remember when they were a shilling.

"Even Pat and me don't know the recipe" says Godfrey. "Richard Borrowdale, Fred's son, comes in once a week to buy his meat and his sausages and says they're as good as ever. There's no better recommendation than that."

Later we're joined in the back shop by Jeff Morland himself, now retired. Mrs Borrowdale, he says, told him that Shildon once had exactly as many butcher's shops as it had pubs. "That figure was 26."

If the Cards had been dealt for Old Maid, there'd have been plenty of Mr Beef the Butcher. Godfrey's uncle Ronnie had a shop in Spennymoor, another uncle worked for a butcher in Shildon. Nat, a colourful character who'd been a tank driver in Burma during World War II, opened his shop at the bottom of Main Street around 1960. It was compulsorily purchased in 1968 when the council talked of widening the road, a compensation condition that they weren't allowed to trade for a further two years. Godfrey worked as a meat inspector instead. The road never was widened.

Far from the usual round of pork pies, polony and pigs' trotters, the new shop gained a reputation far beyond the town boundary, not least for game, including venison, the deer very likely stalked and the birds quite possibly shot by Godfrey himself – though on the day of the glorious phone call he'd been selling bangers not bagging fliers.

"It's been a terrible year for grouse" he says. "Two years ago was the same, the ground so hard that little bits and pieces of insects couldn't burrow through it, so the young grouse starved. It's a very funny thing, is nature."

Nor does he any longer head for the Highlands in search of venison. "There's a lot of roe deer locally now. Just yesterday a chap came in with a deer for me to cut up. A fortnight before that we had the health inspectors around – they were over the moon, five stars."

Variety, quality and Borrowdale's sausages help ensure that – "thankfully" – business remains pretty brisk. "It's quite good but we'd never do as well with just Shildon folk – all those supermarkets opening up at Tindale Crescent, all the farmers' markets just there for the day. Pat and I sometimes look up and down Church Street to see how many people are about. You can look both ways, the main street, and maybe count four or five."

Alex has joined them in the business, often there at 4am to bake pies, prepare meat and (of course) to make sausages. Like her dad, much of her spare time's taken up with pointer dogs – "a family obsession" says Godfrey.

The moron on the motor bike may suggest occasional lawlessness – "bits and pieces of aggravation" says Godfrey – including the time just days before Christmas 2022 when their windows were smashed. The culprits then turned odious attention to the

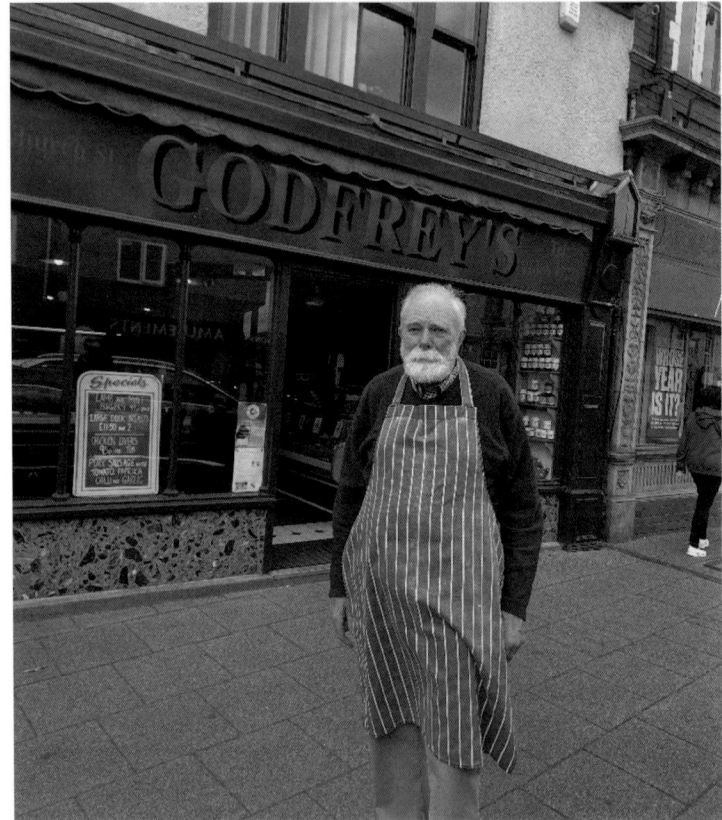

Butcher's boy: Godfrey Card

butcher's over the road, somewhat alarmed when the owners emerged with knives. "They weren't going to do anything with them" says Godfrey. "They just happened to be working out the back and that was what was in their hands. The idiots sharp scarpered, though."

Chapter fifteen

Great great expectations

Jane Hackworth-Young, Timothy Hackworth's great great granddaughter, is a fervent campaigner for Shildon's heritage, for wider awareness of the Stockton and Darlington Railway's place in world history and for Hackworth's acknowledgment at the bright blazing centre of it all.

"She still remains the town's most vociferous advocate" wrote George Turner Smith in his *Railway History of New Shildon*. It runs in the family.

Chiefly, immutably, the feeling persists that Hackworth gains insufficient credit as the hand that rocked the cradle of the railways and that those most posthumously (if unwittingly) responsible for the childnapping are George Stephenson and his son Robert. "It has been debated historically and to the present day whether Hackworth got enough recognition for his work" says the introduction to the National Railway Museum's Hackworth archive, thousands of letters and documents collected by family members and held in a vast library known neatly as the Search Engine.

Mike Norman, author of the smartly named *It wasn't Rocket science*, expressed similar views in the December 2023 issue of *The Globe*, the Friends of the S&D magazine named not after the infamous pub in Shildon where the early engine drivers peed away their pay but after one of Hackworth's best known locomotives, the one which hauled the first cargo train to Port Darlington, later known as Middlesbrough. "There is a tendency for George Stephenson to be placed at the head of the queue with Timothy Hackworth standing in his shadow

and well behind" Norman wrote. "Only a man at the top of his profession could do what Hackworth did."

Hackworth's youngest daughter Jane – she who improbably attended the Roman Catholic finishing school in Belgium after earlier education at the Young Ladies' Seminary run by her sister, Prudence Nothingale, in Penrith – was among early family champions. Born in 1831 in Soho House, the newly occupied Hackworth home in Shildon, she married George Edward Young, the Wesleyan Methodist minister in Darlington, in 1853. "Thereafter" notes the NRM archive, many of Timothy Hackworth's children, grandchildren, ancestors – presumably they mean "descendants", a common mistake – and friends campaigned for (Timothy's) recognition.

She died in 1914. "Jane Young appears to have been involved in research about her father for most of her life" says the archive.

Prominent among fellow combatants was John Wesley Hackworth, the 16-year-old entrusted with that perilous mission to Russia, who in 1849 – the year before his father's death - challenged Robert Stephenson to a locomotive building competition. The gauntlet appears not to have been returned.

Even in the mid-19th century, a time when Disgusted of Tunbridge Wells was probably still just mildly dissatisfied, John Wesley Hackworth wrote frequent letters to the newspapers protesting at those, says the archive, "who he thought were preaching historically inaccurate notions in relation to those who were involved with early railway development."

Among family successors were George Robert Young, whose masterwork Timothy Hackworth and the Locomotive was published in 1923, has been reprinted on momentous occasions in S&D history and (who knows) may well resurface in 2025. Born in Bishop Auckland in 1860, he was the son of the former Jane Hackworth and her minister husband.

"The story has been written to present the real circumstances in truer perspective" Young noted in his preface, adding that there had been many biographies of his grandfather's contemporaries and accounts of early railway history. "The share taken by Timothy Hackworth in establishing the steam locomotive assumed such microscopic proportions that there was a danger his work might be ignored altogether."

Similar fears may have assailed Reginald Hackworth Young, Robert's son, when with his 26-year-old daughter he headed north to Shildon in 1972 after reports that Soho House and much else of a historic and cherished nature – not least the coal drops, now a listed building – were to be demolished to make way for a relief road. Soho House should on no account, of course, be confused with the American-owned private members' club chain of the same name.

Reginald Young, known as Rex, was himself a distinguished engineer credited with designing for English Electric the first cooker with electronic oven and gas hobs. His daughter was Jane Hackworth-Young.

Born in London in 1948, a lovely and a multi-talented lady, Jane readily agrees to a chat in the Spring of 2024 despite the predations of long Covid. "It's horrendous" she says. "It's been two years and I've actually got worse in that time. Every morning when I wake up I wonder if I really want to get out of bed. I'm just so, so tired. The doctor said it sometimes goes after two years but what if it doesn't? I fear I'm stuck with it."

Brought up in the capital, she left school at 16 with eight O-levels but no thoughts of an engineering career. "Girls didn't in those days" says Jane. "It just wasn't considered." Vividly, she remembers the head teacher telling her mother that her daughter wasn't very bright but that it didn't matter because she was pretty and shouldn't have much trouble in finding a husband.

"That's probably why I never got married" says Jane, with a little, slightly sardonic, laugh.

She worked for an insurance broker and then as a secretary for Donald Albery, later Sir Donald, the theatrical impresario said in his Wikipedia entry to have done much to translate the adventurous spirit of 1960s London onto the stage. "Luckily he seemed to like me" says Jane and swiftly she assumed greater responsibility. Without suggestion of name dropping, global celebrities like Fonteyn, Olivier, Gielgud and Richardson again have their moment on stage. "It was a wonderful life" she says.

Thereafter she became director of the British Theatre Association, worked as an administrator at the Russian European Trust, had two terms as a Labour councillor in Hammersmith and Fulham and became a familiar figure on picket and protest lines.

It was on an NUM line that she was nearly arrested, she recalls, and on a Women Against Opencasting demonstration that she walked along the cordon of police officers with a collecting tin. "Every one of them gave something, they were quite nice" she says.

Her great great grandfather would certainly have approved of her Labour party membership, perhaps been less comfortable with the fact that, far from being a zealous Methodist, she's not even baptised. "My father just didn't engage with religion,

Relatively inspired: Jane Hackworth Young

didn't encompass it" she says.

In Shildon in 1972 and thereafter, she and her father had meetings with Walter Nunn, a long serving Labour councillor and man of strong principles whose brother-in-law was Sid Chaplin, the author and playwright perhaps best remembered for *Close the Coalhouse Door*. Walter kept a good allotment, too, though the wine cellar was ever empty.

"I liked the town. I was amazed that they'd kept Timothy Hackworth's gravestone so well and that, even back then, so much was named after him" says Jane. "My father had done a lot of research but wanted more doing. The council wanted to help - the will was there but the money wasn't."

It was Walter Nunn who, at a time in the 1970s when the Gateshead Metrocentre was no more than a glint in Sir John Hall's aquiline eye, had worked with developers on Steam City, a visionary retail park on the Brusselton edge of the town which, not least when real hardship came with the wagon works closure, could have transformed Shildon's fortunes. Look now at the burgeoning retail park a mile or so away at Tindale Crescent.

The Northern Echo devoted its entire broadsheet front page to the planned development. Sadly, there were those with less vision and fewer principles than Walter who ensured that it didn't go ahead – and neither did the proposed road through Soho House. George Smith (who's interested in pursuing a biography of Jane Hackworth-Young) writes of her father's "tireless campaigning" against the proposed road and of a man "sufficiently familiar with the trappings of government both local and national" to know those with the right levers to pull.

Jane recalls it a little differently. "Walter just said they ran out of money." Whatever the case, it came as a huge relief.

Three years later, to mark the Stockton and Darlington Railway's 150th anniversary in 1975, the near-abandoned Soho House had been transformed into the Timothy Hackworth Museum, greatly and enthusiastically supported by the pioneer's family and opened by the Queen Mother. Modest – minuscule – in comparison to Locomotion, to follow 30 years later and less than half a mile away, it nonetheless represented victory.

In 1977, father and daughter were involved in a serious car crash in which Reginald Young was killed. "They thought it was me who was the goner at first" Jane recalls. "I had to have my spleen removed and suffered a few broken bones but I survived. My father already had TB and then they discovered cancer. Sadly, he didn't make it."

In 2002 she finally acknowledged the curlew call of the North, if not quite to Shildon then to Teesdale, 20-odd miles to the west and, says Jane, absolutely glorious.

At first she had a house with a stable and three horses in Mickleton – "I know, the mad woman" – before moving to a cottage at Rokeby, alongside the A66 and then in 2022 further downsizing to Cotherstone, a village west of Barnard Castle that, in her later life, had also been home to that solitary daleswoman Hannah Hauxwell.

One of those house detectives would at once discern that the current place is owned by a book lover, and that her first love is railways and their history. On the wall are S&D-related paintings – "originals" – by celebrated local artist John Wigston, on the table a library book by Horrible Histories author Terry Deary, who lives in Co Durham, called *Dangerous Days on*

Victorian Railways in which a chapter talks enthusiastically of Timothy Hackworth. "Beneath that bald dome lay a steam powered brain" it says.

She also runs a bridge club, paints, loves gardening, plays 5s and 3s dominoes in the Teesdale League – "we got promoted from the B division and won the cup" – and until Covid was an enthusiastic long distance walker, twice having completed the 260-mile Pennine Way. Though the illness compelled her resignation as vice-president of the Friends of the Stockton and Darlington, that energetic and high-viz group which aims to secure a legacy for the length-long line, she continues actively to support the S&D and its first locomotive superintendent.

It's a pretty small room in which we drink her coffee, George and Robert Stephenson perhaps the elephants in it. Jane's slightly guarded. "I'm enthusiastic about correcting things, righting wrongs, giving due recognition to those who deserve it. People get left out, don't they? When I was a child people said that George Stephenson built the first steam locomotive but they were going around 20 years before that.

"There are so many books, so many histories, which do a great deal of harm to the cause. There was a television programme with about 40 mistakes. I've just stopped watching."

Locomotion museum describes Hackworth and George Stephenson as "friends and rivals". Would she agree?

"Timothy Hackworth was always a very polite man. I don't think he disliked George Stephenson but he didn't like the way that George would rush at things. Hackworth was meticulous, he always wanted to get things right. I think in their lifetime there was respect, it was afterwards that they were supposed not to get on."

Many of the locomotives built by Stephenson, she says, were designed be her great great grandfather. "I wouldn't say they were close friends but I think they had a pact, a working understanding."

Picket lines notwithstanding, she accepts that some of the Co Durham collieries had to close – "the conditions were inhumane" – but insists that Shildon Shops could have been saved. "There were orders out there. It was political; they didn't try hard enough. Shildon was quite a poor town to start with. I'm afraid that it's struggled after that."

Might the bicentennial celebrations offer a catalyst for renaissance? She pauses, smiles – not so much knowingly but perhaps suggesting that I should know. "The three councils (Co Durham, Darlington, Stockton) seem to have missed a big opportunity so far. It's such a shame."

There'll be steam traction, she says, at Locomotion, at the Preston Park Museum near Stockton and at the re-born Darlington railway centre now called Hopetown – "ridiculous name" says Jane, a view with which *The Globe* wholly agreed – "even the selected font was more akin to a Wild West saloon than a Georgian railway."

And Shildon has Locomotion, once said to be the site of the world's biggest marshalling and now home to one of its biggest railway museums. "As we like to say at the Friends, Shildon wasn't the first at anything but it brought everything that had been designed and planned together" says Jane.

Long or the short of Covid, she hopes to play an active part in the celebrations. "My driving ambition has always been to secure for Timothy Hackworth the recognition that he deserves. It still is."

Chapter sixteen

Bruss stop

Though Brusselton is just half a mile from the former wagon works, and thus from the heart of Shildon, it's likely that most Shildon folk have never been there and that many might struggle to know how to find it.

Known to its friends simply as Bruss, it was the summit site of the stationary winding engine – steam powered – which from day one of the S&D drew rope-hauled coal-laden chaldrons up the 1,960-yard incline from the Gaunless Valley before gently (it was to be hoped) letting them down again to where Locomotion and luminaries awaited.

It was the site from 1834-1968 of a colliery that at its peak in 1960 employed 366 men and killed far too many of them. It had an engineman's house, still standing, around which were built North Terrace and South Terrace and the little Wesley Methodist chapel where two or three were scripturally gathered together to hear John Littlefair set out on a preacher's pilgrimage.

It remains home to Brusselton Wood, growing since Roman times and abundantly rewarding exploration, was close to the site of Brusselton Tower to which a little cautiously we shall return, and since 2014 has been subject of care and attention from the Brusselton Improvement Group – Brusselton is a BIG deal – which supposes the Incline a "Georgian engineering marvel" and seeks to protect and to cherish the area's railway heritage and legacy.

Robert Young liked it up there, too. Though acknowledging that the site of the first railway works was "a damp, dreary unpromising place, wanting in any attribute to make it a desirable place of work" he insisted that the "wonderful beauty" of its surroundings unfolded from the heights of Brusselton "can be destroyed neither by railways nor collieries." Nor has it been.

Brusselton's bairns used to walk across the fields to Timothy Hackworth school. Memory murmurs that there was a Brusselton lass in our class of 50 – Elizabeth Wright, possibly – though we had little interest in the opposite sex at Timothy Hackworth Junior Mixed (an indifference, it should be swiftly be added, which was entirely mutual).

A bit like the Grand Old Duke of York, save that the chaldrons might not strictly be said to have been marched up to the top of the hill before being marched back down again, the Brusselton Incline was also said, a little optimistically, to be home of the world's first railway signalling system. A tall pole at the bottom had a disc fixed to its top. When the disc was spinning the wagons were ready but since it was more than a mile away from the engineman, that worthy gent was given a telescope with which to discern the go-ahead – all very well in broad daylight but more problematical in a familiar south Durham murk and yet more difficult at night.

Timothy Hackworth, who in 1831 had devised a more powerful 80 horse power stationary engine, also designed a system of bells and whistles not easily understood by 21st century authors but reputedly a great deal more effective. The incline remained in daily operation until 1856, superseded by a new branch line which ran from the north of Shildon Tunnel to St Helen Auckland, but was maintained until the 1880s, lest the tunnel become blocked.

Mostly occupied by pitmen, North Terrace had 42 houses, South Terrace no more than eight, together home to more than 200 people. The admirable Chris Lloyd in *The Northern Echo* a few years back thought Bruss "a pretty wind-blown place with panoramic views" and reckoned that many houses had had little shops in their front rooms – Stablers stocked essentials from the London and North East Tea Company, Mrs Turnbull sold tins of paraffin with which to keep the lamps burning, the Wards had a couple of cows to provide milk and the Dunns – the Shildon area had abundant Dunns – sold coal.

As with proper sanitation, electricity came late, though it's recorded that by 1953 someone identified as "the parson" had gained a television and everyone crowded in to watch the Coronation (and possibly the FA Cup final a couple of weeks earlier.) North Terrace was demolished in 1971.

The Durham Mining Museum's website records 13 fatalities at Brusselton colliery, two in 1966 – one killed by a cutting machine, the other struck by derailed tubs – and none before 1905 when a 21-year-old incline attendant was also struck by a runaway tub. The collection of names is by no means complete, it again adds, an inarguable if melancholy assertion.

In 2002, more than 30 years after the pit's closure and despite opposition from residents and conservationists, UK Coal won permission to opencast the site, known as Southfield and said to hold 580,000 tons of residual coal. Not only was the site a haven for deer and badger, it was claimed, but for our old friend the dingy skipper, perhaps on the wing from Shildon sidings and perhaps not quite so elusive a butterfly as might have been supposed. UK Coal built special hatching boxes for them, extracted 6,000 tons of coal a week, planted 130,000 trees and were gone. Southfield looks lovely.

Brusselton Tower, about 800ft above the sea, was known when we were kids as Brusselton Folly – an older term for a summer house - though initially said to have had a very serious purpose. It was only one moonless and distinctly muddy night in the 1970s that the true extent of the folly became apparent.

The story has it that the octagonal tower was built by Cuthbert Carr, a 17th century Sheriff of Newcastle who for many months led resistance to the marauding Scots' siege of the city before finally the walls fell and many were killed. Spared, Carr moved south to St Helen Hall, near West Auckland, the tower reckoned a lookout against further unwelcome Scottish incursion. Its ground floor was said to have mosaic tiling and to be used for dancing, the "sumptuous" dining room above popular with local gentry and the immediate area frequented by picnic

Straight and narrow; North Terrace in 1967

125

parties. That things didn't always go according to plan was recorded in a remarkable report from the Durham Advertiser of July 21 1865.

"Picnic at Brusselton: A picnic and gala under the auspices of the New Shildon Saxhorn Band was held on the grounds of Brusselton Folly on Monday when upwards of 500 attended and amused themselves in the different games provided for their entertainment, consisting of cricket, turzey etc but the chief attraction seemed to be dancing, which was joined in and kept on till dark. Refreshments including intoxicants were provided in the grounds, the latter of which we regret to say having been rather too freely indulged in by the band and officials, so much so that towards the latter part of the day many of them got intoxicated and their conduct became of the most disgraceful character.

"The bandmaster getting enraged at one of his party, addressed him in the most violent terms and using the most inelegant language he could choose to the disgust of all present, threatened to leave the platform taking with him his books, but on secondary consideration returned and the dancing was resumed. The day was beautifully fine and had the affair been properly conducted, and intoxicating drinks not indulged in, a most pleasant afternoon might have been spent."

Carr married Anne Byerley of Middridge Grange, scion of the Bulldog Byerley family to whom an earlier chapter referred, and was reputed to have had dug a two-and-a-half mile secret tunnel, via Brusselton, between their two homes. Co Durham has so many supposed secret tunnels, truth to tell, that it's a wonder the whole county palatine didn't long since collapse in a subsided heap.

By the 20th century the Tower had fallen into disrepair – subsidence? – a *Northern Echo* reader in 1930 calling for remedial action. "Children can no longer play within its gaping walls" he wrote. "The wind moans where laughter once rang." It remained a popular picnic spot, the more visually imaginative given to claims that they could see Saltburn in one direction and the Irish Sea in the other and no matter that the Pennines might have obscured things a little.

The folly disappeared in 1961, demolished by Shildon builders Syd and Maurice Parks allegedly on the orders of the Ministry of Defence who supposed it a strategic landmark in the event of the Cold War warming up. One of Gerald Slack's admirable books on Shildon and its environs records that, just as the folly was knocked down before it fell down, a waterproof, reinforced concrete underground nuclear fallout monitoring post was built just yards away.

One of 1,563 throughout the land, some still visible, it was erected to accommodate three Royal Observer Corps folk and a fair bit of equipment. "Thirty years after the collapse of the Soviet Union it is sometimes easy to forget about the impact of the Cold War, and the shadow of nuclear warfare under which people lived" writes Gerald. Probably not because the Cold War was prone to global warming, the monitoring station was decommissioned seven years later.

It was also on that exposed site that I found myself on a dark (and perhaps stormy) night in the 1970s. More sensitive readers may consider a trigger warning in place.

Ineluctably, George Reynolds has been mentioned before. He was a local criminal, a sort of celebrity safe blower, who'd recently opened a coffee bar and night club in Shildon but who

Running track: artist's impression of Brusselton engine house

retained some questionable associates. One was Tony Hawkins, a burglar from Willington whose speciality was Co-operative stores, perhaps in the belief that they paid dividends and usually through the front door. Tony had failed to answer his bail and an arrest warrant had been issued.

About two o'clock one morning George, ever the dramatist, rang to say that Tony was anxious to hand himself in but first wanted to give me his side of the story. Protest about a manifest need for beauty sleep was unavailing. We met shortly afterwards, drove in George's Thames van – Hawkins impatiently concealed beneath an elderly proggy mat in the back – to the former site of the Tower, approached through the sort of glorious mud in which one or more of Messrs Flanders and Swann's hippopotami might happily have wallowed.

Confessional complete, George tried unavailingly to reverse the van. The fugitive and I pushed, rear wheels caking us head to foot in clarts. So it was that, about 4am, we presented ourselves at Bishop Auckland police station where the fresh faced constable behind the desk looked casually up from his copy of *The Tiger.* "Oh hello, Tony, we've been expecting you" he said.

It was folly personified.

For a fairly small fee, the Ordnance Survey will produce customised maps, two-and-a-half inches to the mile, of any location in the land. Mine, a birthday present, is labelled *All routes lead to Shildon* (which, of course, they do) and has my picture - caveat emptor - on the cover.

Here's the curious thing, though: even at two-and-a-half inches to the mile, scaled up almost to include a decent-sized haystack, there's no mention of Brusselton. There's Brusselton

Wood, Brusselton Farm, Brusselton Lane but not so much as a 6pt pirouette for poor old Bruss.

Undeterred, and on the first glorious day of what latterly is termed meteorological summer, we set off nonetheless on one of the many walker-friendly footpaths that now traverse a delightful area. Off the map maybe, uncharted territory perhaps, local knowledge must prevail.

The start of the two-and-a-half mile road north-eastwards from Royal Oak to Shildon was originally Dere Street, where Roman legions marched without so much as expectation of a pint in the Railway Institute or a kind word from the centurion. To the west, probably predating sundry Ceasars, Brusselton Wood was the sort of place where you might expect to find a piggy-wig stood and with a ring in the end of its nose. Edward Lear would have supposed it trulgy.

We head eastwards from the road, where the reclaiming open-casters have been as good as their wooded word. Where there are clearings there are views of Shildon itself. "It's a bit like one of those Georgian prints of the Promised Land" says Sharon, warming to the place in the afternoon sunshine and reprising almost simultaneously lines attributed to John Wesley – but actually spoken by Christopher Hopper, one of his assistants – as their preaching party headed on one of fairly frequent forays eastwards into Weardale.

The promised land from Killhope Top

I now exult to see

My hope is full – oh glorious hope –

Of good spice cake and tea.

There are cabbage whites but no dingy skippers, the latter perhaps unable to blend with their multi-coloured surroundings. There are sonorous skylarks, foolish pheasants and, close to Shildon, there are peewits, known informally if not ornithologically as lapwings and offering a further reminder of the way things were.

Surveying the likely route of the Stockton and Darlington in 1821, John Dixon – great-nephew of Jeremiah Dixon, the Cockfield lad who jointly surveyed the Mason Dixon Line which ultimately divided America's northern and southern states - had been distinctly underwhelmed by the area where the railway works would be established and the nascent New Shildon take form.

The site was a wet, swampy field, Dixon told the *Bishop Auckland Herald* in 1863, a likely place to find a snipe or a flock of peewits. Robert Young's impressions had been similarly bleak, as we have noted, but things were to change. "As has happened a thousand times since in other districts, the railway came along and a new town sprang into existence."

The peewits, had they flown for centuries, might hardly have recognised the place.

The walk takes us past High West Thickley Farm, firmly on the map, the temptation to take home a few logs to help keep home fires burning in later months perhaps fortunately outweighed by the impossibility of lugging them. The smartish phone claims that it's 17 degrees, sometimes cloudy and that we're in Bishop Auckland. The first part's simply inaccurate – the sky a perfect blue – the second simply scandalous. This is Shildon, dear – as near as dammit, anyway. What is it with Bishop?

The only downside is that, wherever 21st century humanity may penetrate, so also does evidence of 21st century slobbery, of litter from Costa Coffee and, co-laterally, its countless commercial cousins.

So on to Brusselton, navigationally non-existent, past the restored stone setts by which thousands gathered on that morning in September 1825 to watch the train of 13 wagons hauled the 1,960 yards up the incline from St Helen Auckland before being lowered the 880 yards to Shildon, and history.

"All sorts and conditions were there" Young wrote. "Some were riding, some driving, some on foot, friends and enemies – the former to see a great triumph, the latter the collapse of an absurd scheme."

A home-made sign at the entrance to the half-hidden hamlet announces that children are playing and, probably without authority, seeks to impose a 10mph limit. Grass verges are newly, verdantly, mown. A George VI post box, now the only formal amenity, announces a 9am daily collection and advises on how its apps might be used. Not even the great triumvirate of Stephenson, Hackworth and Edward Pease might have understood an app.

Though Brusselton itself is a cul-de-sac, a path follows the old trackbed down to the Shildon bypass and towards the site where Locomotion launched the new age. Out the back of the enginemen's houses, still occupied, is the former S&D reservoir, now home to New Shildon Angling Club and to a truly delightful nature reserve, almost undiscovered but open to the public.

On the gate are notices about subscriptions, membership responsibilities and, more alarmingly, Weil's disease, spread in rats' urine and not the sort of thing upon which to dwell on so idyllic an afternoon. This is paradise regained, and it's barely half a mile from Shildon.

We fall into conversation with three angling club men, friendly chaps, among them 75-year-old Fred Wright whose father moved from Fulham to a job at the Shops when Fred was ten. When he was 13 they moved to Brusselton, a place that he's never left, never wanted to and remains pretty sure that he never will, though he worries about talk of creating a formal three-metre wide cycle path from the village down to the bypass. "We get motor bikes as it is, there'll be racing cars next" says Fred.

He's also heard that the stone setts at the east of Bruss, erroneously believed to be S&D originals, are to be removed before the bicentenary. "I remember them being laid about 40 years ago" he says. "It was a community service lad, they'd drop him off every morning with a pick, a shovel and maybe a sandwich and pick him up again at night. The stones came from South Church or somewhere."

We walk round the pond – "a heap of mud if it hadn't been for us" – marvel at its attraction and at its anonymity. Fred's a nice chap and a good talker: in the hope of another afternoon like this one, we arrange a return before the summer's much older. Good spice cake and tea may be optional.

No 1 Engine House sounds like it might be the home of a small town United States fire station, but is much more important – more historic, anyway – than that. It's Fred Wright's place in Brusselton, evidence of its former status clearly visible out the back. S&D 150th anniversary mirror above the stove, imaginings abundant, reflection seems almost obligatory.

The 40ft radio mast in the garden might also have a ring of the fire department about it, but Fred's also a ham – helps pass long winter nights – fellow enthusiasts around the world are sent a postcard with an 1875 image of the semi-derelict winding engine on the front and a brief history on the back. "On September 27 1825 the local committee and other proprietors of the Stockton and Darlington Railway Company met here to inspect the winding engine. They then embarked upon an 'elegant covered coach' and were lowered down the incline to the Masons Arms public house in Shildon. Here a 'superior loco motive travelling engine was employed…."

Elegant? "Well, probably elegant for that time" says Fred.

The hurly-burly long done, only vestigial evidence of the long and winding railroad, it's glorious up there on a serene July morning. Though a sign advises that the footpath remains closed, the creation of a cycle route up from the Shildon bypass is complete. "I don't mind but just don't understand all that expense" says Fred. "I doubt if we see two or three bikes a week up here, maybe there'll be a few more for the bicentenary."

Fred's dog Toby – "typical terrier, one word from me and he does what he wants" – is first to the back gate in greeting, his subsequent 90 minutes spent eviscerating a teddy bear. Toby's teddy has endured multiple eviscerations. *Last of the Summer Wine*, appropriately, occupies daytime television.

Fred came to North Terrace as a 13-year-old – no relation to Elizabeth Wright, who shared that cramped classroom at Tin Tacks – married and moved to Northumberland for seven years in the 1970s – returned to the Engine House where contentedly,

singly, he remains.

His dad had been a navigator and bomb aimer on Lancasters and was awarded the DFM, though Fred insists it was Dakotas, not Lancasters, which won the war. "They were the planes that carried the fags and booze for the troops." Wright senior came north looking for work, found employment at Shildon Shops and a home at Bruss. Fred had been a grammar school boy in London, was told that Bishop Grammar wouldn't accept him in mid-term and instead attended the boys' secondary modern in Southland Gardens, now only for juniors but still known to Shildon folk as the Council School. They were two years behind London, he insists.

The late John Hope, a contemporary, went on to keep goal for Newcastle United, Sheffield United and others but was forbidden by the headmaster to play for the school team until he could recite *Miller of the Dee* by heart. *Miller of the Dee*, he liked to recall, was an exceptionally long poem.

"We'd walk every day, whatever the weather, over the fields and up past the cemetery, then walk home again for our dinner with still time for something to eat" says Fred. "These days you see all the mothers dropping the kids off in their SUVs – in Brusselton there was only my dad and one other person even had a car and he had a lot better things to do than take us to school in it."

Brusselton proved an adventure playground. "We roamed everywhere – fishing, shooting, rabbiting, riding our bikes. We built all sorts, had amazing bonfires, so big they'd scorch woodwork half way down the street. It was a real community, a self-contained little community with not an empty house. We loved it. When I came back in 1979, North Terrace demolished,

Catch: the nature reserve

there were only two families I knew. All the rest were strangers."

Nemesis came in the rubicund form of PC Tommy Trebilcock, the fabled Shildon police officer recalled elsewhere. "Tom had a Triumph motor bike and we just had our push bikes" Fred recalls. "By the time we got home if we'd been up to mischief he'd be waiting on the doorstep, clip around the ear and that was it, no further action. Mind we were still a bit scared of him, Tommy, but I suppose his bark was worse than his bite."

There were also a few scrapes at Bishop Tech, where wagon works apprentices and colliery learners were taught side by side, including the occasion on which Fred and a mate turned a hose on pit lads smoking (as then carcinogenically was permitted) in the common room. "Back at the works we got suspended for two weeks. On the way out of the hearing one of the gaffers whispered 'Well done, lads'."

Part way down North Terrace, number 32 he thinks, Nick and Nellie Moses had their little shop. "There were no supermarkets in those days, only the Co-op in Shildon. Nellie's was maybe a bit more expensive than Shildon but it was worth it. You could go any time of the day for stuff."

Brusselton colliery was still in full vigour, New Shildon Drift still supported the coal-black economy, the wagon works clattered and banged barely ten minutes walk away. Now at the end of that little cul-de-sac there are just seven houses – six occupied, Fred thinks the other occupant was evicted. Seven houses, a post box, that serenely secret nature reserve and an awful lot of history.

By the summer and autumn of 2025 it's likely that Brusselton will have rather a lot more visitors, winging their way, anxious to witness where it all began. Fred insists that they'll be welcomed. "I get a big annoyed when people talk about the Stockton to Darlington Railway instead of the Stockton and Darlington – Dan Snow did that, so did Fred Dibnah – and I get a bit annoyed by people who think they know it all."

He's also unhappy about the Brusselton Improvement Group's work to reclaim the waggon way from the west. "They cut down a load of trees and shrubs, you can't even go brambling any more."

However persuaded, he insists that visitors are welcomed. "We get a few already and likely there'll be more. I'll natter to anyone – I'm talking to you, aren't I?"

From push bikes they grew into scramble bikes, escapades yet more hazardous. On one occasion he ruptured his spleen, broke several ribs, had his knee cap detached and suffered several other serious injuries. Discharged from hospital, he was referred to fondly remembered Shildon GPs Frank Hutchinson and Richard Malcolm. "I still remember going in and one of them saying '******* hell, not you again Fred. It was the first time I'd heard a doctor swear. I didn't know that they did."

These days he and Toby also keep a paternal (piscatorial?) eye on the lovely lake and nature reserve out the back. "We used to go angling all over Britain but the biggest fish I ever caught was a 23-and-a-half pound carp called Nobby, 20 yards from my back door."

Nobby? "Most of the big fish get a name. There was a record breaker, about 44 lbs, called Clarissa. I think it's in the National History Museum or somewhere now. Good name for a fish, Clarissa."

The engine house, he believes, is even older than the railway itself. So what are the drawbacks of living in an historic house and a hidden hamlet that may soon attract rather more attention than it has for two centuries? The chief problem, says Fred, are the winters. "In 2010 we had two successive days when it was minus 15 degrees, two weeks when it never got above freezing. The lake froze and killed thousands of pounds worth of fish. We just had to throw them over the fence and leave them for Mr Fox.

"There are pictures of my sister sitting on the roof of one of the pigeon crees and all you can see is the little fence on the top – snow right up to there. It's also a wind tunnel from the Gaunless Valley. If it's blowing 30 miles an hour in Shildon it's blowing 50 in Brusselton and all that can also make it cold. We've no gas, they won't put it in for just seven houses and coal's about £500 a ton. The stove's the only heating I have."

Hell might freeze over, however, or at least New Shildon Angling Club's lake might, before he'd consider moving. "Why would I want to leave somewhere like this for somewhere like Shildon where you look out of your window and all you see is another window? They'll have to carry me out of here in a box."

Chapter seventeen

Whit and wisdom

Shildon Methodist Church's website is topped with the most appealing of messages. "Welcome to the ones who are single, married, divorced, widowed, gay, confused, filthy rich, comfortable or dirt poor" it begins.

"Welcome if you are from Shildon or just passing by. Welcome if you can sing like Pavarotti or can't sing a note. Welcome if you're just browsing, just woken up or just out of prison. Welcome if you're more Christian than the Archbishop of Canterbury, or just come to share little Jack's christening. Welcome if you are still in recovery, or still addicted."

So it continues, even publicly welcoming those who've blown it all on the horses and perhaps with a retrospective eye on that sixpence each way that dear old Aunty Betty would smuggle twice a week to Percy Allan's.

"Welcome seekers and doubters, saints and sinners, regulars, visitors, friends and strangers…." it goes on.

Some of it's particularly apt, though not the bit about singing like Pavarotti. I once attended a funeral here when the deceased's son was produced in cuffs from Durham Jail, once when churchwarden at St John's – across the road – had to go seeking a curate who'd slept in for Evensong, once when a nipper was unceremoniously shown the choir vestry door after one particularly unenchanted and audibly excruciating evensong.

Goodness knows what boxes are ticked at today's 2 30pm service but almost all the 15 in attendance are elderly, almost all

female – and, yes, without exception welcoming. It's particularly good to be at church in Shildon and not to be attending an old friend's funeral.

It was Timothy Hackworth, of course, who helped spread Methodism in the Shildon area, though it's recorded that in 1769 the agricultural hamlet – as then it was – had three practising Methodists who gave 7/10d to the church. Whether monthly or annually, individually or collectively, is unclear.

Hackworth travelled many a mile to preach, lived his faith, shared his resources. Though he oversaw the building of a chapel near the Soho Works, it was those who followed who erected huge, square fronted churches all over town – some Primitive Methodist, some Wesleyan Methodist, some simply styled Independent Methodist and some barely 100 yards one from the other. Even when Methodism was formally united in 1932, many – and by no means just in Shildon - kept their distance.

Shildon's "souvenir programme" for the 1953 Coronation carried a half-page advert for the town's Methodist church "Wesley circuit", listing the Main Street, Soho Street, Garbutt Street and Redworth Road churches. That 1932 act of union notwithstanding, the former Prims never got a mention.

Published in 1994, Vera Chapman's evocative little photographic recollection Around Shildon noted that the original Main Street chapel was built in 1877, seated a total of 1,000 of the faithful upstairs and down and with the Sunday School at the back cost £6,000. Barely 100 yards away, a year younger, the Primitive Methodist chapel on the corner of Church Street and Primitive Street held 750 while, Prim and proper, the Methodist chapel half a mile down the bank at the bottom of

St John's Road could accommodate 800. Opened in 1866, the Wesley Methodist chapel in Cross Street accommodated 700, enthusiastically conforming in their non-conformity.

There'd been others, of course, on Redworth Road (later a bookie's) and on Church Street, an "Independent" Methodist chapel on Robson Street, near the former Conservative Club, and another on Byerley Road – now a Pentecostal church. Truth to tell, Methodism had nearly as many places of worship as now there are worshippers.

The church in Main Street, opened in 1976 to replace another on the same site, alone survives. It was chiefly from this congregation that a group of young people called Geordie's Penker recorded that marvellous song to mark the Stockton and Darlington's sesquicentennial – "And who needs Presley when you've got Nigel Gresley, he'll convert you quicker than old John Wesley." Remember?

These days there are no church youth groups, though the hall is home to a weekly coffee morning and to something called a New Age Kurling Club. This afternoon there's probably no one who hasn't a bus pass in his pocket. Disheartening? "We don't get disheartened, we're called to be hopeful" says Alan Lawson, a smart and spritely 81. "You could say we get frustrated, though" he adds.

I'm reminded of the Rev Graham Morgan and his wife Emma, Shildon circuit ministers in the early 21st century, whose patch included the gallant little Valley chapel at Coundon Grange, once next to a pub formally called the Cumberland Arms but known thereabout as the Blood Kit. Graham remained so resolutely hopeful – positively cheerful, indeed – that he published a couple of joke books. I once did a local radio interview

Stalwart: John Littlefair

135

Joker: the Rev Graham Morgan

with him, a poor man's Michael Parkinson to Graham's Billy Connolly, innocent little asides like the number of Methodists it took to change a light bulb. "Five" said Graham, "one to change the bulb itself and the other four to organise the Love Feast which followed". He was also fond of the observations that if God had wanted him to touch his toes He'd have put them on his knees and that if you took life too seriously, you might never get out of it alive.

Graham and Emma were subsequently posted to Scarborough, a place which a Yorkshireman might consider to be heaven on earth and others (after Stanley Holloway) to be nothing to laugh at at all.

It's Pentecost, known popularly as Whit Sunday, the feast of mighty rushing winds and of speaking in tongues, the Church's birthday. "Sadly I haven't had time to bake a cake but that may be to the benefit of your health and wellbeing" says the Rev David Payne, superintendent minister of the ten churches in the Bishop Auckland circuit. These days the circuit has just one other minister, and she's on long-term sick leave.

Before the day's out, David will have conducted services in Etherley, Hamsterley, Bishop Auckland, Shildon, Witton Park and a telephone service, a Covid legacy. "Quite good fun, those" he says.

At Shildon there are good old hymns like *All creatures of our God and King* – ascribed to St Francis of Assisi – like *Breathe on me breath of God*, though not to the tune once so familiar at Tin Tacks – and the more modern *Walk in the light*, to which it's possible to clap though not while juggling a large-print hymn book and a shorthand notebook simultaneously.

The minister preaches enthusiastically and adeptly, likes to saw the air. "So many people today have no notion of God" he says.

Some remember me. "I used to alter your blazers when you and your twin brother went to school and I worked at the Co-op" says a nice lady called Gillian who again stirs memories of Stanley Matthews football boots and of dividend declared.

We talk of places like the Friends Meeting House, the Quaker headquarters, where in the 1950s we had polio jabs and dangerously (if dependably) let the side down while representing Shildon in a road safety quiz.

St John's parish church, which once had three services every Sunday, now usually has one. All Saints, thought of as the railwaymen's church, closed in 1998, Frank Lawson, in one of his little digressions, near-ecstatically recalls the pie and pea suppers at All Saints and, less spiritually, the friend's where mushy pea sandwiches might be savoured on Christmas Eve.

St Thomas's Roman Catholic church now has a Saturday evening Vigil Mass because the one priest who covers a group of parishes can't be everywhere on the Sabbath. The Salvation Army battles gallantly.

Alan Lawson sang in the Primitive Street choir as a teenager, about 40 of them – "goodness knows how many more in the congregation". They did operettas and oratorios, recalls Joyce Hird over the tea and biscuits – "Mozart, all sorts."

Gwen Wharton was just three, she says, when reciting her piece at the Robson Street church. That it was "I am a little soldier, I'm only three years old" is coincidental because it was also my piece when somehow pressganged by Aunty Betty at the same little church. Probably there was a poke of pear drops in it. "I think it was the only one anyone ever knew" says Gwen.

Someone with a smart phone calls up the long gone Fryer Street Independent Methodist chapel, just across the road – "40 in the society" it says but goodness knows how many in the congregation.

Unsurprisingly, Mr Payne has little time to talk before dashing off for his telephone service, a bite of tea and Witton Park. We hope to arrange a chat some other time, but regrettably it never happens.

Few Shildon Methodists may be remembered more affectionately than John Littlefair, a local preacher for 55 years until retiring in 2012 "except in case of illness or emergency". It was surprising, he observed not long afterwards, how much illness and emergency there'd been.

From a long line of Shildon folk, and a former chairman of the town's football club, he'd preached his first sermon at Brusselton, where the little chapel dated back to Timothy Hackworth's evangelical zeal, taking as his text the familiar scripture about two or three being gathered together. He may have overestimated.

"It was dreadful, awful," John once recalled with characteristic honesty though even that may have attracted slightly more of the faithful than one evening at Keld, top end of Swaledale, when only the organist and steward turned out.

Soon, however, John and many more – especially across south Durham – got the message. His trade mark, if a Methodist local preacher may be said to have one, was to remove his jacket during the opening hymn. Shirt sleeve order, he was getting down to business.

Particularly they loved his comfortable, comforting style in the little village chapels like Wind Mill, South Church and Woolley Terrace – now all closed. I'd heard him at Auckland Park back in 1995, a preacher with more visual aids than the average branch of Specsavers. "I'm not really an ogre, just a kindly old man" he assured the bairns at the back.

When the much bigger Newton Aycliffe Methodist church celebrated its 50th anniversary, however, it was John who was invited to lead morning service.

Bless him, he'd also once appeared in my Eating Owt column – Geordie pun – after he and a friend had been asked at a café in Hartlepool if they were pensioners. Told that it was indeed the case, the waitress sliced a dumpling and gave them half each. "I wonder what she'd have done if it had been a fried egg" said John.

When John Littlefair was born, Timothy Hackworth's town had eight Methodist churches. When he died, aged 82 in 2014, there was just one. It was there that we bade farewell to a brilliant man.

The subsequent chapter on cricket notes that the fairground was in town. This was the same Whit weekend, the following day, the shows - for the shows must go on, in latter days even on the Sabbath - still overflowing the football pitch at the bottom of the Rec where far into his 60s little George Elliott would referee local league football while seldom straying beyond the centre circle.

Much the same shape as the ball, only bigger, George was also a director of Shildon FC and the world champion raffle ticket seller. As with Durham prison, none escaped.

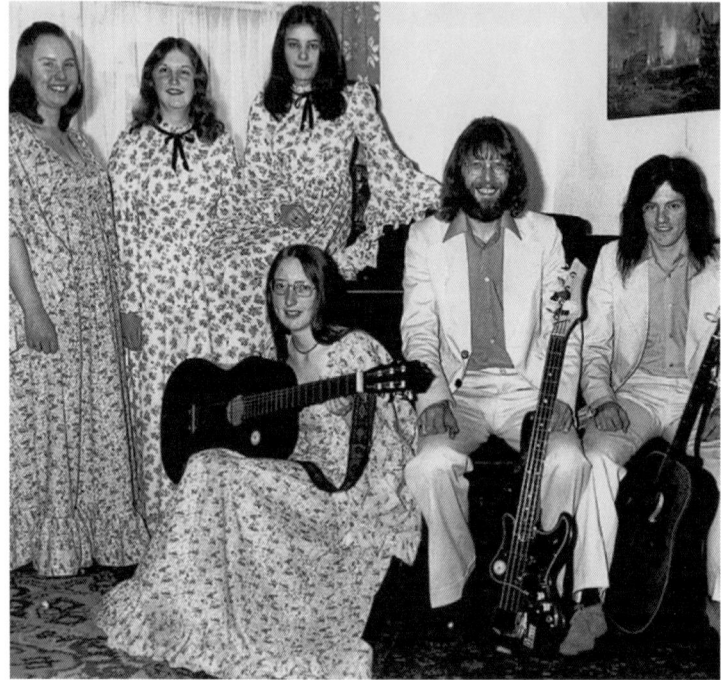

Marbles of the age: Geordie's Penker

Once the fair accompanied Shildon Show, a largely craft-based affair begun in the 1860s that honed competitive edges for miles around and not least in the cake baking classes. It was the bragging rights, not the 7/6d prize, that most mattered, not least in the ceaseless sororal rivalry between mother and Aunty Betty.

As an impressionable 13-year-old I once won a goldfish at the shows, that unfortunate creature in turn presented to Pat Gell, daughter of the Shildon telephonist in the days when even local calls had day and night to be routed that way.   Though not necessarily ungrateful, young Miss Gell wisely decided that there were plenty more fish in the sea.

In many ways the shows have changed little, though in our day there was no need for bored looking security guards at the entrance – as now there are – because no one would have dreamed of pinching your goldfish.

Still you can hook a duck, prize every time, still try to knock over a pile of cans with an effete bean bag, still test the mettle of Wild Bill's rifle range. Only the caterpillar seems to be in hibernation, lost out to a more permissive age. Come to think you can no longer win a goldfish, not in a polythene bag anyway, though the darts stall offers an octopus mood (dunno) to all who give it a throw.

There's a food van called Fat Frank's, the corpulent gentleman not on view, others selling Chinese noodles and Japanese sushi, Greek street food, New York burgers and, bit closer to home, Yorkshire pudding wraps.

It's the charges that have changed most - £3 for three shots at a simple football game, £4 a go or three cars for a tenner on the dodgems where once it was sixpence and a squeeze. At 4 30pm on this Whit Sunday there are more on the dodgems alone – so much for best avoided – than there were in Shildon Methodist church. Perhaps that should remain the thought for the day.

Chapter eighteen

Shops workers

Inevitably there've been some memorable characters among the wagon works workforce. Those I knew well included George Romaines, who became a star in the early days of Tyne Tees Television, Jack Watson – a highly talented all-round cricketer and renowned football scout – and Tommy Taylor, one of that line of champion railway boxers and a man who became a long-serving local councillor, windmill-tilting Lib-Dem parliamentary candidate and honorary Durham County alderman.

Tommy, a delightful man, had been spending part of the night shift removing wax from his ears with a matchstick – many apocryphal, stories abound about how the wagon workers passed the night – when a workmate inadvertently jogged his elbow and half the stick became marooned in the inner workings of Tom's cranium.

They took him to Darlington Memorial hospital where sympathy may have been mixed with incredulity. "Ah" said the doctor, "I see you've come for the match."

Probably Tom had also been around in the 1970s when the BR Boxing Club (as then it was) held shows at the Kings Head Hotel in Darlington and someone thought it a good idea to have topless young ladies perambulating the ring between rounds in a pretty diaphanous attempt to remind spectators how far things had gone. Too far, some supposed.

A senior works manager, whose identity may remain undisclosed but who was a prominent local Methodist, implored me

Not struck: Tommy Taylor

not to put anything in the paper. Unlike the young ladies, the regrettable episode was covered up. Tom died, aged 82 and much mourned, in 2023.

The wagon works fire brigade may not have had much cause for alarm. George Smith records that the first fire engines were horse drawn, then hauled behind a locomotive. Though Shildon fires were few and generally feeble, the crew had been sent off to Hartlepool docks back in 1954 to assist with a major blaze there.

Jack Watson headed both the security and fire fighting operations. You could tell he was a gaffer because he had a white helmet. The other lads wore black.

He was born in High Spen, near Gateshead, served as a police officer in the Northumberland force, had a lengthy and very successful Minor Counties cricket career with both Durham and Northumberland and at the age of 70 claimed a hat-trick for Bearpark, a former pit village west of Durham. "I was so old, the other players kept calling me Mr Watson" he said. The ball remained, mounted, on Jack's mantelpiece in Shildon.

He'd also kept goal for Ashington, on one occasion conceding nine at Grimsby Reserves but still named man of the match. They gave him a box of kippers, though he probably asked for chips on the side. Jack was a six-foot trencherman, familiar in supermarket cafes across the north, was Shildon Railway Cricket Club president until his death but for some reason missed the launch of the club calendar in 2010. "If I'd known there was corned beef pie things would have been different" he said.

Shifted to Shildon, the Watsons had lived near us in Alexandra Street. We'd play cricket with their son Ian in the preposterously pot-holed back alley between their house and Geordie Ellis's scrapyard, though whether the back alley took spin cannot now be recalled.

As a football scout, Jack was so highly regarded that at the age of 89 he was appointed Middlesbrough FC's scouting coordinator, given his own office and secretarial support, which may have been key. Jack was old school, a PC to Jack was a former constabulary colleague and a laptop was something on which to bounce the bairn.

He'd five times been caretaker manager of Darlington FC, twice declined the job on a permanent basis, his 90 birthday celebrated with a big Sunday lunch party at the Darlington stadium built by that other well-remembered Shildon lad, George Reynolds. Probably it was coincidental. He died before reaching 91.

George Romaines was a Shildon lad, born in 1930, the family home in Scott Street, just a short shunt from the Shops. He was another Tin Tacks boy, his mum given 19 shillings a week to scrub the school floors. After leaving school at 15,

*Chiming: George Romaines (on left, with cravat)
and the cast of the One o'clock Show*

George found himself an apprentice electrician in the break-up yard alongside Jack Kasher – who'd survived the Great War trenches, won an FA Amateur Cup winner's medal with Bishop Auckland in 1921 and died while on his way to put on his digits at Old Shildon Club – and Dickie Downs, a former Barnsley footballer who became the only Shildon man to win a full England cap. Dickie's widow lived at the top of Albert Street. We'd deliver milk there before school, pint of TT seven days a week and half-a-dollar tip at Christmas. That the Barnsley mascot in Dickie's playing days was a donkey called Amos may be considered irrelevant.

Nor was he the only Shildon lad to make a name on television. Gordon Peters, born Gordon Peter Wilkinson in Southland Gardens – behind the football ground – was in 1973 given a prime time BBC comedy series. Unfortunately it clashed with *Coronation Street* and was never repeated. Though he had bit parts in countless other sitcoms, though he provided the voices of the Mister Men – the male Mister Men, anyway – and though he trod the boards until shortly before his death, aged 95, in 2022, things were never quite the same.

George had started on 12/8d a week at a time when Italian prisoners of war were still at the works. "They made the sweetest tea ever" he recalled in a biography commissioned by his three sons to mark his 80th birthday.

His flimsy earnings were greatly augmented by the realisation that the boy George could sing for his supper – not least at Spennymoor greyhound track where he could pocket £12 50 a night for crooning between races but knew, knew fine well, when to stop. "Not even Frank Sinatra at his fabulous best could have held the audience once the dogs started being paraded at Spennymoor" said George.

In January 1959 he sang on the opening night of Tyne Tees Television, thereafter becoming a striking star on the *One O'clock Show*, a five-days-a-week lunchtime entertainment which ran for 1,098 programmes over five years. George missed just two. "It was like painting the Forth Bridge" he told me. "The moment you finished one show, you had to go off somewhere to start running through the next."

Though employed as a singer, on one occasion he'd appeared as an "Ancient Briton" on a daily "caveman" sketch called Ug and Og, neanderthal stories fronted by Austin Steele and Jack Haig. The vigilant viewer who pointed out that the ancient Briton had forgotten to take off his wristwatch won two guineas from the listings magazine.

When time was called on the *One O'Clock Show*, George joined the station's public relations department in Newcastle but never left Shildon, settling in Enfield Lodge, near the Rec, about which more in a later chapter. For some reason he never went back to the works. He was 82 when he died in 2012, just days after Jack Watson.

Chapter nineteen

Jewel purpose

John Priestley is 84 at the time of our chat in May 2024, still up and about at four o'clock most mornings – "someone has to wekken the birds up" he says, cheerfully – still at the newsagent's at six to collect his daily paper. Though not getting away all that well – as probably they say in Shildon – he remains articulate, amiable and engaging.

Though it's barely 11 o'clock, his wife Margaret offers substantial sustenance – "just a bite" she says, as Co Durham folk like to understate – and probably if you've been up seven hours you're ready for it.

John was a West Auckland lad, lived out the back of the football ground, drove a bus to Wembley when West reached the 1961 FA Amateur Cup final – "the driver had to pay in those days, but it was only about five shillings" – and wrote in protest to the *Daily Herald* when the BBC stopped screening the second half of the final. "It mightn't have mattered to them in London but up here it was as big as the FA Cup final" he said.

A fitter, and manifestly fit for purpose, he joined the works-force in 1964 and soon afterwards became an Amalgamated Engineering Union representative on the office-based team – two AEU, two NUR, two Boilermakers – which represented the wagon workers. "They called us the Big Six" he recalls. "For a short time after I went we were the Big Seven. I'd no intention of being a union official but they asked for volunteers to put their hands up. No one did, so it landed on John."

In his early days, he says, the biggest problems among the men were frozen finger and loss of hearing. "There wasn't the protection they have today and there wasn't much health and safety, either. Some of the men were almost deaf because of it.

"I served under three works managers and none of them was awkward as you might say. We'd say our piece and they'd say theirs. Most of the time it was sorted out. It was a very friendly place, no one really argued. I won't tell a lie, I enjoyed it."

He was also encouraged to stand for the district organiser's job, held by Darlington-based Harry Hammond, but failed to be elected. "Too many left-wingers on the other side" says John.

Shildon, however, was a town with all of its eggs – or at least the great majority of them – in one brittle-bottomed basket. The announcement in 1982 that the works was to close came as a shock, the engineering union at once at the forefront of efforts to save 2,600 jobs and, perhaps with it, the future of an entire town.

"There were rumours but, honestly, we'd not really seen it coming. We'd just won a big order from the Congo, the high-capacity wagons were going really well, work from Switzerland and all over. If you got a job at the wagon works, you expected to be there for life and your son to follow you on an apprenticeship. Everyone thought it was secure."

Not long before, someone in management had supposed Shildon "the jewel in British Rail Engineering's crown" – the ironic title of a Durham University PhD when the jewel swiftly tarnished. On Facebook, the *Shildon Works story* was divided into 15 parts, with the mildly insulting explanation that they didn't want to threaten attention spans. These days it would have come with a trigger warning, and no telling at whose

Speaking out: John Priestley addresses a closure protest meeting, 1983.
Bishop Auckland MP Derek Foster is on his right.

temple the trigger might have been pointed.

Though a reprieve was announced, few – with good cause – were reassured. The fight, and the fighter, went to London, to Brussels, even to the Conservative Party conference in Brighton.. "Norman Tebbitt asked me to address it, it was a very strange feeling I can tell you" says John. "Tebbitt even said he'd come to Shildon but he never did. He must have got on his bike."

He paid several visits to the House of Commons. "The good thing about the Commons is that outsiders – Strangers they call them – aren't allowed to buy drinks. Even a Tory MP bought me a pint once – I made sure I drank it pretty quickly."

Labour Party leader Neil Kinnock addressed a meeting at the Railway Institute, spoke of being "sorry from the bottom of my being" that he had no good news to bring, told them a unique level of skill and commitment was being rewarded with the closure of the gates. "Government considers that whole areas of the country can just be discarded, and can't distinguish between slimming and starvation.".

There'd also been a rally at the town's football ground and a mass protest march through London for which they hired a train, British Rail unlikely to have made its corporate fortune since every last man among the marchers was on a free pass. "The lads were brilliant" John recalls. "We were shouting – "Maggie out, that sort of thing" – but a police superintendent told me he'd never seen such a disciplined march and offered me the use of a police car for the rest of the day."

He declined. "My place was with the lads. We never once stepped out of line, either physically or figuratively. I was very proud to be with those lads that day. They did themselves and Shildon proud, too."

The BBC also talked of an "impressive campaign". Seldom, their reporter added, had a town rallied so spectacularly to a cause.

With hindsight, would John have done things differently, perhaps called an all-out strike? "I don't think we could have done. If we'd walked out, that would have given them an excuse to close the works immediately and to blame the men. We had a lot of support – the local MP (Derek Foster), the MEP (Roland Boyes), Sedgefield District Council but Mrs Thatcher was determined to close the works" – and like an A4 Pacific (one of those streaks) at the end of a country branch line, the lady wasn't for turning.

"She boasted she'd never been on a train, made a virtue of it, that's how much she cared about the railways" says John. "We had to fight hard to try to get other industries and other jobs onto the site, but Mrs Thatcher was determined to close Shildon."

David Reynolds's history of the Railway Institute comes out in sympathy: "A hard-nosed Tory Prime Minister on a mission to prove that the influence of the trades unions could be broken was never going to listen to their voices or to relent in the slightest."

Others felt similarly. At the reunion to mark the 25th anniversary of closure, local councillor Tommy Taylor – the man with the matchstick inadvertently lodged in his ear – sang *Your cheating heart*. None doubted to whom the cheating heart belonged.

Battle lost, redundant with the rest of them, John became the neighbourhood watch and farm watch co-ordinator in Teesdale, was an active member of the Durham Football Association council and chairman of the Crook and District League. Tony Blair, by then Prime Minister, invited him to a reception in Downing Street. "I told him I couldn't stop for long because I had 20 farmers waiting for me on a reccy that night. They even gave me a van with a blue light on top. I liked that job, too."

He and Margaret now live in Staindrop, about ten miles west of Shildon. These days he rarely gets over that way so reserves judgment on how things may have changed. At the 1999 reunion he'd been less cautious, however. "The day the Shops closed, the heartbeat of the town just stopped."

The most noticeable thing about the vast wagon works site, these days rebranded Hackworth Industrial Park and colonised by all manner of other industries, is that it's all pretty quiet. Whatever shot blasting, powder coating and even diagnostics may be, they're unlikely to require a drop hammer. There are times, goodness knows, when you can almost hear the birds cough.

Many of the buildings remain, none likely to win an award from the Royal Institute of British Architects, some augmented by their new owners. Some of the floodlight towers from the marshalling yard survive, too, a reminder of what might be supposed the not-so-dark ages.

There's a thermo-plastics company, another offering "Innovation through heritage" – which may need further explanation – a third in the business of "road marking solutions." Have you noticed that on the motorways these days every other lorry promotes on its side not haulage or transport but logistics solutions or, more likely, sustainable logistics solutions. It's as if it's the answer to everything.

Another business appears to offer "painless dent removal"; closer inspection reveals that the removal is paintless.

Deli's Diner, signed from the main road, proves no more than a trailer pulled by a car, four or five plastic chairs on the sun-blessed pavement outside. Mandy's Kitchen, on the neighbouring Furnace Industrial Estate – once the site of Furnace Colliery – isn't some re-born pit head canteen, either. It's another trailer.

At the time of passing they've two customers between them. A few hundred yards away, on Redworth Road, a noonday queue forms talkatively outside Betty's chip shop, and it's not even Fish Friday.

The second-most remarkable thing about Hackworth Industrial Park, however, is the number of scrap metal merchants, or recycling companies or in one case a "commercial vehicle breaker and exporter" of which this is the "Durham processing facility." The biggest appears to be Northern Metal Recycling, half-hidden nearby is the home of the Class G5 Locomotive Company, painstakingly building Shildon's first steam locomotive in about 160 years and no matter that the G5 sounds like one of those European summits which politicians and assorted hangers-on so greatly seem to enjoy.. Much more of them, it's to be hoped, on an open day.

End to end-of-the-road, rusting vehicles await the cutters, grimly reminiscent of those 1960s photographs of abandoned steam engines at the North Road works in Darlington, silently sizing their fate. Once there were millwrights and pattern makers, jig fitters, die sinkers, forgemen, blacksmiths and goodness knows what else. Now they cut up cars.

Others arrive on the back of a lorry; a caravan, happy holidays abandoned, has its doors hanging off. If this is make or break for Shildon, the latter seems the more obvious fate.

Run by Durham Business, an offshoot of the County council, the Furnace estate mostly has smaller units. Up the top, trees still in leaf, it's almost verdant. Outside one of the units, a van promotes "amazing" parties with rodeo bulls, hot tubs and the like. All we had 60-odd years ago was pass the parcel and, when things got really exciting, a game of postman's knock.

Getting up steam: the Class G5 workshop

Eager to chat, a couple of chaps from one of the workshops wander across. Sadly, they belong firmly to the "changed for the worse" school and however counterintuitive, however unprofessional, such views are not really to be encouraged.

Among all the good things happening in Shildon, and there really are quite a lot, none may be more exciting, more surprising or – paradoxically – more appropriate than that meticulous construction of a Class G5 0-4-4 steam engine on the former wagon works site.

In the Cradle of the Railways, it's Mike Wood's baby, will weigh 58 tons, measure 37ft, look fantastic, cost getting on £2m and, it's hoped, eventually haul passenger services on the main line. The gestation period, however, makes a hairy mammoth seem positively short term by comparison.

Dr Wood, a train spotter as a lad, had the idea in 2005 when practising as a GP in Spennymoor. Now 74, he still works two days a week at a surgery in Crook – partly, he admits, to help fund his passion. "I just thought there was something missing in steam locomotive preservation" he says. "A lot of preserved locos are Great Western, there's a real dearth of North Eastern Railway engines.

"The G5s were terrific little engines – simple, beautifully proportioned, reliable and good looking. You could almost say they were sexy. I only had very basic engineering knowledge, not much more than a schoolboy, it was something I had to pick up."

The G5 Locomotive Company's website carries the strapline "Recreating a North Eastern legend."

He's also been much involved with the preserved Weardale

Railway, chiefly operating between Stanhope and Wolsingham, owned three Mark 1 coaches on the line – "rot boxes, every time it rained they deteriorated further" – and still owns a single coach diesel multiple unit – "my bubble car" – for which he paid £12,000 and has spent another £90,000 on restoration.

"Someone offered me £2,000 for it. I asked him why he thought I was going to accept £2,000 after all that effort and money and he said it was all he had. I turned the offer down."

The G5 class – class of its own - was designed by the NER's chief engineer Wilson Worsdell, after whom one of Shildon's newer streets is named, 110 of them built at Darlington in the last years of Queen Victoria's reign. All but two lasted into the 1950s, particularly familiar on the lines around Tyneside and on local services between Durham and Newcastle, but by the end of the decade all had reached the end of the line, broken up back where they began.

None had names – "they were humble locomotives" says Mike, wholly affectionately – nor will the new build be christened. Its number, 1759, will follow sequentially from the other 110. Like all the others, too, 1759 will identify – or at least be referred to – as female and without fear of transgendering.

There's an open day on the Shildon site in October 2024. I'd last met Mike Wood there in the Spring of 2013, work seemingly well underway, Dr Wood hopeful that it would be complete by the end of 2014. When George Turner Smith visited in 2017 for his book on New Shildon's railway history they'd still offered the prospect of being up and running within another 15 months.

North Eastern Railway Restoration, the company Mike chaired in 2013, employed ten men – four of them former wagon workers – but was liquidated without debts. Now the G5 Locomotive Company has 220 shareholders, a great many Friends (even "Superfriends") but depends wholly upon volunteers and, little and largesse, upon donations.

In 2013 he'd estimated spending at £1m, now supposes the total to be £1.3m with maybe another £400,000 needed. How much of his own money? "£136,000, maybe £138,000 now" he answers at once.

When last we'd met he'd also talked of his wife's patience and tolerance. Since then they've divorced. Anything to do with the Class G5? "Let's just say it was a contributory factor" he confesses.

Even the hope of steam for the S&D bicentenary has long evaporated. "We underestimated the complexity" says Dr Wood and for a "simple" engine, that's pretty paradoxical, too.

Mike Wood was a West Yorkshire lad, came to Spennymoor with his parents when he was 13 – his father was a GP, too – at a time when steam traction was fast fading from the region's railways. One of his brothers is helping build a working replica of *Mountaineer*, the first engine to work the Ffestiniog Mountain Railway in Wales. "Steam engines are genetic, they just get in the blood, you can't do anything about it" says Mike.

Major parts of the new locomotive, patterns of other parts, are spread around the G5 workshop, each carefully labelled and classified. Bits are identified as eccentric sheaves and slide valves; there's a motion fund, a construction fund, a ten gallon fund. Were it a Lego kit, or at least a junior Lego kit, it would be easy to envisage putting it all together in a day or two, job done. Unfortunately it's not. Dr Wood talks of the little things, company chief executive Tim Taylor of the fiddly bits, all to be put punctiliously into place.

Part of the delay, says Mike, has been because few in the industry have the relevant expertise. "No one had built a rational crank axle since 1952, there's a lack of the right engineering skills. Those who can do it don't want your money, they've got enough work on. There's a huge delay in getting everything done.."

So is the basic principle of locomotive building very much different from Timothy Hackworth's time, men toiling by candlelight with rudimentary tools in oft-freezing workshops? "The Victorians were brilliant engineers" says Mike. "Basically they were producing drawings on the back of fag packets, or would have done if there'd been fag packets in those days, and turning them into steam engines. The principles are still pretty much the same, it's just the tools that are different."

Dr Ian Taylor, chief exec Tim's late father, grew up in Durham, attended the Royal Grammar School in Newcastle, travelled daily between the two by a train usually headed by a G5. He also became a GP and was much involved with the G5 project. His other passion was visiting Co Durham's pubs, all 750 – at the time, nothing like so many now – ticked off. "He really did it, I still have his map" says Tim, a chemistry graduate who sells kitchen utensils and breathes steam.

Unlike Mike Wood, Tim believes that the allure misses a generation. "It's like beards. Your fathers had beards, we don't, all the youngsters today have beards. I don't know why it should be." To him, he adds, it's a glory project. "The G5s were a stunning piece of engineering, a wonderful piece of equipment, the proportions lovely. It'll be fabulous to have one in steam again. We'll get there."

That Shildon folk appear thus far to have shown little interest may be because the project's little publicised, the company's base – prosaically Unit 8S – is concealed near where the wheelwright's shop once turned a shift. "We had the mayor a few years ago, a woman from Durham County Council once but that's about it" says Mike.

We're sitting around a handsome table that once served the waiting room at Gateshead East station. One of many cupboards overflowing with books – railway books – came from Gateshead East, too. Such their attention to detail, they probably also know the whereabouts of every book

The completed locomotive will need extensive trials, probably on the North Yorkshire Moors Railway, before being cleared to haul passenger services on some of the region's preserved railways – the NYMR, the Aln Valley, the Weardale, the Wensleydale – and later, they hope, on main line specials. "These little engines could do 60mph hauling five or six coaches between Newcastle and Middlesbrough" says Tim. "She's not going to worry about 25mph on the Wensleydale."

As now they see it, Mike Wood could be almost 80 before his dream comes true. What might happen then? "I'm an optimist, a glass three-quarters full man. This is an ideal heritage project and we'll have done the hard bits" he insists, "after you've built one it's much simpler. We'll probably build another."

Chapter twenty

Part of the reunion

Forty years to the day since Shildon Shops formally and fune-really fell silent, a reunion is held at the Railway Institute. It's Sunday June 30 2024, one or two houses in Redworth Road showing their colours for the forthcoming general election – unanimously for Labour's man – one or two more flying the flag for the national football team. One seems rather more likely to be successful than the other.

A couple of old Shops workers compare notes on the way in, not about welding, wagons or whatever but the number of pills each must swallow every morning in order to hold body and soul in symmetry.

The first chap says he takes ten every morning. That's nowt, says his mate, perforce he must pop 13. "Tek nee notice" says a third gentleman. "They'll be starting on who has the most bits of medical kit inside them soon." Truly it is a sign, a symptom perhaps, of changed times.

ITV North East, what folk still call Tyne Tees Television, had carried a piece a couple of days previously, included a 1984 clip when closure was imminent. "Shildon Shops is Shildon's heritage, why should they let Mrs Thatcher take our heritage away?" a lady asks helplessly before pretty much answering her own question.

"If Mrs Thatcher says it has to close, Mrs Thatcher closes plac-es. Look at Consett."

Beneath a chapter heading "The siege of Shildon", the splendid brochure produced four decades later to mark annihilation's anniversary reiterates the thought. "A hard-nosed Tory prime minister was never going to listen to their voices or relent in the slightest."

The main hall's thronged, the bars bouncing. Jane Hackworth Young, at once encountered, still talks of closure – "tragic, just tragic" – while enthusiastically seeking signatures on a peti-tion to save the original station buildings at Heighington, three miles up the line, said to be the world's first.

There are folk who recall my dad and his iron horse, who re-member my Aunty Betty ("didn't she like a game of bingo at the Hippodrome?") who talk of Uncle Jim and Aunty Jenny, Lambton Street locals, who sang their hearts out with the Op Soc and who danced in step, too.

There's a guy who bears a marked resemblance to Russ Abott but probably isn't since the comedian may never have got his hands dirty at the works, another who's come from Finland, though he has to make his excuses in order to reach Broms-grove before nightfall. What Bromsgrove has that Shildon hasn't it's impossible to say. There are old men with children, grandchildren, maybe yet younger generations, and the great thing is that pretty much all of the bairns seem fascinated.

In the main hall there's an exhibition of wagon works memo-rabilia and artefacts, from bells to bogies and from blue boiler suits – one size fitted all? – to the BRSA leek club donations box. A *Daily Mirror* cutting, dated January 1984 and by-lined Neil Kinnock – then leader of the Labour Party – is headlined "End of the line for our men of iron."

Another cutting shows Roy's Rolls, the *Coronation Street*

Lying down on the job: the reunion effigy

café, a Shildon Shops wagon plate prominent then as now on the wall. The idiosyncratic Roy Cropper is said to be a train buff, so probably knows the Shildon story, too.

An elderly poster promotes a Christmas Eve dance festival at the Institute – "ladies ninepence, gentlemen a shilling" - another advertises a concert, not just any old concert but a grand concert, attractions including Evelyn Simpson (elocutionist), Mabel Lee (mezzo-soprano, Shildon) Jessie and Arthur Cass, comedy duettists and Arthur Broadbent (Darlington) said to do "character sketches". Admission sixpence, reserved seats a shilling.

Between times the 2,500 or so workforce turned out or mended around 800 rail vehicles each week, alone producing 11,083 merry-go-round wagons between 1965-83. When the music stopped, the order book was full, that's what really narked them.

There are books, too, some to buy and others – like Ron Spedding's 1988 memoir of a working life at the Shops – simply for reliving well-thumbed history. Ron spent 42 years at the Shops and had, he confessed, a sort of love/hate relationship with the place. "I have been known to praise and defend it on occasions and have also cursed it and the day my father put my name down to work there.

"It was at Shildon Shops that I learned a trade, made and developed lifelong friendships and enjoyed the true meaning of that word….The Shops was a community, a very large family of proud people."

Ron had also recalled the wartime years when women – albeit in those unalluring and distinctly asexual boiler suits – were added to the workforce and the subsequent effect, perhaps co-incidental he disingenuously supposed, on washing and toilet facilities. "Previously washing one's hands was frowned upon and the conditions were primitive.

"They consisted of battered tins or buckets, each jealously guarded by four or five men, representing a group or unit. There were hundreds scattered throughout the site. The men would take turns to go to the smiths' shop or forge and return with a piece of red hot steel or iron. This was dropped into the tin or bucket containing cold water and, hey presto, hot water for the use of."

The gentle touch, they not only gained basins (hands, for the use of) but a marked and doubtless welcome improvement in toilet facilities which hitherto had most kindly been described as communal. "The seating consisted of one long plank running the full length of the building and divided into eight cubicles, each one partitioned with accommodation for one person."

In the old pit terraces, similar netty-and-not-nice provision was made at the bottom of the yard, known as two-holers (or, of course, multiples thereof.)

Ron Spedding continued: "The water channel also ran the full length of the building and carried the water below the seating in a slow continual flow. Sometimes when the toilet had a full house, some joker in the top cubicle would use the flow of water to play a practical joke, setting fire to a piece of newspaper and then laying it in the slow moving water to float past and beneath each seat in turn". The imprecations flowed rather more quickly than the water did; the management conveniently built amenity blocks instead.

Among the Railway Institute's own treasures – there are many – is an 1833 poster, when Hackworth was still superintendent, addressed to those in the employ of the Stockton and Darlington Railway Company at New Shildon and laying down stipulations for their service. A man who turned up more than a quarter of an hour after the bell rang would lose a quarter of a day's pay, a man leaving his work without giving notice to the clerk or foreman would be fined one shilling as would any workman swearing or using abusive language to his shop mates. Any man found drinking would be considered to have forfeited his situation.

Terms and conditions (as now they might be supposed) were little less draconian in 1867. The working day would be from 6am to 6pm except on Saturdays, when knocking off time was one o'clock. No one was allowed to take firewood off the site, smoking would be punished by a ten shilling fine for a first offence and dismissal for a second, the use of "profane or improper" language "strictly cautioned against."

So at length it went on, the curious thing about so comprehensive a code of conduct that most of the early workforce were reckoned illiterate, so might hardly read and learn. The Sunday lunchtime lads sup their ale and consider their own situation in the summer of 2024. Maybe, they agree, things aren't so bad after all.

Perhaps the day's most surprising exhibit is the sleeping bag laid – solemnly, somnolently – on the main hall carpet, a nod and forty winks to the widely held belief that the wagon works night shift was given to a little surreptitious shut-eye and a matter to which we shall return over a pint. The sleeping hag is occupied by a pale faced effigy who appears to be wearing ear plugs and by the effigy's teddy bear. The sound of gentle snoring comes from the direction of the bag. Investigative journalism reveals the bear to be the culprit and no matter that the snoring appears to be coming from its navel. Bears are built differently, as any child knows.

The bar's so rich in reminiscence it's barely possible to hear the Sabbath dominoes shalt-not shuffling. Such the demand for pies in the main hall, it's suggested that they may have to be restricted to half-a-pie-per-person. The Institute's working on a ten-year survival plan – many more days like this and the problem will be resolved in the space of a Sunday afternoon.

The anniversary brochure also carries a piece by dedicated and ever-helpful Shildon historian Alan Ellwood on annihilation's aftermath, lamenting that the jewel in the crown's closure came despite a full order book. "The town today is much changed from how it was in 1984 and much poorer for it. It feels in many ways like it has never fully recovered" he writes. The bar lads put it more bluntly.

What's changed? "It's a s**thole, that's what's changed" says Alan Coates, quaffing his lager. Chiefly, echoing Paula Nelson at Shildon Alive, he points the finger at what he terms exploitative landlords, exacerbated by estate agents' frequent findings that Shildon is the cheapest place in the land in which to buy property, a dubious distinction shared sometimes with Ferryhill, a few miles north, and with Horden on the Durham coast coming up on wretched rails.

"They'll do up houses on the cheap, rent them out for more than they're worth, attract people who can't afford to live down south but who aren't really comfortable in Shildon, either" says Alan.

He'd started at the works as a 15-year-old – "left school at 14, really" – following his dad who'd daily cycled the 20-odd miles each way from Thornaby. He knew it was a good job, says Alan.

He'd lived in Lambton Street, too, recalled days and nights (as do many) when there was no need to lock the front door. "No one would come in, not without knocking. We'd even leave the door open when we went to bed.

"The Shops was a great place to work, lots of camaraderie, though there didn't seem to be a whole lot of health and safety in those days. You took risks and there didn't seem anyone who wanted to stop you."

Richard Skilton, his mate, also worries about Shildon. "Look at all the rubbish in the back streets, it's a sign. You ring the council, they say they'll come, they don't. I really worry about what's happening to this place. The rail trails are brilliant, but the rest of the town leaves a lot to be desired."

Beneath the headline "Refugees are being dumped up north"- and the sub-heading "Families sent from London are being put in homes with no gas or electricity" – a series of *Northern Echo* articles three months later highlighted the issue. "What we are seeing is very concerning, vulnerable people are being transported hundreds of miles from their support networks and being abandoned in an area that doesn't have the experience and well-developed services to integrate them into the community" said new Bishop Auckland MP Sam Rushworth, the face on those election posters.

Durham City MP Mary Kelly Foy joined concerned voices. "It's absolutely abhorrent that London authorities are not only discharging their duties by relocating people out of the city, away from any support network they may have, but they are putting vulnerable families in properties that are simply not fit for habitation."

The following month the *Echo* told of a young mother, all her life in the Hillingdon area of London, who'd been told by the council that unless she and her young child moved 250 miles north – to Horden – they'd be on the streets within days.

Ms Kelly Foy was aghast. "It's little more than social cleansing" she said, though even that reaction may have seemed restrained compared to Chris Bailey of the Action on Empty Homes charity. North-East towns like Shildon, he said "were becoming London's leper colonies."

Elsewhere in the Institute they're talking football, remembering the successful Shildon BR side of the 1980s and, much the same time, the all-conquering Shildon Works Juniors. The BR, as all knew them, had won an Auckland and District League and Cup double in 1981, beating Ferryhill John Dee (it's recalled) 2-0 in the final at Bishop Auckland's ground, well-remembered men like Eddie Sharp and Dennis "the Fridge" Ferguson. "That team would have beaten any Northern League side" insists Ronnie Keller.

What of those occasions when blind eye seemed turned to shut-eye, when sleeping on the job seemed to be taken lying down (though not, necessarily, with a teddy bear?) "There were some good jobs to be had at the works but they were hard and dirty jobs" says George Jary. "I'll tell you what it was, there was only a certain amount of work you could do each night, only 110 per cent of what you were allocated. After that you might get your head down for a bit; it made you worked quicker, and better."

"It's what these days you'd call an incentive bonus" says Ronnie Keller. "They broke all kinds of production records at Shildon Shops. Maybe you got an hour's kip, but it worked."

At the heart of it all is Dave Reynolds, now a vigorous chairman of both the Institute and of the Shildon Heritage Alliance group, an impressive portfolio for a Bishop boy. In 2019 he'd overseen a film called *The full works*. Now he's working on Made in Shildon, a new documentary which should be finished in the autumn. At four o'clock, Institute still lifting, few rushing home for the five o'clock kick-off, he gazes approvingly around. "A sad occasion" he says, "but it's been a canny day."

Chapter twenty-one

Anniversary waltz

Those around the Stockton and Darlington Railway have always been keen sumptuously to celebrate their anniversaries. Shildon wasn't always invited to the party.

The old town, truth to tell, sometimes seemed like the little boy who Santa Claus forgot. Might it even have been centre of global attention in 1975 had not the Wagon Works yard been the only remaining area of railway real estate big enough to accommodate the coruscating Cavalcade?

The first real milestone was in 1875, the occasion pretty much hijacked by the burghers (spellings may vary) of Darlington. The Lord Mayor of London was invited, the Lord Mayor's trumpeters turned out – late – the town was vividly decked and hundreds from across Britain and beyond banqueted in a marquee on the cricket field.

One of many banners proclaimed "The pick, the hammer and the locomotive, the source of England's greatness."

Shildon was ten miles and half a world away, save that the North Eastern Railway gave men with ten or more years service half a day off, possibly a free pass to Darlington, and for some of them a "plain dinner" in the evening.

A locomotive exhibition was staged at the North Road Engine Works, three or four of them built in Shildon. One, No 1033, was even named *Shildon*. No 10, *Auckland*, was said to have been built by Timothy Hackworth himself but in reality was an imposter (or what schoolboys of succeeding generations would

have supposed a swizz.)

No 10 was actually No 26, *Pilot*, built in 1848 by Alfred Kitching. In his 1974 book on Stockton and Darlington anniversaries, the prolific railway author Ken Hoole notes that two Kitching locomotives were available and none of Hackworth's. The decision taken to pass off *Pilot* as *Auckland* in Hackworth's imagined honour, though whether that upright gentleman would have approved is questionable. "As the names had been removed, it was simply a case of painting a new number on a rather decrepit engine" wrote Hoole, laconically. And still they called it *Auckland*....

By the time of the centenary celebrations of 1925, Stockton was also in on the act, starting point for a huge cavalcade attended by the supposedly great and possibly good. It ended at Darlington. Shildon remained ten miles away, though the LNER laid on a special train for workers and their families, may even have let them use privy tickets but failed, plain or otherwise, to lay on dinner.

The event took place on July 2, not September 27, so as to fit in with the meeting in Britain of an international railway conference and better to accommodate the timetable of the Duke and Duchess of York, the future King and Queen. Historians suggest it was a meticulous, magnificent and many splendoured occasion, railway staff and other lesser mortals involved in the procession issued with umpteen instructions including the directive that laughing and loitering were strictly forbidden.

Finally having reached Darlington, VIP guests were given a tour of the Faverdale works and of another locomotive exhibition before being wined and dined, the Faverdale paint shop glossed into a banqueting hall for the occasion and the menu including veal roll centenary, roast duckling a la G Stephenson, gourmandises a la Puffing Billy (honest), stuffed tomatoes a la Pease and strawberry melba Stockton and Darlington. Thereafter guests headed to their various homeward trains, on which dinner was served. Stockton's programme is said to have been yet more ambitious.

To mark the centenary. *The Northern Echo* produced a very splendid 84-page souvenir, the front cover vividly decorated with railway themes and the back occupied by an ad for Lingford's Baking Powder, said then to be just 64-years-old but born and raised in Bishop Auckland. To mark the occasion, beneath images of Edward Pease and George Stephenson, there was also a poem by Reginald Gray, the editor.

Divinest tongue of Shakespeare, Turner's brush

And Purcell's organ swelling down the ages,

Free-speaking Hampden whom no force might crush

Se England writes her fame in the world's pages.

No less their gift who, in the change of things

When pastoral counties of their ancient soil.

Laid on industrial altars offerings,

Fashioned this miracle of wheel and coil.

Who saw in these historic fields of Tees,

Of all the throng and long is dead,

These two men's engine puff and groan and wheeze

And knew the old life over, saw rails spread.

From shire to land, from land to continent

To make all earth their iron monument

Other advertisers included Gilbey's Invalid Port ("4/9d of all retailers"), Waterman's pens ("37 years with one nib"), Tiger Sauce ("millions of bottles sold annually, fivepence ha'penny"), Kompo ("for colds"), Lifebuoy soap ("your unseen health eye") and Stockton Co-operative Society which boasted 24,737 members and a £770,170 annual turnover.

There were no advertisers from Shildon. In Shildon, without even the accompaniment of Lord Prudhoe's Band, they probably raised a glass in the Cross Keys and were done.

The centenary of George Stephenson's death had been marked in 1948 by an exhibition of stationary locomotives at Manors station in Newcastle and by functions in Chesterfield, the Derbyshire town near which he lived.

Not (for once) to be outdone, Shildon staged a number of events two years later to mark the centenary of Hackworth's passing, including a visit from the 15-year-old Railway Queen

Ton up: the 1925 cavalcade

(somewhat curiously described in the centenary brochure as "versatile"). The occasion, it added, would not be complete without her, though perhaps the other Queen, the King's wife, was washing her hair that night. There was also the placing of a wreath on Hackworth's grave in St John's churchyard, a service with bands and choirs in the Recreation Ground, a Sunday open day at the wagon works and a week-long exhibition of models, as we have recalled, in the Scout Hall in Church Street.

I remember the Scouts Hall, indeed was briefly one of Baden's boys, riding along on the crest of a wave – on the back of someone's scrubbed-clean coal lorry - in the days that the Scouts carnival saw the streets lined up to 15,000 people, more than the town's population. More of that later.

The Hackworth event had been organised by a committee of 27, including T H W Cruddas, the works manager, and Hartley Appleby, the station master, he with a liking for signalmen's sandwiches. The brochure, price one shilling, offered abundant opportunity to extol the great engineer, starting with the wordy observation that the booklet would be found "a not unworthy record of the enterprise and gentlemanly characteristics of so worthy a man."

Then it became really unequivocal, with particular genuflection to *Royal George*, Hackworth's 1827 locomotive which pioneered the blast pipe. "Timothy Hackworth has the exclusive right to the high honour of being inventor of the locomotive. No one else can claim a title to that appellation."

Both the railway and its locomotives were described as female, though whether Mr Jemmy Stephenson employed similar language must forever remain a matter of historic uncertainty.

Among the truly remarkable things about the momentous Cavalcade of Steam, Sunday August 31 1975, is that without the ever-patient help of the local studies staff at Darlington library I'd barely be able to remember a thing about it.

Still it takes time for the microfilm librarian to change the reels, as probably they said in former times at Shildon Hippodrome, a chance myopically to peruse the shelves. There are ten or 11 books about George Stephenson, or George and Robert Stephenson, one of them by celebrated (and celebrity) biographer Hunter Davies sub-titled "A biographical study of the Father of the Railways".

Next to the Stephenson archives is a volume about the animals, mammals and reptiles of North-East England, an interesting exercise in cataloguing but these guys know what they're about. There appears to be nothing about Timothy Hackworth.

Back in the 1970s I wrote *The Northern Echo's* John North column, a five-days-a-week diary to which, freakishly, we shall also return. On the occasion of the great Cavalcade, however, there was only one person who was going to chronicle events for the self-styled Great Daily of the North, one who knew Shildon's railways like his own back yard – which effectively they'd been 20 years earlier – and probably only one who knew that "sesquicentennial" meant 150th, a little knowledge shamelessly showboated.

"Timothy Hackworth wouldn't have liked it" the cavalcade account began, "not on the Sabbath, anyway."

Durham Constabulary and British Transport Police deployed 220 officers on the ground and a chief inspector in a helicopter, perhaps he who spotted that five lengths of track had gone missing near the sidings. A local man, identity optional, was said in the time-tested phrase to be helping with enquiries.

Sixteen 12-coach diesel multiple units ran a shuttle between Shildon and the main line at Darlington, the bloke who sold Sunderland rosettes outside Roker Park football ground had changed allegiance and exorbitantly flogged Stockton and Darlington Railway colours instead.

Guests included the actor Kenneth More and Eric Treacy, the railway-fired Bishop of Wakefield. Alan Pegler, Flying Scotsman's former owner, provided the commentary. The great poet Sir John Betjeman had also hoped to be in Shildon, doubtless waxing lyrical, but was unwell. Very definitely there was Jim Sutton, an 88-year-old retired railway fireman from Hurworth

Place, near Darlington, who'd been a special guest at the centenary celebration as well.

Others had travelled overnight on the 1 15am sleeper from Kings Cross to Newcastle, £9 50 second class return including full English at Newcastle Central. Thereafter a day return from Darlington to Shildon was 40p.

The other curious thing was that, though more than 300,000 people from across the world thronged Shildon and the lineside towards Darlington, the *Echo* (price 5p) gave up just 200 words of its front page for the epochal occasion, the rest remaindered to page five, the journalistic equivalent of Shildon sidings.

The broadsheet front page told instead of "ten o'clock terrors" – London bombers – of continuing protests to free George Davis and of claims by shadow defence minister Bill Rodgers that the Labour Party was being infiltrated by "Trots". Back then it was easier for a camel to pass through the eye of a needle, as the Good Book has it, then to get regional news onto the front page of *The Northern Echo* but at least the ad for Binns store – "Save £100 on musquash coats" – was local if still far out of reach.

Coats that had been £340 were reduced to £240. Cavalcade or no, probably not everyone rushed at once.

Save for an invitation to "test drive a Mercedes Benz of your choice", page five was wholly given over to the bright-burnished occasion, its success yet more greatly assured because Newton Aycliffe councillor Jill Frise had withdrawn her threat to lie across the line in protest at spectator charges and spent Sunday digging up spuds in her back garden instead.

That she had been lambasted in an Echo leader had nothing

Full steam: part of the 1975 cavalcade

to do with it, she maintained, though the change of heart was perhaps fortuitous. Mrs Frise was rather a large lady and would have taken some shifting.

Otherwise all went well, the gentlemen of Aslef – as ever driving a hard bargain – having agreed to work an extra Sunday shift in return for double time. What's that phrase about the more things change the more they stay the same? Led by the replica of Locomotion One, tailended by the prototype High Speed Train, the 34-locomotive cavalcade travelled at 4mph, taking two hours to pass the throng. Five engines terminated at Heighington, Locomotion put on a low loader and taken back to Beamish Museum in north-west Durham, whence it had come. The remainder steamed off to Darlington.

Most of the engines had been on display at the well-decked wagon works the week previously, indelible old names like Sir Nigel Gresley and Princess Elizabeth, Mayflower, Green Arrow and Flying Scotsman (sponsored, let it be noted, by Scottish and Newcastle Breweries.) No. 910, a little North Eastern Railway tank engine, had also taken part in the 1875 and 1925 celebrations, though in 1888 had blamelessly been at the centre of controversy.

Back then, railwaymen were allowed to adorn their engines with paintings of wildlife and the like. Someone dressed 910 with a painting of a lady in (shall we say) a state of undress, perhaps not unlike those risky, risqué maidens at the boxing tournament. Management got the picture, too, such titillation forbidden forthwith.

Nothing so scandalous in 1975, though Fenchurch caused a minor sensation when someone appeared to have whitewashed her coal and *Railway Magazine* (35p) supposed the High Speed Train not just to have been dirty but "filthy dirty", stirring suggestions that amid such coal-fuelled company she might have been supposed a pariah.

Former Great Western locomotive Raveningham Hall caused jollity by playing Ilkley Moor Baht 'at on its whistle, a Yorkshire melody thought previously to have been the preserve of diesel multiple units, Sir Geoffrey Boycott and the Brighouse and Rastrick Brass Band.

In *Railway Magazine* a page of letters paid tribute to a "magnificently successful" event, while Caithness Glass advertised a set of six S&D glasses with "full colour design" for just £3. "A truly memorable day" the mag concluded and so, memory moistened, it was.

Headed "Of mutants and monkeys", the John North column on September 1 1975 – perhaps one I'd written a little earlier – had also originated in Shildon, or to be precise, back at what North-East folk call the shows. It concerned 71-year-old Harry Chadwick, who toured with one of those once-familiar freak fairs proclaiming exhibits like six-legged lambs or cows with three tails, or whatever. All, of course, were "alive", or had been, or would have been in a more innocent age.

Trouble was, Harry and his lady wife Rosie had had enough of freak after freak week after week, wanted to retire but couldn't for the life of them find a buyer. His son, Harry grumbled, had been born and raised among freaks but seemed to have found his spiritual home on the ghost train. His daughter ran a bingo stall. None of the grandchildren had shown an interest, not even in Tupper the five-legged goat – wasn't Tupper the tough of the track? – which, apparently unimpeded, had fathered 37 kids.

The cat with six paws had also been confined to quarters, Harry said, because the folk offering goldfish as prizes had lost rather more than anticipated. "I could have an elephant with six heads and some woman would still want to see the bloody cat with six paws" he said. Worse yet, the four-legged hen had rolled over and died. It was some week, some year, for Shildon.

Chapter twenty-two

Football field

Sunday dinner at 30 Albert Street was on the table by 12, sometimes even earlier and the washing up in hand before the opening strains of *Two-Way Family Favourites*. With the exception of the last Sunday in April, tea – John West's pink salmon, tinned pears in season – would be served at four. The last Sunday of April was different.

The last Saturday was the day of the FA Amateur Cup final at Wembley, victory in the 1950s and early 1960s perennially claimed by Northern League rivals Bishop Auckland or Crook Town, once even Willington and, near enough, West Auckland.

After a celebratory Saturday night in London the victors would catch a Sunday train from Kings Cross, alight at Darlington, climb with their beribboned trophy aboard an open-topped double decker and head triumphantly homeward. There's even a story about the Bishop Auckland players falling in on the train with the blonde singer Kathy Kirby and adding further to the weekend high notes, though that need not concern us. Always, or so it seemed, the homeward route led through Shildon. Always, or so similarly it seemed, generous hearted Shildon folk would throng the Hippodrome corner in good natured but envious salute. The tuna and the tinned pears went cold.

Though Northern League hegemony seldom seemed threatened, on the few occasions when a southern team won the thing, their return journey – or so memory compels – would still lead past the Hippodrome corner. For all of us it was a rite of passage and we tried hard to be stoical: next time, we assured ourselves, it would be Shildon.

Probably I was five or six when first setting foot on the Dean Street football ground, 3d admission and a further twopence should access be sought to the celebrated pagoda grandstand, its two-plank paybox guarded by a two-legged Cerberus called Snack Davis, Horatio in a flat cap. None knew, nor posthumously knows, how he came by "Snack", but the likelihood seemed that any child trying to sneak in without his twopence might be eaten, with chips, for tea. Even for league games there'd be a couple of thousand in, the roar audible across the town.

Not that match attendance was mandatory. The Saturday afternoon matinee at the Hippodrome was a persuasive counter-attraction, cheap bench seats at the front but jam jars no longer acceptable in part exchange. There'd be a cartoon from Looney Tunes – there probably couldn't be today - a main film which was almost always a western, and as finale the latest instalment of the serial to the invariable accompaniment of frenzied foot stamping as the cavalry crested the hill. On windfall days we might manage a twopenny lolly from Lindsey Walker, the ice cream man, or an everlasting bar, eternally fraudulent, from the little sweet shop at the bottom of Main Street.

Gradually, however, football won. They were the Railwaymen, the club logo a representation of Royal George – Hackworth's most celebrated locomotive – and, as the headline writers liked feebly to suggest, the Railwaymen were on the right lines.

Save for the pagoda grandstand, and by executive accounts the purple-plush boardroom beneath it, the ground was pretty basic. The gent's in the corner was a corrugated iron structure with soakaway sanitation most kindly termed antediluvian and for those over 5ft tall offering little chance of privacy. The terraces were overgrown, the tea hut tepid, the stand inviolate. We loved it all, of course, sacklessly and ceaselessly smitten.

In 1959 we reached the Amateur Cup quarter-final, around 8,000 said to be squeezed into Dean Street, drew 1-1 with Walthamstow Avenue – robbed. robbed – and lost the replay in Essex. The following season we marched to the FA Cup first round, drew 1-1 with Oldham Athletic at home - see under "robbed", above – and again lost the replay. Two years later we once more reached the FA Cup first round, again drew Oldham and on Bonfire Night – Saturday November 4, Sundays still sacrosanct - went down 5-2 in Lancashire after George Sinclair had headed us into a tenth minute lead.

Back then, and strictly until 1974, footballers at Northern League level were amateur, entitled only to legitimate expenses. Whoever coined the term "shamateur" had it in one; it was the age of the little brown envelope.

Stan Wilson, a Teesside teacher who in later life tilted at parliamentary windmills for the Liberal Democrats, once told me about his Shildon debut in the late 1950s. After the match he joined the queue at the treasurer's table to claim expenses, was asked how much and quoted the five bob train fare from Redcar. The more experienced chap next in line was asked the bus fare from Spennymoor, told them £3 and was duly paid out.

By the time of Stan's second appearance, the train fare from Redcar had shot up astronomically.

There was another FA Cup first round appearance in 2002-03, a 7-2 defeat at Notts County, the team managed by Ray Gowan, an excitable Londoner, and the club chaired by Gordon Hampton, a local businessman who dyed his hair purple to match the colour of the team's shirts and perhaps to reflect the patch. In 2012-13 we reached the two-leg semi-final of the FA Vase, the competition that in 1974 had replaced the Amateur Cup,

lost 2-0 in the first leg at Tunbridge Wells on a pitch on which a hippopotamus might happily have wallowed and after 30 minutes of the home leg led 3-0. Wembley was an hour, and a long lifetime, away.

We lost, the only time in 70 years support that I found it impossible to accept that football was only a game. Truly shattered, I sought six-pint solace in the Three Tuns. The anguish eventually eased. One day, I decided, we'd still be atop that bus.

The Dean Street ground is much changed, and much for the

Stalwarts: (LtoR) Barry Murphy, John Atkinson, Jeff Ridley, Susan Clarkson

better. since those formative days of the 50s. These days gentlemen may even refrain from soaking the corrugated iron. It's a Thursday morning in August 2024 and four of the great stalwarts – John Atkinson, Susan Clarkson, Barry Murphy and Jeff Ridley – have gathered in the guest room to reminisce and to reflect.

Outside in the sunshine the pitch looks in first class fettle, though it's envisaged that it will soon be replaced by an artificial surface in order to maximise its use in the community, the focus of much of club chairman David Dent's effort.

Individually and collectively they are loyal, long serving and lovely, seemingly little burdened by a combined 320 years of supporting evermore, though John's not – as they say in these parts - getting away too well and Barry, as they might never say in these parts, is becoming a bit mutton jeff.

They also worry about the town's perceived decline. "It's no longer a nice place to live" says Susan "I wouldn't dream of walking out on my own at night." Nor, she adds, would she dream of living anywhere else.

It's been a bad week for the footballers, too, a home defeat in the extra-preliminary round of the FA Cup – which the Railwaymen were probably never going to win, anyway, not if Arsenal and Manchester City had anything to do with it – followed by another Dean Street defeat in the league in which two home players were sent off and a third banished to the sin bin, during which ten-minute period of venal servitude the other lot scored three times.

"It was awful, the worst discipline I've ever seen and one of the worst performances" says John. "I hardly slept all night."

They remember happier times, talk of stalwarts like Bill and Joan Clarkson, Susan's parents, and like Edith Aisbitt and her husband Bill – "Uncle Aisbitt" Susan calls him, affectionately. For many years Joan ran the tea hut with Edith; Bill was a long-serving club chairman and groundsman, seemingly ever-enshrouded in purple pipe smoke when such indoor indulgence was legitimate.

They also remember Syd and Mike Armitage, father and son, and little George Elliott, who could sell raffle tickets to the Pope (and probably had). Syd Armitage, who had a couple of shops in the town, was a long-serving club treasurer; Mike, an accountant and my friend from our first day together at Timothy Hackworth infants, was for 40 years an extraordinarily dedicated and wonderfully efficient club secretary and later a member of the FA Council. The very best of men, his sole flaw was an incorrigible liking for John Smith's Smooth.

John, 91-year-old patriarch of a Newton Aycliffe company which makes staircases, has been club president for 45 years, succeeding Cecil Attwood OBE, chairman of the Dufay Paint group which had headquarters at All Saints. For many years after the factory's closure, the No 1 bus automaton still announced the stop as Dufay, just as strangers might even now hear of the Hippodrome and wonder where they're getting off.

John's car, registration JA55, stands outside the ground. He paid £3,000 for the plate, has turned down £50,000, perhaps not as locally prized as Graeme Scarlett's SH11DON but globally envied, nonetheless.

He was born in Middlesbrough – "Manitoba Gardens, they called the area Little Canada" – moved to Newton Aycliffe when his father took over the business there. "Just the fifth permanent house in the new town, not even any roads or sewers" says John. He worked for the TSB, joined the War Office – "if I told you what I did I'd have to shoot you" – played junior football with members of the Clough family. "Brian's first team was Grove Hill Methodist Juniors, not many people know that" he says, inarguably. Upwardly mobile, he joined the stairs company and moved to Shildon after meeting his wife Sheila, a Shildon lass.

That he has heavily financed the football club, more than once probably saved it from extinction, is no secret. Only the amounts remain confidential. "A lot of it has officially been loans" says John. "I never wanted it back and I never expected it back. It's the people you do it for, there've been some wonderful people here."

There was one occasion, however, on which terms and conditions applied. "I was only 80 and I told the manager before the Vase semi-final that if we got to Wembley I wanted a place on the subs' bench, even if I only came on for the last 30 seconds and got one kick." Defeat by Tunbridge Wells relieved club and manager of a dilemma.

Barry, 80-odd, has proved no less munificent in his 50-odd years with the club. He points to a sign high on the wall near the gate – "The Murphy Family Turnstile Block" – indicating yet another piece of what-goes-around-comes-around means of parting a man from his money. "That was another £1,000" he says. Though his shareholding is large, it's unlikely ever to make his fortune or, indeed, to finance the next round of drinks.

"I've always been interested in buying shares" says Barry, still at the ground most mornings. "I suppose you could say that I'm here so often because I'm keeping an eye on my investment."

Susan was eight when asked to help on the gate, remains at the receipt of custom 50-odd years later. "Bob Morley the gateman liked to go out and watch when the match started so he left me in charge" she recalls. "The gateman got paid in those days and he gave me a Mars Bar at half-time, that was my wages. I still love it, you get to meet people, nice people, find out what's going on."

Sometimes her parents would take her into an empty dressing room. "I remember there were huge baths, so big I couldn't see over the top, but even just to get into the stand area you had to get past Snack Davis. You could write a book about Snack."

Jeff wasn't really a Shildon lad at all – Close House is a mile away, bottom of Eldon Bank – but collected pools money in the town. "I knew every street" he insists. "I liked the Shildon folk." He was football club vice-chairman for 27 years and edited the *Town Crier*, Shildon's free newspaper. He's 80, too, still trying to master dominoes. "Football gets in your blood" he says over morning coffee. "None of us is going to stop supporting now."

Asked a lifetime highlight, both John and Susan nominate the FA Cup tie against Notts County one November Sunday afternoon in 2003, though for different reasons. "It was the first time I've been in a Football Lague boardroom and the hospitality was amazing, roast chicken and chilled Chablis" John recalls. "We lost 7-2 but I still nearly missed the bus home. I didn't want to leave."

Susan? "My mam was too poorly to travel but on the morning of the match I came around the corner into Dean Street with my dad and there was just a sea of people, about a dozen buses lined up. He'd never seen so many people supporting Shildon,

Plateful: Graeme Scarlett

he was very proud that day."

Barry remembers the Durham Challenge Cup final against South Shields in 2019, 600 supporters following the Railwaymen to Sunderland FC's Stadium of Light. "I think we were the first Northern League club to play on that ground. Everything just clicked that night. Billy (Greulich-Smith) scored the winner."

In the 1930s, the side including well-remembered local lads like Alf Wilde – Wacker by both nickname and nature – and Harry Nicholson, the team won the Northern League championship five times. It didn't happen again until 2016, the title clinched with a 4-0 victory – Good Friday lunchtime - at Bishop Auckland, the dear old enemy. That's Jeff Ridley's

stand-out moment. "We came back here to the clubhouse and I was dancing with John Atkinson, jigging up and down. There can't have been any women. By five o'clock there wasn't a drop of alcohol left in the place. It was one thing to win the title – but at Bishop, that was really special."

Crowds now usually disappoint, between 200-300. Part of the problem is that the town with an estimated 16,000 population in the 1930s now has around 10,000, many of whom have few roots and little money. When briefly the club was promoted to the higher Northern Premier League, admission rose and gates fell. "People just couldn't afford it" says Susan. "Youngsters aren't as interested and the older folk are becoming unwell, or don't like the cold or are just dying."

Another regular topic is whether limited resources should better be spent on the team – no longer shamateur, pretty well paid – or on the ground. "The chairman's spent a lot of money here and it looks great" says John Atkinson, "but personally I'd rather see more spent on the team."

Norman Smith, the most dedicated of volunteers, puts his head around the door. "What this club really needs" says Jeff "is ten more Norman Smiths."

Each of the quartet still dreams, as do many more born within the sounds of the Shildon Works buzzer, of a maiden Wembley appearance – none more ardently than John Atkinson. "I'm 91 and it's been a long time coming" he says, ever cheerfully. "I just wish they'd get a move on."

Tuesday August 24 2024 wasn't a particularly good night for Shildon FC, either, losing 2-1 to Redcar Athletic – a fourth successive home defeat. After the 9 30pm finish, club chairman

David Dent had done what needed to be done, said what had to be said and driven the 40 miles back to Whitley Bay.

The following morning he's back in Shildon for a quick catch-up with his 91-year-old dad – retired painter and decorator Sid Dent, who'd been at the game – and promptly at nine turns up for a chat over breakfast at the George Samuel Brewery taproom, where the wagon workers tea and toasted all those shifts before.

The journey from north Tyneside has become greatly familiar, even when – as the night before – there'd been roadworks and diversions substantially to extend it. In truth he is the personification of the adage that you can take the lad out of Shildon, or wherever, but you can't take Shildon out of the lad.

For different reasons, both of us need to weight watch – the chairman because of a stroke a few years back, the inquisitor for more obvious reasons. One of us has toast and jam, no butter, the other the full English, toast and butter. No guesses.

So what had been defeat's aftermath? "I don't usually go into the dressing room after the match but I did last night and I congratulated them" says David. "We played really well against a good side with a big budget and were very unlucky to lose. I get very emotionally involved because I'm a supporter first and foremost. We'll still be in the mix at the end of the season."

He and his wife Diane, the club treasurer, became involved with the Railwaymen in 2017, the club website now topped with the mantra "Inspiring people to be the best they can be" and tailed with the statement that the club is "under the significant financial control and ownership of David and Diane Dent." So much for my three-and-a-half shares.

Diane's from Wallsend, a few miles inland from Whitley Bay – doesn't suffer fools gladly, her husband concedes, doesn't like football but supports Shildon. "She gets it, she's down to earth, she knows why we're doing this. Wallsend's a bit like Shildon really, lots of people who can't afford to live on the coast or in the middle of Newcastle."

Much has changed on their watch. The nationally loved Dean Street ground, originally a cycle track, is transformed with impressive new dressing rooms, new floodlights, new hospitality and meeting facilities and a synthetically surfaced pitch near the entrance for school and community use. The clubhouse beneath the old "pagoda" stand remains the most convivial, most congenial, in football. Were there a picnic table table, Dean Street might be near the top of that, too. The main pitch is expected to acquire a "plastic" surface shortly, allowing much wider use by the community – and, of course, more income. Many other activities, particularly for children during school holidays, take place.

In 2021-22 the team was promoted from the Northern League to the second tier of the Northern Premier League but two years later was relegated whence expectantly they'd come. "That's my biggest regret, we shouldn't be in this league" says David. "I tend to blame myself."

So why do it, why with Diane spend so much time building a community club and so many hours on the road? "I might no longer live in Shildon but Shildon will always be part of me" he says. "I always wanted to do something for the community and that's why I came back to invest in the club. I was aware of the gap in the town between those who have and those who haven't. If they took Shildon out of me I'd be lost, I really would. I also wanted a home for my dad, something he could be part of, something to live for. I'm still a Shildon lad, really."

The family had moved to Alexandra Street when he was five, the youngster taken to matches by his dad. He recalls Boxing Day derbies against Bishop Auckland – "I think we beat them 5-1 once" – and a 5-0 win over Penrith ("Tommy Tinkler scored all five"). He attended Council school and then Sunnydale, left (to parental dismay) at 16 and worked briefly for his dad. "I got to paint the dressing rooms at Dean Street, at the time it was my dream job" he recalls. He was a goalkeeper, played as a youngster for Shildon United in the Auckland and District League, turned down the chance of Northern League football with Shildon. "It was the worst decision I ever made" he concedes.

Belatedly he went to university – "the first member of our family to do so" - gained a good degree, qualified as a chartered surveyor and by 35 was a partner in the international project management company Faithful+Gould. Three years later he started his own project management consultancy, clients including Sunderland FC whose former chairman, Bob Murray, remains a close friend and advises on Shildon projects. Irene Hays, chair of the Sunderland-based Hays Travel group, is another associate. "I've worked with some very influential people and I've turned to them for help" says David.

"It resonates that the Foundation of Light has been a catalyst for the whole city (of Sunderland) and works on numerous levels. Smaller scale, perhaps, but I want the same sort of benefits for Shildon, a real bridge for the community."

The stroke compelled reappraisal. He sold the business and set up as a consultant, clients including Liverpool University. He's also a consultant to the Football Association. "I had no interest at all in going back to work. In any case we'd been taking on work that I wasn't really comfortable with" he says. "I only work with people I want to work with and now I don't have 40 or 50 mouths to help feed, the way that I did before.

"To this day I don't know how to stop. I'm supposed to be semi-retired now but I work every day. I don't mean financially, but I just need to do something. I've set an agenda for the next three years, after that it might change.

How has the old home town changed? "It's never recovered from Shildon Shops closing, has it? The main street's in a bad way, too. I want the football club to help in any way that it can and I spend quite a lot of time on it."

Any chance that he might move back home? "Not while Diane's alive."

The stroke may have changed his outlook, he concedes. "I don't feel cheated, I feel blessed, I was given a second chance. With Diane's help, I really hope it can be taken, and for the benefit of Shildon" – and they looked like being there or thereabouts at the end of the season.

Chapter twenty-three

Cricket field

Every cricket ground in the land which runs close to a railway line – and even in post-Beeching days there seem to be an awful lot – carries in its personal holdall the story of the big-hitting batsman whose massive swipe lands in a passing coal truck, ends at Battersea Power Station (or somewhere) and thus becomes the biggest six in the game's long and illustrious history. Some might suppose it apocryphal; cricketers as one swear to its eternal and individual verity.

At Shildon it's no different, though the supposed destination – Doncaster – falls a little short of expectations. Surely they can envision further than that.

Founded in 1913, the "railway" cricket team played on a field at the back of the Shops, became Shildon NER, then LNER and after nationalisation Shildon BR – which is what they were until the Shops shut and which, to many, they remain. Formally they're now Shildon Railway, as is the football club on the adjoining field.

Formed in 1954, the footballers marked their 50th anniversary in 2004-05 by winning the Durham Alliance League double and three other trophies, beat 10-0 a team from the National Union of Rail Maritime and Transport Workers – an occasion followed by a civic dinner – but soon afterwards fell upon hard times. Alan Morland, the secretary, wrote to other clubs with railway connections – Crewe Alexandra, Doncaster Rovers, Horwich RMI – seeking help. Only Doncaster Rovers came good, sending a framed picture of a B17 steam engine named after the Yorkshire club. No one had ever called an engine

Shildon, not since Timothy Hackworth's time, anyway.

John Ryan, the Rovers chairman, had himself been a train spotter, made millions from cosmetic beauty clinics – his 100,000 clients said to have included the former Page 3 girl Melinda Messenger - and still had a huge model railway in his garden. "Doncaster supporters gaze upon their team like many may fantasize about Melinda" a *Guardian* sports reporter once, improbably, wrote. "In both cases there is little chance of scoring."

The British Railways Sports Association moved to the club's present home, appropriately at the end of Hackworth Street, in 1955. Outdoors it accommodated football, cricket, tennis and bowls, with weight lifting and tug-of-war teams, too, and some dab hands at whist.

We'd wandered down to the BR as bairns, the cricket scorebox in the corner about the size of a matt green dog kennel – OK, a medium-sized dog kennel – with little hatches which opened outwards and on which kids, tins boys, would hang numerical updates in return for a surreptitious spam sandwich at the tea interval.

Folk also recall the scorers' wondrous wagon wheels, by which they mean clever little diagrams of the areas of the ground in which runs were scored and not the chocolate biscuits of that name which, allegedly, roll in ever decreasing circles.

Back then the only men in Shildon who wore helmets were Tommy Trebilcock and his mates at the police station; back then the only sledging took place down Elephant's Trunk; back then (as we all know) the sun shone daily, dawn to dusk.

By 1955 the BR had two teams in the Durham County League

spearheaded by Northumberland and Durham all-rounder Jack Watson – the man who also led the wagon works fire brigade – appointed club professional on £600 a year, enough back then to buy a small car. "Mind, we made him scrat for it" John Raw, secretary for 50 years, once colloquially observed. Jack was joined down the years by still-remembered local heroes like Fred Brownless, Les Coward, Joe Hook, Keith Hopper, Ken Stainthorpe and Bob Whaley, known universally as Tweet. Long before Twitter, was invented or Elon Musk decided that X marked the spot, why Tweet? "I think" says someone in the clubhouse, "it was because he liked a little chunter."

Along the ever-appealing branch line from Darlington, joined by a small group of Americans who talk of Shildon railroad station and wonder why the train has no seat belts, I'm on the BR boundary again for the match against Hartlepool II in the North Yorkshire and South Durham League third tier, which Shildon lead. Behind the rope where once a box Brownie might from a distance have muttered and shuttered, a photographer with a long lens the size of a bazooka fires dozens of frames every minute.

Much else has changed, not least that the scorers sit with their laptop computers in front of the pavilion, proceedings remotely updated ball-by-ball not just to the unmanned electronic scoreboard on the opposite side of the ground but to pretty much anyone in the world able to hit five or six smartphone keys in the correct sequence.

Today an incoming batsman may be greeted with the words "Oh, hello?" – the insidious inference that a rabbit may soon be caught in the headlights – or on one occasion with the observation: "Are you No 10? The No 11 must be terrible." There's no swearing, audible offensive language punishable under league rule by a two-match ban.

Another, rather more regrettable, change is that there are no longer cricket teas. "Covid did for that" says Railway stalwart John Brennan, Mind, he adds with unintentional appropriateness, they were becoming a bit of a chew, anyway.

I'm joined by John, a retired primary school head teacher, and by 78-year-old club president Jim Robinson, a tins boy back in the day – "Mind, you had to do as you were told" – whose father had a long and distinguished BR career interrupted by a couple of years coastal cricket at Blackhall. "He was ticed by some feller called Watson" Jim recalls.

He'd started on the tins on the old ground out the back of the works, made his second team debut there – "I can't have been above nine" – was joined over the years by his brothers Mel and Keith. "The old ground was quite a long way, pit heaps on one side of the path and great piles of wheels on the other, that's unless you knew the farmer and could cut across the field. I can't really remember what the facilities were like, but they wouldn't have been up to much, that's for sure."

The new place had two jettisoned railway carriages, oddly romantic but possibly third class, which served as changing rooms. Alongside the cricket field was a little hut called the Slip Inn, where they might manage a post-match pint. It remained part of the British Railways Staff Association, covering both the Institute and the sports ground, until the Shops shut. "You paid something like sixpence a week. It was pretty good value for a tanner" recalls Jim Robinson, whose father died, while still playing, in 1964.

"Closure changed everything" says Jim. "When the wagon

works was going strong, if anything went wrong here or there were any repairs needed doing, you just rang them and someone came over, all work guaranteed. We had a full-time grounds-man, too."

John Brennan also remembers those days admits that they hadn't the money to do all they'd like to have done. "It was quite difficult" he concedes. The pavilion and clubhouse had opened in the late 1960s. "I remember coming over here with Dean and Chapter seconds and thinking what fantastic facilities they were" says John. "It was the sort of place that everybody wanted to play."

Decline followed the works closure, the club obliged to leave the Durham County League when unable to raise the required second team. Nor were matters helped when, in 2013, a groundsman inadvertently treated the grass with something very different from nutrient, much of the field blackened and NYSD admission postponed.

"Things were at their lowest ebb around that time" says John. "I was chairman, secretary, treasurer, second team captain and helping out on the ground. At one time the committee was pretty much me and Jim. If it hadn't been for Jim, there wouldn't be a club."

The seconds string also included Alan Ramsey, like John at the time in his 50s. The next oldest was 15. "We couldn't even go for a pint after the match" John recalls, "we had to take the kids to MacDonald's. Things began to turn around when we were lucky enough to get into the NYSD League."

Jim's brought his scrapbooks, the programme for Jack Watson's memorial match in 2016 including a tribute they'd asked me to

Great all-rounder: Jack Watson

172

write. "Jack Watson was a good lad" it began without fear of contradiction. "If not a native Shildon lad then a Shildon lad by affectionate adoption, and that made it even better."

Asked the most memorable moment of his own career, Jim at once recalls a 1960s match when K R Hopper had joined Crook as professional. Jack Watson, he again, was bowling for Shildon, "I'd been pressed into service as wicket-keeper and we had Keith stumped Robinson, bowled Watson. Jack was very pleased about that."

And K R Hopper? "Not quite so pleased, I think."

The sun's so hot that we're chatting in the clubhouse shade, "finest hour" scorecards framed on the walls alongside photographs of former overseas professionals like fast bowler Chris Matthews, who played for the BR and Australia in the same year, like Willie White, Shirlon Williams and Wilkin Arvind Mota.

There's also a photograph of umpires Harry Dobinson and Dickie Mackerel, both former BR men. Dobbo, a wonderful character known without civic authority as the Mayor of Hunwick, had on one occasion walked to the middle and called "play" before realising that he'd left the ball in the dressing room.

Perversely, the merry May weather is also a reminder of the stormy day that Bishop Auckland estate agent John Armstrong, playing at Shildon for Etherley II, broke his collar bone when a sight screen was blown down on top of him. Out of harm's way, he thereafter fielded in the slips.

Outside there's now a veranda, chiefly occupied by players' families. That there aren't many bums on seats elsewhere may primarily be because there aren't many seats for bums upon which to be parked. Tins binned, the electronically empowered scoreboard hums quietly to itself as if pottering about in the back garden, an advert on the front for Comtek IT Services suggesting a wholly different generation game. These days you can't even be rebuked (there were other terms) for walking in front of it.

In the distance there's the sound of what travelling folk call the shows, confirming the long-held belief that the shows must go on. The traditional view of All Saints church seems obscured, however, or perhaps the church has gone away for the day.

The ground looks immaculate, chiefly due to John Brennan's TLC, though the area behind the fence in the far corner is a wilderness of the sort in which 40 days and 40 nights might penitentially be spent, access denied because it's believed that the remains of Timothy Hackworth's Soho Works are buried beneath and thus subject to a preservation order. Hackworth's cottage is little more than 50 yards distant, so close that – had cricket reached Co Durham's 19th century working classes and not just the toffs of Raby Castle – the great engineer could have broken off from digging his potato patch, leaned querulously against the fence and invented the first critics' corner, an' all.

A deep fielder gazes over the fence into the jungle. "Lots down there" he supposes.

Lots of what? "Well, I didn't mean dead bodies" he says.

Nearby strolls John Young, for many years a Shildon player and who still lives somewhere out the back. The best player he played with, he says, was Fred Brownless. The fastest was Chris Matthews, the Australian pro. "I don't know what it was like to face him as a batsman, but I'd be standing at third man and still be bloody terrified" he says.

Matthews played three tests, took six wickets at 52.6 and never returned to Shildon. "Stuart Broad's dad in the Ashes series hoiked him all over the park" John recalls.

These days they don't employ a professional, nor pay anyone else. "We did have a little incentive scheme but the players said they weren't bothered" says Jim. £90,000 in hard-wrung grants has helped develop the ground, though they still shop second hand for equipment.

The Railway have scored 176, dismiss the Hartlepool lads for 113. Mutually applauded from the field, the teams head for the Saturday evening clubhouse fast filling, where there's bingo and an inevitably "fabulous" vocalist. John Brennan concedes that things for the cricketers are looking as good as they have for a long time. "It's in pretty safe hands at the moment."

Back along the path between ground and railway embankment, I'm the only passenger awaiting the 8 31 to Saltburn, the PA system playing Saturday evening music of a sort unlikely to be heard at the great BR bingo ball. The diesel multiple unit's exactly to time – there've been no coal trains this way for long years now, hundreds of six-hit cricket balls lost in the mythological mists alongside them.

Impossible to walk around the BR ground without again recalling K R Hopper, a Shildon lad who played both cricket and football for his home town and for Durham County, a 20th century incarnation of the biblical adage about a prophet not being without honour except in his own back yard.

Keith was born and raised somewhere near the Shops – Scott Street, memory suggests – sang in All Saints church choir. "It was funny playing in your home town team because everyone thought they knew you" he once told me. "I'd be going to church on a Sunday and they'd cross the road, like in the parable of the Good Samaritan, if they thought I'd had a bad game the day before."

Another Tin Tacks boy, he'd played for the LNER second team – on that field behind the wagon works – when just 12, though as an adult he usually contested a higher level, for many years into his 70s for Bishop Auckland where he became club chairman. As a footballer he was coveted by Chelsea and West Ham United, played for several Northern League clubs, once scored seven for Shildon in a match against Stanley United but was roundly, perhaps rudely, informed that it should have been eight.

Unalone, he worried for the future of club cricket, despairing of a younger generation. "Youngsters today want everything instant – instant coffee, instant sex" said Keith. "Their attention span's so short they can't even watch a 30-minute television programme without a break in the middle." He took skiing holidays until 75, sang with Shildon Amateur Operatic Society, umpired assiduously. Great lad, Keith died in 2016, aged 83.

There was a second cricket team, Shildon Town, playing in the long-disappeared Mid-Durham Senior League at a time when almost every village had a side – maybe even a second string – and the Mid-Durham had three divisions.

Town's team in the 1960s included Geoff Hill, who taught us semi-colons and things at Bishop Auckland Grammar School and who because of a permanent limp was known universally as Chester, a nod to Chester Goode, Marshal Dillon's loyal sidekick in *Gunsmoke*.

Why Mr Ibbotson was nicknamed Cosher, Mr Robinson got Ichabod and Mr Bibby answered to Isaiah are different stories entirely. Suffice that Cosher carried a length of Bunsen burner tube in his jacket pocket, though not for purposes of O-level chemistry, and the explanation for Isaiah was apocryphal going on absurd.

Town played on Thompson's Field at the top of Eldon Bank, an area which an Ordnance Survey map might have identified as rough pasture but which not only served the cricketers of Shildon Town but the raggy-trousered footballers from the streets, including our own, round about. The eponymous Mr Thompson appeared usually to be pretty good about the persistent juvenile trespass, possibly because he was seldom there.

To the north was a pond, oft-frozen in winter but at other times home to newts, possibly even of the great crested variety. These days a zealously protected species, the newts of the late 1950s led a rather more endangered existence at the jam jar laden hands of the kids from around Albert Street.

Behind the wooden fence on the eastern side of the field were Waverley Terrace allotments, where my dear old dad had two plots in a bid to keep the family fed and where a chap called Gordon French kept a pig and grew apples. Though mildly interested in the occasionally pugnacious porker, we – led astray by Dennis the Menace and by the *William* books – were particularly attracted to the apples.

Thus it was that, one summer evening, a few of us 11-year-olds pitched camp on the cricket field side of the fence, about five yards from the apple tree, the larcenous intent barely more obvious had we worn horizontally striped jumpers, carried bags marked "Swag" and posted a large notice: "Scrumping in progress, do not disturb."

First thing the following morning, Mr French disturbed us nonetheless, his accusation that we'd been at his apple tree vigorously denied. A dozen discarded gowks may have offered instant incrimination, but Gordon had been crafty – he'd scattered soot around the base of the trees and demanded to see our shoes. For black hand gang read black-foot gang.

Though it may not have been supposed the crime of the century, even in 1960, he dialled Shildon 6 (if not 999) and reported us to the constabulary. While we escaped with not even a chiding, much less a hiding, it seemed prudent thereafter to take apples from the fruit bowl – these weren't even ripe – and to stick to trainspotting.

Chapter twenty-four

Brassed off

If music be the food of love, as someone-or-other observed in *Twelfth Night*, then Shildon may be the least romantic place in Christendom. Once brass-buoyant, bands have fallen silent. Unless it is football followers chorusing (after the Beatles) that they all live at the top of Eldon Bank – musically discordant and factually awry – choirs are little heard either.

Back in the 19th century no social occasion, no march through the town, seemed complete without the New Shildon Saxhorn Band, recalling one of my old mum's quaint old phrases – she had many – that it wouldn't be a show without Punch. Sometimes they'd march in step with the Town Band or the Temperance Band from which soberly it seceded.

An insatiable first, David Reynolds's history of the Railway Institute, records that in 1922 the Shildon Orchestral Society, mostly comprising railwaymen, performed a concert embracing everything from *Orpheus in the Underworld* to Charles Ancliffe's military waltz *For valour*. Another orchestra, strings attached, was based at All Saints church.

Then there was the North Eastern Railway Band which became the LNER Band and then (of course) the British Railways Band, though it was no doubt one of the colliery bands which shattered the seven o'clock slumbers every Durham Big Meeting day. There was a Wesleyan Band and later there was the North-East Industries Band, also based in Shildon.

Few summer Sundays might pass without a concert on the Recreation Ground bandstand, large crowds gathered round in the seemingly permanent sunshine with their Shippam's paste sandwiches and bottles of tap water. Then there was the Band of Hope, of course, though that was something else entirely (and no doubt had optimistic adherents of its own.)

There were operatic groups in both Old and New Shildon, perhaps merged into the once-vibrant Amateur Op Soc which held sold-out annual shows at the Hippodrome until film rights sold out to bingo and they'd to catch the No 1 bus to Darlington Civic Theatre. Among the bit-parters in *Oliver!* was the young Kevin Stonehouse, a Shildon lad (or was it Eldon?) who'd been an apprentice at the Shops, played football for Blackburn Rovers, Darlington and others and was an international scout for Newcastle United when he died, aged 59, in 2019.

Stoney, a lovely man, had recalled his musical youth at a Shildon FC talk-in two years before his death. "One of Fagin's lads, it's what you did in those days" he said. "These days they smash up bus shelters"

Once, come to think, I bagged a walk-on part in *Paint your wagon*, wholly forgettable musically but memorable for something that happened backstage and which must remain forever behind the scenes.

A different note, admittedly, but at St John's Youth Club in the sometimes swinging but seldom sinning sixties we were periodically entertained by The Warriors, a band – a group they'd have been back then – led by John Saxby, whose parents had the fruit shop in Church Street, with some of his mates from Barnard Castle School. Then there were the juvenile jazz bands, uniformly epitomising all that's inexplicably said about smartness and carrots – what's so smart about a carrot? - on parade not least for the annual Scouts' Carnival.

Marching on: the Salvation Army band

Old-timers at the Institute danced for generations to the Tommy Smurthwaite band. Bob Murton, who'd started at the Shops when 14 and became chief draftsman, led an ensemble known as The Imps when they played at the Imperial at Darlington and the Bob Murton Band pretty much everywhere else, a musical interlude which clearly did him no harm.

Aged 104 when he died in 2014, Bob had played bowls at Sunnydale Leisure Centre until beyond his 100th birthday, perhaps the country's oldest active sportsman and still up and down like a green baize bluebottle. "My knees have gone a bit wonky but there's nothing wrong with my eyesight, I can still read a bias, still play a canny bowl" he said – beneath the neat headline "Old men's marvels" – on the occasion of his centenary and, since he was 100, the munificent bowls club gave him life membership thereafter.

Now there seems barely a toot. "It takes an awful lot of money and an awful lot of commitment to form a good brass band. It's just become uncool" says Graeme Scarlett, though hopeful that – a bit like that steam engine reserve supposedly buried beneath a hillside in Somerset or somewhere – a brass band may one day again march through the town.

Graeme's other passions include vintage buses – he also returned The Eden, once familiar throughout south Durham, to the roads. Outside his house sits a car with the registration SH11DON, surely the world's most coveted. Not for sale, he insists.

Dave Reynolds accepts the contribution of a brass band towards community cohesion but points to the difficulty of finding, training and keeping enthusiastic musicians. Kelly Ambrosini, his partner and fellow town councillor, plays with a band at Dunston, near Gateshead, getting on 40 miles away. A bit like Northern League footballers, are musicians now the subject of transfer fees? "Certainly a band has to make it worth your while" says Dave. "I wouldn't say transfer fees, but you can definitely claim expenses."

Graeme's a Shildon lad, took piano lessons at primary school, turned up at a Town Band practice where he asked Ernie Bennett, the conductor, if he might have a bash at the drum kit. Erne declined, doubtless politely, gave him a cornet instead. Graeme plays it still – a solo, all too often, these days.

He became band manager, organised a "mini-concert" atop Blackpool Tower, left after what he terms a clash of personalities, started the North East Industries Band. "We called it that

Music men, Tom Bulch and George Allan

178

rather than hope for one big sponsor" he says. "£25 apiece for a lot of little sponsors would have worked very well."

Now they've pretty much disbanded, too, though the instruments remain in store behind premises in Church Street and a few of them gather periodically for what Graeme calls a blow-in. "We'd borrowed people from the Thornley Colliery band, got some old uniforms from the Amoco brass band in Stanley because we couldn't afford new ones, said we'd pay for them at Christmas after we'd played for a bit of carol singing.

"I suppose what's happened is just a sign of the times. Brass bands have declined all across the North-East, though the situation's a bit better in Yorkshire. You have to turn up for practice two or three times a week, maybe practise more at home, then give up a day for a concert or a competition somewhere. Younger people have lots of other things calling them, older people have families. There's a lot of hard work in brass banding."

Ever attuned, Dave Reynolds had helped form a choir at the Institute, progress disrupted by Covid and later by the teacher's illness. "Shildon has a wonderful musical tradition" he says. "I'd love there to be a revival; somehow I can't see it."

Shildon's brass band heritage is personified in Tom Bulch and George Allan, born just 15 months and two long terraces apart in the 1860s. Bulch, from Strand Street, was the son of a locomotive fireman – then known as an engine loader – Allan's father was described as a master tailor. The family lived in Chapel Street.

Both youngsters were blacksmiths at the railway work until Bulch and three others decided to seek their fortunes in Australia, "between two and three thousand people" at the railway station to see them off. All, added the *Middlesbrough Daily Gazette*, were members of the Shildon Temperance Society and much respected in their native town.

Bulch became a noted composer and conductor, set up a music publishing business, played piano for silent movies when things got a bit tight and is credited with "accidentally" shaping the music for *Waltzing Matilda*, that testament to swagmen, billabongs and coolabah trees which became Australia's unofficial national anthem.

George Allan never got much further than Pears Terrace, so close to the railway works that he could have nipped home for his dinner, but became known as The March King after composing music like *Knight Templar* and *The Wizard*, still played by brass bands around the world. Very much more might be said but Dave Reynolds, that man of very many passions, spent four years researching and writing *The Wizard and the typhoon*, a wonderfully comprehensive and always entertaining 550-page account of the two men's divergently parallel lives which resonates yet and warrants much better than to be plagiarised. It's available from the Railway Institute, or through Amazon.

At the Salvation Army, at least, the band plays on. Many in attendance may be Smiths or Dunns, or children or in-laws or best friends of Smiths or Dunns. All are Christian soldiers of the top rank. Chris Smith, the bandmaster, points out a band room photograph, circa 1988, with 35 musicians. Now there are about half as many – "when they're all here" – but still blowing strong.

Ken Smith, Chris's dad, led the Songster Brigade for four decades. Vince, Ken's brother, studied at the Royal Academy of

Music, did national service with the Band of the Scots Guards, was Salvation Army bandmaster for a similar period to Ken.

Chris not unreasonably supposes that the decline in brass bands had coincided with the closure of the pits and the decline in other traditional industries. Music's very important, he says – "but I would say that, wouldn't I, I'm a music teacher."

I'd last been to a service in the citadel, appropriately in Cross Street, five years after its opening in 1995 – the golden jubilee celebration of the Songster Brigade, founded by Madge Longhurst, a young lieutenant in her first posting. By the millennium she was Major Madge Eugene, returned for the anniversary of a choir that had sung everywhere from the Over 60s club to the Royal Albert Hall. "You could walk down the streets and hear the men (at the Shops) literally going hammer and tongs when I was here" she said. "Now I don't think I could find my way around any longer."

Another lady at that service had been a clippie on United buses in the days when it was possible to travel from Shildon to Bishop for threepence, maybe even twopence ha'penny, so long as you fibbed about not being over 14.

Back in the year 2000 it had been a glorious day, shirtsleeve order including the little lad with "Beckham 7" on his back. Since this is the month of July in the sodden summer of 2024 it's altogether less clement. "If I'd known it was this cold I'd have worn my thermal vest" says a cheery lady of 90. Many others are in Army uniform, though bonnets went out with bustles and bows. Others just wear (and need) a double-knit Army cardigan.

The service begins with the band accompanying that splendid

hymn *Great is thy faithfulness*, a very good start. About 40 are gathered, Captain Amanda Smethurst observes that few youngsters are present – "but we have quality" she adds. It's announced that the previous day's summer fair had raised £992 – a total later to be revised above four figures. "I did my bit, all those bacon sandwiches I ate" says Chris.

The only problem's that the hymn words are projected onto overhead screens and, as with the blackboard at Timothy Hackworth Juniors, I struggle to read a single word.

Captain Norman Armistead, Shildon's commanding officer 25 or so years back, had come to see me one morning at work. I'd wondered if he might fancy a bite to eat and thus we adjourned to the Raby Hunt at Summerhouse, a few miles west, in the days when it was just a country pub and not a Michelin-stellar restaurant.

Captain Armistead, of course, remained strictly teetotal. It was only half way through his sausage and mash that he remembered he'd said he'd be home for lunch and hurried to ring his wife from the phone on the bar. Had he simply mentioned that he was having something to eat in the pub, there probably wouldn't have been a problem. Norman, however, felt obliged to reveal the identity of the devil with whom he was sharing the long spoon.

The scriptural phrase about falling among thieves came at once to mind, but Captain Mrs Armistead doubtless forgave him in the end.

The Shildon corps is said formally to have enlisted in 1911, followed shortly afterwards by a visit from General William Booth, though one of Frank Lawson's books claims that it all began on May 4 1879, 32 attending a prayer meeting the following week and the first officers chosen that December. Vera Chapman's little book *Around Shildon* carries a sepia photograph of a Salvation Army soup kitchen during the General Strike of 1926, a feed-the-five-thousand mission in which they were by no means alone. Fred Smith, Ken and Vince's dad, is prominent on a 1947 picture of the young people's band.

"You don't have to be musical to be in the Salvation Army but I suppose it helps" Ken once said. "There are still people who don't think it's Christmas until they hear the Salvation Army band playing carols."

Another old band photograph had included eight-year-old Derek Dunn, still playing cornet 70 years later. He remembers that the band was commissioned on Empire Day, can't recall the year but knows that they marched through the town and ended up in the canteen at the Alfred Morris Furs factory, a perhaps improbable occupant of the Dabble Duck industrial estate. Regular engagements include Remembrance Day: he's played Last Post for 50 years or more.

Captain Smethurst preaches about contentment. Three days after the general election, contented or otherwise, there are prayers that the new Prime Minister may have wisdom, insight and discernment. Whether or not those prayers appear thus far appear to have been answered is not, of course, a matter which should concern us. The songsters sing vigorously, the band plays out, over coffee we talk about the Army's other activities and about the manifest need for their presence in Shildon.

Twice a week they run a food bank, on other occasions family groups, youth clubs, keep fit, bible study. Derek Dunn – "really, really good with those who are struggling" says Captain

Smethurst – isn't the first to highlight the problem of incomers from other regions arriving in Shildon after learning that it has the country's cheapest housing, or perhaps not having much say in the matter. Many have no money, no furniture, no work and not much hope; many arrive at the food bank "a bit high" on drink or drugs. None is turned away, none – as at Shildon Alive – is judged. "They see on television about the cheap housing and they come anyway" says Derek

A few weeks earlier he'd encountered a chap with a serious alcohol problem, out of hospital and pledging eternal abstinence. "He was walking down the street with two carrier bags, clanking. He told me he wasn't drinking as much. That was as good as it got."

"There's a lot of need in Shildon but a lot of support, a really good social network" says Captain Smethurst. "The churches work together and with others. It's good; yes, I am content."

On the second Wednesday of July 2024, Hackworth Park is the venue for the Shildon Big Brass Bash, part of the Durham Brass Festival promoted much to its credit by the County Council and, like all the best things in life (with the possible exception of pork pie) it's free. There are just two problems. One's that the mid-July weather again more closely resembles mid-November, the other that England's footballers are simultaneously playing the Netherlands in the semi-finals of Euro 24.

No contest, then.

"All those who say there's nowt to do in Shildon should be getting themselves down here tonight. They might even realise what a lovely park we have" says county councillor Shirley

Quinn, a true local champion, gazing across at a huddled, hooded gathering of barely 100.

The optimists have brought picnic baskets, the pessimists parkas, the realists umbrellas. The five bands shelter in a row of conically-topped tents which rather resemble those at a medieval joust. There are food stalls with names like Acropolis, presumably Greek, Zen-thing – no presumption – and Hedgehog Bakery which is a disappointment because it doesn't sell pies. What else are hedgehogs for?

Based in Durham City, the week-long brass festival has gigs across the county, some styled Big Brass Bashes and some Little, held on what cricket folk would once have called outgrounds. It all leads up to the Miners' Gala though these guys aren't Colonel Bogey men, nor Floral Dancers, and probably can't play a note of Gresford, that great memorial to the pitmen. It's what might be called modern brass, swinging in the rain.

Another difference between Hackworth Park and the Big Meeting is that there's no sign of Mr Ian Lavery MP, that indelible champion of a vanished industry, or for that matter of that ubiquitous chap from the railway union who pops up whenever there's a tub to thump, but maybe they're at home by the fire watching the football.

The promotional literature describes the bands as "eclectic and energetic", which is pretty much spot on. They've names like Das Brass (from London, not Germany), Rajasthan Heritage, Heavy Beat Brass Band and Young Pilgrims. Briefly I wonder if Young Pilgrims might be some sort of junior Salvation Army band and might essay a few verses of *He who would valiant be* – No 515 in *Songs of Praise*, the well-thumbed hymn book at Tin Tacks – but these are shorts-sporting lads from Glasgow.

Food of love: brass in the park

Briefly too, I wonder what Timothy Hackworth himself, a man who hardly dared even sing *Keep your feet still Geordie hinny* outside the confines of Soho Cottage lest it upset the Sadducees, might have made of all this.

"We love rain in Glasgow" says the Young Pilgrims leader, clearly speaking from drookit experience, as the weather worsens.

It's eclectic indeed, more Tijuana than Tindale Crescent Club, more New Orleans meets New Shildon. Truth to tell, none of the tunes is familiar save for what briefly appears to be a snatch of *Baa baa black sheep*, and which proves a black sheep in wolf's clothing.

It's also belfry practice night at St John's church, a few hundred yards up the hill, evoking youthful memories of the days when George White, the rather rotund tower captain, also led the 1st Shildon Scouts. Bells bow to trumpet and trombone, inverting lines from *Crown him with many crowns* – "Look how the heavenly anthem drowns all music but its own." Rajasthan Heritage probably don't know that one, either.

The bandstand's illuminated. Rows of fold-up wooden chairs mostly unoccupied, may have been kept around the Rec since the distant days when Mr McCutcheon, the park keeper, so optimistically rang his bell to signal close of play. Shrouded in waterproofs, an elderly couple obdurately occupy their chairs, reminiscent of one of those old seaside postcards on which the picture is similarly bedraggled and the caption's about coming to Blackpool for fresh air and sunshine. A black-and-white terrier sits motionless, ears cocked, back to the music, for all the world like Nipper, entranced by His Master's Voice.

The bands are brilliant, boisterous, embodiment of all that *Wind in the Willows* supposed about little wet and water rat. Last up at 8 30, the Oompah Band may have the short straw. It's pouring, Harry Kane has equalised from the penalty spot, better yet to come. Almost all have departed for football and – quite likely – for fireside. It's been a greatly enjoyable and wholly different evening, a happy band, nonetheless.

Then there's a big surprise. The Ofsted report on Thornhill primary school, enthusiastically embraced in the book's foreword – "behaviour is exemplary, pupils feel safe and happy at this school" – also noted that Thornhill not only had a brass band but that the band had twice played at the symphonically celebrated Sage in Gateshead.

Might I join a rehearsal? "Certainly" says Samantha Overfield, 18 years at the school as teacher, deputy head teacher and now head.

It must be 50 years since last I set foot in the Council school, as then it was usually known, back in the days when a boys' secondary modern shared an upstairs/downstairs site with a junior school and the head might demand that John Hope learn *Miller of the Dee* by heart or be excluded from the school football team.

"Welcome" signs on the gate are in several languages, one of which may be Mandarin, another Urdu.. On the fence another sign promotes the Walk to School Challenge – "improve your health, protect the planet" which these Brusselton boys had done all those years ago, and still gone home for their dinners.

It's late November and the school's not yet decked for Christmas, though the town itself is starting to look festive. Signs in windows enjoin "Santa, stop here", fairy lights anticipate Advent, a giant inflatable dinosaur – the scriptural significance of which is not immediately obvious – stands in a little garden at the back of the football ground.

The school's quiet, none shouting or being shouted at. As at Timothy Hackworth, that may be the biggest change of all. Prominently placed, a "compliments folder" records exactly what it says on the cover, everything from a note from the bus driver on a school outing – "fantastic bunch of kids" – to appreciation of the Chinese New Year workshop.

On the walls are little aphorisms – "If you can clue it, you can do it", "Impossible is just an opinion". Another message suggests that the Ofsted inspectors, much maligned, clearly had a point.

Miss Overfield had herself learned the trumpet at primary school, gave it up, regrets it. "We try to offer enjoyment in every single session" she says. "Some of the children have very difficult home lives. School is a place where we can build trust, introduce new experiences, A lot of the children enjoy singing. It's about listening, too, about mental wellbeing. Music's a different outlet, there's a lovely sense of togetherness. We have one little girl who struggles a lot with reading and maths but absolutely loves her music."

Not just brass band bonding, the school recently bought half a dozen "small" violins, too.

Though musical language is universal, almost all children have English as their native tongue. The signs on the gate, says the head, are to remind them of a wider world. "We aren't very diverse at all; the signs help create awareness of a multi-cultural world."

It's 3 30pm, band practice well underway in one of those multi-purpose school spaces that serves as assembly hall, dining hall, gymnasium and goodness knows what else. As these days they may rarely say around Shildon, they're giving it what fettle. "That snare drum sounds a bit snary" says Fiona Casewell, a peripatetic music teacher, as a little lad bashes away like a 21st century Dave Brubeck (of whom, of course, he is unlikely ever to have heard)

There are around a dozen of them, almost all boys; most read music. "It's not that hard" she insists.

Miss Casewell, born into a brass banding family in the pint-sized county of Rutland, also conducts Spennymoor Town Band and has a youth band, a bright burnished brass band zealot. "That's not a bad description" she concedes. "There's so much that can be gained by playing an instrument, lots of positive experiences, but mainly it's fun."

She's joined by Nathan Minns, a former Thornhill brass band pupil, who's now studying music GCSE at King James I School in Bishop Auckland. "I still love brass bands" he says.

The band rehearses *Let me entertain you*, which I don't recognise, and *Last Christmas*, which I do. "I'd love for some of them to carry on playing after they leave here" says Fiona. "It's not necessarily about being the best player in the world, it's about making friends, making music, perhaps maintaining traditions. Brass bands are part of our heritage, part of Shildon's."

Samantha Overfield has gone back to attending to the million-and-one matters which form a queue outside the modern head teacher's door. No need to blow her own trumpet, Ofsted and these bairns do it for her.

Language school: the sign at Thornhill primary

Chapter twenty-five

Rec and running

The playground area was formally just one small part of the Rec when we were kids – sticky slide, creaking plank, spider's web, teapot lid, sluggish swings – but in truth we played just about everywhere.

We played football wherever there was space for two coats and a kickabout, cricket with one of that central avenue of trees as a wicket – tree stumps, as it were – golf in the too-short days when there was a putting course next to the bandstand, marbles wherever a small hole might be dug or, more likely, imagined.

No one had termed the phrase all-weather pitch. Everywhere, absolutely everywhere, was an all-weather pitch to us lot and not much deterred by ice and snow, either. We'd even have played dominoes in the hallowed rest house had not its elderly occupants erupted at our every insolent appearance.

The Rec's attraction notwithstanding, just about the only thing we didn't play was truant, or nick as more colloquially it became known, though (as an earlier chapter has mentioned) it would have been a poor timekeeper indeed who set his watch by Tom Coates's class.

Perhaps the most reliable sign of the time came when Mr McCutcheon, that put-upon park keeper, emerged at sundown to ring a large handbell, the bell tolling that shortly he'd be locking the gates but a warning routinely ignored unless there were fish and chips for tea. Poor Mr McCutcheon's would very often go cold

The Recreation Ground had formally been opened in 1912, a large and manifestly gleeful procession – many on pumped-up velocipedes – making its way from Byerley Road, then called Shildon Road. The history books, sadly, fail to suggest the route. Probably it's four decades since it was renamed Hackworth Park, a welcome genuflection to the town's most distinguished citizen, and probably things have changed a bit.

The new playground's almost futuristic, the stuff of A-level design and technology lessons. There's another playground, aimed at younger children, next to the tennis court. On one of the grassy banks there's an installation for something called Parkletics, which talks of apps and of QR codes and on which I've never yet seen a soul.

Now a global phenomenon, parkrun – for which lower case must always be the case – covers 22 countries across all five continents, around 1,250 events in the UK at 9am each Saturday, for which Christmas Day offers no ease-up and provides no exemption. Described simply as a time trial, the 5k (3.1 mile) event began at Bushy Park in London in 2004, devised by Paul Sinton-Hewitt, said to be a bit fed up after being incapacitated by a sports injury. There were 13 runners and three volunteer marshals. Ten years later Sinton-Hewitt was appointed CBE for services to grass roots sport.

There are parkruns in prisons and on beaches, in the grounds of stately homes and around reservoirs. There are runners who travel Britain and beyond to tick them off, like those who "collect" Wetherspoons pubs, those who essay a sort of parkrun A-Z. "There's a Zuyder-something-or-other event in Holland" says Neil Wood, race director of the Shildon event. "People seem to love that one."

They're off: the Timothy Hackworth parkrunners

Notice boards around the park advise of much else that's happening thereabouts, from Fun4All to Mobile Adventurers to Active Shildon. Still, says Neil, there'll be plenty of folk in Shildon who'll never have heard of parkrun – "and those who won't know we have this beautiful park, either."

He's a Shildon lad, grew up in East View Terrace – overlooking the Dean Street football ground – watched games from his bedroom window. Involved with the Shildon parkrun since being timekeeper at the first event 11 years ago, he's very content to be there so long as none expects him to break sweat. "They made me do athletics at school. I hated running, still do" he says. "I'm very happy just to do the administration."

Perhaps the best thing of all is that weekly participation is free, the organisation funded both locally and nationally by grants and sponsorship and in turn giving back to the community with events like food bank collections, food banks having taken the place in towns like Shildon of Barclays and their brethren.

America, says Neil, is among the countries where it's been relatively slow to catch on. "The Americans are a bit suspicious, they can't believe that they're getting something for nothing. Look at the cost of going to the gym these days. This way you keep fit for nothing."

It's largely non-competitive, seen as a personal challenge. The first home isn't called the winner but the first placed finisher, the tail-end Charlies are sympathetically described as walkers, not runners. "The only person you're competing against is yourself" says Neil, 64.

The website's strong on safeguarding and on safety. "Some sections of the course may accumulate mud, leaves and puddles after rain" it warns. Oh, right. The injunction to entrants to ensure that they're fit enough to walk, jog or run 5k may also be an exercise in back protection. There's also a warning about Lyme disease, as there had been at the lovely nature reserve in Brusselton.

At Shildon the course record's 16 minutes and 16 seconds with an average 29 minutes 32 seconds. Nationally the men's best is 13:45, the women's 15:13, the average 29:12. A chap called Fauja Singh recorded 38:39 the day before his 101st birthday.

It's July 2024, Shildon's 487th event, the day of the English football team's European Championship quarter-final against Switzerland. Participants of all shapes and sizes (and several extra-outsizes) are gathering near the Masonic Hall. All seem in good spirits. Most wear something approximating to running kit, a couple are clad in the cross of St George. "I didn't know it was clowns' fancy dress day" says someone cheerfully. No offence is taken.

It's Daniel Tatum's 100th event, His mum's baked a celebratory lemon drizzle cake to add to the refreshment table at the finish. "Danny's mum's lemon drizzle cake is to die for" someone says, a curiously fashionable phrase.

Volunteers, usually a minimum 14, have arrived early to set up and marshal the course, a few hundred yards along the Black Path – the Surtees black path, this one - followed by a three-lap park circuit and a final Black Path way to the tape. Set-up gear's carried in something akin to one of those trolleys familiar at garden centres (and which might, indeed, have been cadged from that source.)

Cancellation of the Spennymoor event – the council needed

the park for something else – has brought extra participants to Shildon; a total 99 they reckon. Event director Jamie Reilly addresses about ten Shildon virgins, the term to be interpreted purely athletically, of course. "Run, crawl, walk, whatever you want to do, we're just delighted to have you" says Jamie. "They can dance it if they want to" adds Neil, as an aside. Babies in buggies are welcomed, too.

Jamie also has a word about the ascent through the park – "the famous Hackworth Hill, or undulation as we call it" – and about the bollard immediately in front of the starters, there to prevent vehicle access to the Black Path. "Watch out for it. It might dent your time and something else as well" he says.

They're marshalled at the bottom of the park by 77-year-old George Cawkwell, non-com while his hip replacement settles down but determined soon to be up and running again. George calls some flower, others pet, one or two gorgeous (to which one young lady's response is "Thank you, handsome".) Even the tail-end Charlies seem to be going at a decent lick, though one young lady makes no secret of the fact that she's sneaking a short cut. "She's only cheating herself" says Neil. By no means for the only time, Jack Warters is first home, his 18:23 equalling a personal best.

Cliff Pickering, among the later (shall we say) finishers, has a remarkable story. Now 68, he'd suffered an aortic aneurysm the year previously, spent 13 hours in theatre and three days on a ventilator, now eager both to show off his scars (as folk in such situations tend to be) and to praise the coronary care team at James Cook hospital in Middlesbrough. "Professor Owen was brilliant" he adds. "They said that if I hadn't been quite fit I mightn't even have got to the operating table. I have to build it up gently, but they're happy for me to be running again."

He crosses the line yards ahead of an elderly lady pushing one of those shopping trolleys which seem almost to double as a walking frame. At once she feels the spirit of the thing. "You didn't beat me by much" she says.

Diane Wood, Neil's wife, is in charge of refreshments back at the Hub – lemon drizzle cake alongside flapjack and, appropriately, rocky road cake. The coffee mugs carry a Masonic message, the Masons keen supporters of – if not necessarily participants in - such events. All profess thoroughly to have enjoyed the morning: like the Stockton and Darlington Railway, this one could run and run.

Chapter twenty-six

Gaining the plot

My old dad had two jobs – a number please GPO telephonist in Bishop Auckland by night, on his bike by day to collect club money for the Provident – in an assured attempt to keep us in the style to which we wished to become accustomed.

As earlier recalled, he also had two allotment garden plots, side-by-side on the Waverley Terrace site, chiefly given over to vegetables - spuds one side of the straight and narrow little path, greens the other – plus a couple of little flower beds, a rhubarb and custard patch and a rather ramshackle shed to which he could retire quite literally to get his pipe. I once knew a pipe smoking retired priest in Cockfield whose garden shed bore a sign, a present from his wife, proclaiming it "The Shrine of St Bruno." It would no less canonically have graced my old dad's.

It's fair to say that in those industriously green fingered endeavours he received precious little assistance from his boys, particularly the marginally elder son, though we usually turned up when he tried to beguile a bonfire, enthusiasm similarly smouldering.

It's a sunny Sunday morning in July 2024 and I'm again standing outside the Waverley Terrace allotments, making a note that the old wooden fence which in former times might have struggled to deter a snagger bashing two-year-old has been replaced by an 8ft steel structure akin to the maximum security wing at Frankland prison. A female voice ruffles the reverie.

"Can I help you?" asks Sandra Watson, 77. standing by her back gate. Indeed she can.

It's Philip Robinson's allotment, not Sandra's, has been for the 40 years since my dad died, she merely the minder. Sandra has both keys and conscientiousness. "You don't need Neighbourhood Watch when you've got Sandra" says Philip, when he turns up a bit later. "You don't really even need a fence."

"He fills my freezer every year. It's a fair exchange" says Sandra.

Philip's only there to cut a cabbage for dinner, just as his green-fingered precursor would have done all those Sabbath mornings since. Incorrigibly, instantly, I'm reminded of the old joke about Bella blethering to Bertha over the garden fence, somewhere in the Durham coalfield.

Bella says she was sorry to hear about their Bill, wonders what happened. Bertha replies that he was cutting a cabbage for their dinner, the knife slipped, he slashed his wrist and bled to death before anyone discovered him.

"That's just awful" says Bella. "What did you do next."

"It *was* awful" agrees Bertha, "I had to open a can of peas."

An Insatiable First, the history of the Railway Institute, records that as early as 1846 the committee was keen to provide allotments but were frustrated not least because others had the same idea. "J Smithson Esq has set aside two fields at Chapel Row for the purpose of spade husbandry and has let them to the miners" reported the *Newcastle Courant*. "They are working very industriously at their little plots when not employed in the pits."

When finally the Institute gained land of its own, members dug in no less enthusiastically and are thought to have supported the first Shildon Show in 1860. Allotments were provided behind the present building in Redworth Road when it opened in 1912, though the land was subsequently sold for a car park and for housing.

It's also said that the Institute created allotment land on the spoil heap created by the excavation of the Prince of Wales tunnel – Tunnel Top – though by the time we were young all that grew there was a golden profusion of dandelions, or pittley-beds as my dear old Aunty Betty indecorously, diuretically knew them.

Eric Thompson, a wonderfully gifted artist who grew up on Fir Tree and now has a studio in Bishop, painted loads of sledging kids on Tunnel Top, a skimpy wooden fence again guarding against a fearful, fateful drop – bit of artistic licence, maybe, but not very far from the truth.

In 1952, the Urban District Council's surveyor talked of his dream that the town would become "the garden city of the North", a theme he maintained seven years later. These days the town council website lists ten allotment sites, two of them community gardens, with getting on 500 plots between them. There'd have been 11 but the 3.69 acre Sunnydale allotment gardens, leading off Green Lane, had been auctioned off the previous November by Savills, the posh people's estate agency. Not quite what the visionary surveyor had in mind, perhaps, but green and pleasant, nonetheless.

It's along Green Lane that the Sunday morning starts, and a bit hard to know what's going on. A large paddock with a couple of smart looking portable homes is identified as 46A Stable View, a sign on a fence nearby depicting a rather angry looking dog. "I can make it to the fence in 2.8 seconds, can you?" it says.

What? Don't they know that I was once third – OK, joint third – in the Timothy Hackworth Juniors egg and spoon race?

Boulders block the lane to vehicular traffic. Another sign warns that dogs are running loose and presumably not in practice for the greyhound derby. Behind high hedges there are suggestions of further development but little of spades in the ground. Julie, a nice lady at the town council, confirms the following day that there are no allotments there now.

An allotment tenancy agreement has no fewer than 34 clauses ranging from what might be kept there – hens, rabbits, no cockerels, no dogs, pigeons by written consent – to not being allowed to burn anything save for horticultural waste and even then only between October-March and with the tenant in attendance throughout. My dad's bonfires would maunder on unattended for days, the very antithesis of the adage about no smoke without fire. Besides, who'd have sought the number (please) or pedalled Shildon for the Provident?

The council's terms and conditions also enjoin that gardens be kept clean and "reasonably free" from weeds, that they should be left in a "reasonable" condition and that holders must not cause or permit nuisance or annoyance. If the stipulation included Sunday morning Radio 1, there'd be a bloke at Waverley Terrace out on his ear.

Julie says that in a town of around 10,000 people there's still a waiting list of a year or so for a garden. Most of the sites are familiar, or can be found, but Graham Terrace isn't even on the

Crees great and small: Auckland Terrace allotments

map – "just off Dale Road" says Julie – and Brickyard Allotments is a puzzle, too. That one's near South Street, she says, close to where the wagon works (and, presumably, a brickyard) used to be.

It may not be the next garden city, nor take second place in a Chelsea Flower Show beauty contest, but it seems to me a growth industry much to be encouraged, and to be commended, too.

The Gardeners Guild, which sought through bulk buying to offer cut rate plants and equipment, has folded, even so. Local leek shows, where once the best in show might win a three-piece suite and tenth prize a telly, seem also to have perished, or at least to have been slashed. The *Town Crier* in 2011 reported that the Waverley Terrace Allotment Society's show had gone ahead despite a spate of vandalism just a few weeks earlier with both polytunnels and vegetables "systematically" attacked. In 2015 it was still going, still growing. It's not now.

Wilf Tray, who reported leek shows for the *Town Crier* and was himself a champion grower – "couple of wins at the Grey Horse, couple at the Royal George, once at Elm Road Club" – recalls that the days of three-piece suite talk are long gone. "Towards the end it was mainly beer vouchers as prizes. The shows were still good fun, but they were very bad for your liver."

Back on his allotment Phil Robinson surveys some good looking leeks. "They're just for the table or the food bank now" he says. "There's not the interest, but the vandals haven't helped." All the plots are taken, he thinks – "but there's a difference between being taken and being worked."

There are four-legged vermin, too, though the tenancy agreement urges vigilance. "There were hundreds of rats when I came here, there's one in my trap this morning" says Phil. "I sharp fettle the little buggers."

Once they could keep pigs on Waverley Terrace, probably a couple of horses and a ferret or two. Now the effort seems chiefly horticultural, more greenhouses, huts and shacks – a shed load, it might be supposed – than a month on Greenham Common. Many also have polytunnels, unheard of in my dad's day. Probably there's also a joke about polytunnels, polytunnels and parrots, but one's enough for now.

Two flags fly from a pole on one plot, outside another gate a bin's piled high with beer cans. "It kills the slugs. They don't like Smith's Smooth" a chap says, perhaps mendaciously, though the slugs wouldn't be alone in their distaste.

Another guy, friendly in a Fast and Furious t-shirt, tells of the recent time that he took pods of peas home for the grandbairns' tea. "You plant them, you love them up, you nurture them and the kids don't even know what they are. They think peas come in a tin from Aldi." He grows rhubarb, too, though it seems imprudent to ask where his grandbairns think the custard plants are cultivated.

Signs warn that the gardens are now smart allotments, protected by smart water, forensic devices and CCTV. Gordon French effectively protected his apple tree with half a bag of soot. Sandra Watson talks quietly, ruefully, of kids who gather up the top end – "motor bikes and drugs"

Annual rent for a plot is £30, including water supply and insurance. "Last year it was just £25" says Fast and Furious, a little ruefully, but it still seems the bargain of the century.

Phil had thought that there might still be a leek show at the Fox and Hounds, 200 yards away, though that's unlikely as once again the Market Place pub appears closed. A subsequent Sunday stroll reveals that the Timothy Hackworth has also – however temporarily – hit the buffers. All these pub closures must be driving Shildon lads to drink.

The Auckland Terrace site has just 17 plots, little obvious activity and even less security. One plot's guarded by the sort of rope with which a playgroup might skip, another has an eviction notice on the gate. Auckland Terrace West, past the reservoir and harder to find, has notices warning that the allotments are patrolled on a regular basis, that trespassers and offenders will be prosecuted and that thieves should beware, though of what or whom isn't clarified. There's also a number for Newton Aycliffe police station – perhaps because it's quite hard to find someone at Shildon police station these days – and there's something about coronavirus, too.

A shed has two weather vanes and signs about single file traffic, another (honest) appears to be topped with a crucifix, perhaps a shrine to the patron saint of allotment growers or perhaps once more to St Bruno. Then round the corner there's a cree, glory be, then two crees and then three. These are not ordinary pigeon crees, these are positively palatial, lofty lofts like a penthouse for high flyers from within which comes the gentle coo of contentment, like the man of the house snoozing after Sunday dinner.

The curious thing this Sunday lunchtime is that not one of the 54 plots appears to be occupied by humanity, not even to cut a cabbage – and as was noted earlier, they'd struggle to be down the pub.

Then on to West Road – 62 plots, more notices, even a key-code lock (which, happily, isn't set). A sign warns that only two visitors at a time are allowed in a garden, which makes it sound like the maternity ward at Darlington hospital. In the next field another notice urges not to feed the horses since they're on a special diet, but then again aren't we all.

The West Road allotments seem the most appealing of all – a bolthole, a refuge, a horticultural haven hidden in plain sight not 100 yards from the main drag. Again the range and imagination of structures is extraordinary, nothing like those posh greenhouses they used to advertise in *Radio Times* and, a little more sadly, no sign of those once-ubiquitous LNER goods vans, multi-purposed after ultimate derailment.

One shed rather resembles a Swiss chalet, albeit a chalet that's seen better days. Another might double as a ranch for a cowboy down on his luck. It's lovely. Critturs that may not immediately identify as hens or rabbits also have a home down here, indeed wander to the fence seeking sustenance, and are doing no one any harm.

The funny thing is that once again there's not a soul around, but if Shildon's assiduous gardeners are all at home enjoying a home-grown dinner, it strikes me that they've earned it.

The Fox is open again, though the "For sale" sign remains outside. The agent's website invites "offers in the region of £125,000" but adds that the upper rooms "are uninhabitable in their present form." A notice on the door still warns that the pub's patrolled by a security firm. It's just about my first visit since Percy Jackson was licensed to sell beer, spirits and what not, and how many moons can it be since a publican was last called Percy? Wasn't Andy Capp's local licensee called Percy, too, or was that the rent man?

It's Wednesday August 21, cool and cloudy, among the eight or nine lunchtime customers several elderly gentlemen who believe it proper to wear shorts. Is there still a leek show, I wonder, or has even the last of them been deracinated? "Certainly there is" says the friendly landlady, the only problem that it's in August 31 when I'm on holiday.

Who runs it? "Paul Pecker" they agree in the bar. "What's Mr Pecker's real name?" None knows, nor if Paul might be any relation to Peter, who picked a peck. Eventually I leave a card, ask that the gentleman give me a ring. A despatch from the trenches depends upon it, but I never hear a peep from Mr Pecker.

Chapter twenty-seven

Scouting report

St John's church had several youth groups back in the 50s and 60s – one the Eleven to Fifteens Fellowship, known as the ETOFFs and with its own discordant song to the tune of *Hi-ho-Hi-ho it's off to work we go*. A little later there was a branch of the Anglican Young Peoples' Association of which, though titularly qualified, I was a hopelessly ineffectual chairman.

Around 1965, however, we made shocked national headlines after conducting a somewhat spurious survey which concluded that 50 per cent of Shildon's under-18s regularly visited the pub. The North Home Service, as then it still was, even sent the well-remembered reporter George Lambelle to interview me, tape recorder the size of a sideboard. We met, inevitably, in the pub.

Much the most memorable moments, however, came at the end of our GCE O-levels in 1963 when the Rev Geoff Clarkson, a conscientious curate, organised a week-long youth club trip to Biarritz on the sun-blessed French Riviera and with a day outing, as you do, across the Spanish border to San Sebastian, bull fighting country not easily confused with Seaton Carew. Mixed party, mixed blessing, we stayed in a school, spent the days on the beach scoffing elephantine amounts of apricot doughnuts and the evenings in the little tabac at the end of the road, smoking noxious French cigarettes and drinking aniseed spirits.

Only one of us, incorrigibly, forewent the fags in order to afford the English language newspapers when they arrived 24 hours late.

We were 16 going on 13– most of us, anyway – still innocents abroad. Nothing much else happened - not to me, anyway, though the 21st century adage about what goes on tour stays on tour probably applies. Geoff Clarkson later became chaplain of the infamous Feltham Young Offenders' Institution in west London, said in St John's parish magazine at the time to hold around 400 boys – "many of them subnormal and emotionally unstable." Geoff, the mag added, faced a tough uphill job, though compared to taking two dozen Shildon adolescents to the south of France, Borstal was probably a doddle.

Briefly, I was a bare-kneed Boy Scout, too, the Scouts' carnival one of the town's annual highlights. Thousands, several thousands, lined the streets as a dozen or more immaculately attired juvenile jazz bands, a veritable kazoo's who, escorted as many flat-bed wagons bearing elaborate tableaux – known, sink or swim, as floats.

Easy as falling off a lorry? Memory suggests that no one ever did. Had they done, they'd just have climbed back on. Health and safety hadn't been invented – and falling wrong, in sixties Shildon, was something else entirely. Nor would it be right to recall the identity of one of the youth club ladies who did indeed fall wrong or that of the father though, confined to barracks, he missed several Sunday lunchtime card schools as a result.

As a church youth club member I was once dressed up as a bishop, though not right reverend at all, as a boy scout I was pressganged to promenade as a Sea Scout, a bit like an extra from *Captain Pugwash* and expected to sing about riding along on the crest of a wave while dancing something akin to a rather hobbled hornpipe. Never a float, we sank. One Christmas there was also a scouts' dance, predictably ending with the Drifters' hit *Save the last dance for me*. She didn't.

The scouts hall in Church Street is long demolished, now the site of the Original Factory Shop or some such. The Shildon B-P Scouts – boys and girls, Beavers and Cubs, too – meet together on Friday evenings in the Methodist Church hall, multi-roomed and wholly fit for purpose. They're boisterous, for boys will be boisterous, the girls no less enthusiastic.

Grace Wade, coming up 18 and a member since she was five, is studying criminology and related subjects at Darlington College, hopes to become a leader and to go on to university. "I feel I can be myself, anything I want to be when I come in here" she says. "As soon as you walk in here, you feel safe."

Shildon? "There's not really a lot to do. I feel that the park has been taken over by chavs, if you know what one of those is. I don't much like going out on my own after dark. You have to be careful."

The B-P Scouts formally split from the Scouts Association in 1970 when, as their Wikipedia page puts it, "it was felt that the Scouts Association were abandoning the traditions and intentions set out by Baden-Powell in 1908."

The B-P Scouts own website expands: "The aim of our Association, as stated by Lord Baden-Powell himself, is to promote good citizenship and wholesome physical and mental development and training in habits of observation, discipline, self-reliance, loyalty and useful life skills.

BP's planning and foresight still hold true today, it continues. "We preserve Lord Baden-Powell's original ideas in our programme and methods as much as possible while progressing with the times and keeping up to date with the very latest technology, child protection legislation, first aid standards and safety in outdoor education."

A full-page ad in Shildon's 1953 Coronation brochure – "The Boy Scouts – the finest youth organisation for your sons" – pretty much presaged it. "Developing good citizenship by forming their character; training them in habits of observation, obedience and self-reliance; inculcating loyalty and thoughtfulness for others"….and so, clean in thought, word and deed, it went on.

Still the cubs chant the dib-dib-dib mantra, still offer allegiance to Akela – the Grand Howl, apparently it's called – still they wear caps and neckerchiefs, still the scouts have ranks of sixer and seconder, Shildon's sixer acting as a sort of necker checker. Still they promise on their honour to do their duty to God and the King, still have much the same ten principles, still learn how to light a fire using friction and navigate without a compass. Still a scout smiles and whistles in all difficulties, still is thrifty, still (as we were saying) clean in thought, word and deed. Still, of course, they're prepared, still there's much talk of *The Jungle Book* and its characters from an age when Mr Kipling didn't make cakes but wrote exceedingly good books.

It may be a jungle out there, but in the church hall it feels very different. These days in the Baden-Powell Scouts, everyone wears the trousers and no one runs the gauntlet.

Jeffrey Allison was a Shildon lad who took his scout training to extremes, becoming when 73 years old the first sailor to circumnavigate the Arctic in an anti-clockwise direction – 10,335 nautical miles over five months at sea, 40 days without setting foot on land, cheered by an occasional tin of peaches. "Just like when we were kids" he thought, though in Albert Street (it may be recalled) we had pears.

Troopers: Beverley Watkins (front, centre) with Shildon scouts and cubs

Raised on Drybourne Avenue – posh end – from 1938, he remembered a German bomb dropping on what folk called the Store Field. "I expect they were aiming for the Wagon Works, missed as usual" said Jeff, further recalling that he and his pals got there before the police did. "They took a belt of machine gun bullets and started a fire in a field next to the Recreation Ground. We were hiding behind a fence about 30 yards away. Fortunately they didn't go off."

He attended Timothy Hackworth school, roamed free – "you'd go off on your own with a bottle of water and a sugar sandwich" - gained his Queen's Scout award with the Spennymoor troop. "I remember being taken to Ferryhill Station for my Queen's Scout night navigation test. You just opened the door and off you went, guided by the moon and stars. I'd learned all that at Shildon."

At 24 he became under-manager at Middridge Drift – "there were some rough old Shildon lads" – going on to head a successful quarrying firm before developing, with his wife Prue, the upmarket Middleton Lodge estate and hotel near Scotch Corner, even posher than Drybourne Avenue. It was later taken over by one of his sons.

The Arctic adventure – "like a logical chess game between him and the receding ice" Prue had said – came two years after a similar voyage had ended when he was arrested by the Russians, fined 4,000 roubles – "not much" – for not having the correct paperwork. Back home in 2013 he looked south, eyeing the opposite pole for his next big adventure. Very sadly, he became ill a few months later and died, aged 75, in 2013.

Formed in Shildon in 1912, said on their website to be open to everyone from five to 105, the 1st Shildon (St John's) troop merged in 2023 with the All Saints troop. They're led by 54-year-old Beverley Watkins, happy in an age of equality still to be styled group scoutmaster. "That's the tradition" she says.

Brian Ellis, her late dad, became a Queen's Scout – his tasks including to climb a mountain in the Pyrenees – and himself was group scoutmaster. Angela, her mother, was also involved. Brian died ten years ago from a brain tumour - Beverley's brought his shirt, keen to explain his badges. Both her daughters are also involved with the group, one as cubmaster and the other an occasional visitor from London.

Beverley, who works at a school in Sedgefield, is also a national commissioner for Beavers but is wholly unpaid. "People think it's just a couple of hours on a Friday night but it's many other days, too, sometimes all over the country. I love it, I love taking these kids camping, love watching them develop, love seeing them have quality time together. Sometimes we have to have discipline, because we don't want accidents to happen, but a lot of this is about education, about getting to know the outdoors, about fun. I particularly like it when parents say thank you. That means a lot."

Mind, adds the GSM, she still has a bottle of wine cooling in the fridge every Friday evening back home in Newton Aycliffe.

Her dad worked at the Shops, like many others turned down relocation when they closed. "He didn't want the upheaval" says Beverley. "He got a job eventually but it was hard and Shildon became a ghost town. Losing Sunnydale Comprehensive School had badly affected the community, too. This is a safe place for children to go. They aren't roaming the streets, not getting into mischief as some do when they're older. It isn't for everyone, we know that, but there are a lot of good reasons for being here. If we weren't around, I don't know what some of these kids would do."

Immaculately uniformed – "I don't like scruffy scouts" says Beverley – a near-nine-year-old called Darcey comes over for a chat, talks of how much she enjoys camp fires, sports days and making things. She enjoys singing, too, snatches a few bars of Ging-gang-gooly, a more improbable survivor from earlier times.

What of Shildon? "There are an awful lot of food places" she says, and the group scout master joins in the laughter.

Each age group has its own programme, carefully planned. Each member has his or her own file, detailing things like allergies, medical conditions, whether they can be photographed, all sorts. Every leader has a Disclosure and Barring Service (DBS) check and has a list of qualifications.

A bit autumnal for outdoor pursuits, and the minister might object if they set fire to the church hall, the groups engage in all manner of activities best described as fun. Even the youngest, the Beavers, learn first aid – "recovery position, how to call 999, that sort of thing." At the end, each group's called formally to attention – "Shildon, Shildon 'shun" – and does it very smartly. They salute, say a prayer, recite the promise to do duty to God and the King. The little ones, at least, are given a bag of what formerly were called sweets and now appear to be ket.

The Group Scout Master says she wouldn't be anywhere else, thinks that Lord Baden-Powell would be happy with what's going on – "but I'm still going to enjoy that glass of wine."

Chapter twenty-eight

Happening to a vet

The Veterans' Hub meets once a month, third Wednesday, in what's still known as the Rest House in Timothy Hackworth Park. A blue plaque outside records that the building was opened in 1926 for "social, community and educational purposes" and so, true to purpose, it remains.

The attendance sheet's limited to name and rank though all of those informally on parade could at once declaim "number" if asked to provide it. There's a retired major who's married to a lance corporal, a former captain, a sergeant major. I'm asked to sign but leave the "rank" space blank. It probably wouldn't do to write Poor Bloody Infantry, the status suggested in the book's first sentence.

It's coincidental that The Times this very Wednesday morning should carry a lengthy obituary of John Clegg, the actor who played the public school educated Lah-di-dah Gunner Graham in the 1970s sitcom *It aint half hot mum* and who became a constant target of bullying Battery Sergeant Major Williams. Clegg was also a public school boy, also a private.

Not only is there no rank at the hub, but for many of those in attendance military service is so long ago that they even remember the warrant officers with something approaching affection.

The Hub's another town council initiative, started in April 2023 and led by Glenn Gibson, the council's direct works manager who was in the Territorial Army with the Royal Electrical and Mechanical Engineers and drinks dutifully from a REME mug. "We noticed that there were quite a lot of ex-military in the town but nothing specifically for them" says Glenn. "The Ministry of Defence might tell you that there aren't many vets in Shildon but there are and many of them need support. We try to encourage them to talk about any problems they may have. Mental health is very important, there are lads of all ages with issues. This is somewhere they can chill."

Sometimes there are talks, sometimes outings, on one occasion a chance to view Glenn's collection of replica American Civil War weaponry, about which he's passionate. Shildon Alive provides food, the council hot drinks. This morning someone's brought some rather large cucumbers, though there seems little demand for them.

They're affable, convivial, friendly. Someone tells a joke about an Englishman, an Irishman and a Scotsman but inevitably I've forgotten it. Dogs are allowed.

Outside on the veranda a little group gathers for a chat and, in some cases, a fag. Former Royal Signals staff sergeant Dave Toleman sits in a state-of-the-art mobility scooter, his dog alongside. Timothy Hillary, Shildon born and raised, was a sergeant in 7th Para; Peter Quinn, cigar smoking town councillor, served ten years with the 1st Battalion Light Infantry including three tours of Northern Ireland; Paul Wood, youngest and quietest, was a private in the Green Howards. Firstly, however, there's a little interlude….

I'm sitting on the steps, pondering how on earth to get up again, when Lesley Coley (as was) comes up the path with her grandchildren. That she is 67 is a rather stark example of how time flies. Lesley was one of the Methodist church music group Geordie's Penker which in 1975 recorded Iron Road to mark the Stockton and Darlington's 150th, what some folk call the sesquicentennial. Remember the wonderful lines?

And who needs Presley when you've got Nigel Gresley

He'll convert you quicker than old John Wesley....

Jack, her occasionally short-fused father, served with me as a churchwarden at St John's. Jean, her mum, was a church stalwart, too. They lived on Salisbury Terrace, near the Hippodrome. The six Geordie's Penker members are scattered across Britain, says Lesley, who still sings in a choir. "I'd love to get us together again for the bicentenary but I can't see it happening."

After their parents' death, Lesley and her brother Graham sold the house. The place where we'd monthly put together the parish magazine over nothing stronger than Nescafe became, perhaps more addictively, a cannabis farm. "No one might have known but a rival gang smashed all the windows to try to get at the crop" she says, adding that her dad would have turned in his grave.

Not in my experience he wouldn't. Jack would have risen from it and, one by one, he'd have flattened the lot of them.

Reminiscence among the veterans is far ranging, from fatigues to fags – "rationed to just 120 a week at the NAAFI, not even 20 a day, luckily you could buy some cheap off non-smokers" – and from spiders to sergeant majors (which should not, of course be supposed synonymous.) "We'd go hunting for camel spiders, size of a dinner plate and with legs as thick as your thumb" says Tim.

Unalone, he supposes that Shildon has changed. "I remember when everyone helped one another out. They don't any more.

Great beast: Shirley Crabtree

We were brought up to respect people; you don't get that, either."

Sergeant majors? "They were all right really, you could talk to them" says Dave, particularly recalling Sgt Major Shirley Crabtree, better remembered as the rotund wrestler Big Daddy, named after his father – a professional Rugby League player – at a time when it was chiefly a boy's name. Charlotte Bronte's novel Shirley rather changed things, Shirley Temple put the tin hat on it.

"He was a beast of a man" says Dave. "Whatever they say about wrestling being faked, you wouldn't have wanted to mix with Sgt Major Crabtree."

Did they call him Shirley? "No chance, we called him Sir."

Peter Quinn emphasis the importance of the group. "We went through a lot but still people forget. Don't get me wrong, you make some good mates in the Army but when they come out a lot of the lads are on their own. I was fortunate that I came out with a home and family to go to, many don't and it can be very difficult."

Most have fallen out, gone home, by 1pm. Some will be back in the park on September 28-29, joining Royal British Legion colleagues for a sponsored sleep-out to help homeless ex-servicemen. Dave Toleman, dog trotting alongside his scooter, is among the last to leave. "These Wednesdays are a chance to talk, to let it out" he says. "You'd be surprised how many military just don't want to talk at all."

Chapter twenty-nine

Honours, even

Before the town council's monthly meeting, November 2024, I'm presented by Coun Shirley Quinn with the Town Mayor's award for what effectively are services to Shildon. Clearly they haven't yet seen the book. "I know he doesn't live here any more but he does" says the mayor, only slightly paradoxically. "His heart's still here, anyway."

Most present applaud generously. Peter Quinn, the mayor's husband and fellow councillor, is unable to join in after breaking his arm when falling over the family pet, fresh impetus to the warning to beware of the dog.

The award's greatly kind of them. Shirley also agrees that I can stay for the council meeting and the committees which follow, inevitably drawing comparison with the days of the old Urban District Council, on which I served from 1970-73, the most vocal of five titularly Independent members alongside 15 representing the Labour party. Until local government reorganisation in 1974 – "reorganisation" may be the second most dreaded term in the English language, after "replacement bus service" – urban districts had responsibility for housing, public health and sanitation, planning, many roads and streets, refuse collection, lighting and much else.

When four councils were merged to become Sedgefield Borough, and when subsequently Durham County Council became a unitary – if not a unity – authority, accountability appeared ever more remote. These days the "town" councils are pretty much parish councils, responsible for parks and sundry other grass roots, commendably community conscious.

Back in the early 70s, meetings could oft be fractious (and no matter that it was usually me at the dissonant heart of it all). Now things appear altogether more friendly, more informally formal, less political and thus more effective. There's a sartorial shift, too: I'm the only bloke in the council chamber who's wearing a tie – and, come to think, the only one who calls the meeting leader chairman. To others, both the occupant and the piece of furniture he or she occupies are, unisex, "chair".

There's also a scandal, a real stinking scandal, but we'll come to that in a moment.

At the start of the meeting there's a police report – in the Shildon and Eldon patch over the previous month there've been 19 burglaries, 18 offences of theft or shoplifting, another 18 of criminal damage and 13 of what's termed "violence." It seems an awful lot and there are concerns – by no means for the first time – that the thin blue line may be in danger of diminishing yet further.

Coun Dave Reynolds tells of a recent case of off-road motor biking on grassland near his home. He'd taken "clear" photographs and then rung the police. "The call handler couldn't have sounded less interested if he'd tried" says Dave. "He said no one could come. People won't report things if that's the reaction they get."

There'd also been unwelcome activity at the Civic Hall, across the road from the council offices, where a bunch of kids between 10 and 12 years old had gone into the gent's, blocked the basins with toilet paper, turned on all the taps and, like the taps, ran. Soon water was pouring from the front door, CCTV of all that had been given to the police as well.

Having heard back nothing postdiluvially, the clerk was asked to write to the chief constable requesting a greater police presence in the town. The chief will probably recognise the handwriting. It all seems a bit more serious than pinching Gordon French's pippins.

Members are also concerned about the future of the Sunnydale Leisure Centre, County Council run, not least after the County Council contentiously closed the adjoining Sunnydale comprehensive school, since demolished and the site now frequently visited by those politely termed travellers. "Unauthorised encampments" says the mayor, who thinks that the well-used athletics track across the road from the leisure centre may yet be its "saving grace".

Shirley's also worried that, less than a year before the bicentennial climax, derelict buildings on the visitor route between Masons Arms crossing and Locomotion museum remain ruinous. She means the long closed Commercial pub – what larks when run by the late and lovely Dorothy Howard – the old shop site of Bert Withers the butcher and the former Armitage's shop. All are privately owned. "We'll be a laughing stock" says the mayor.

Committee meetings follow, briefly and briskly. Stuart Joyce, the Civic Hall manager, reports a better-than-budget year, talks of forthcoming Christmas attractions which include three nights of the splendidly named Tess Tickle. Ms Tickle – is that a permissible personal pronoun? – is a drag act, apparently accompanied by the Dragettes. What on earth would the late Walter Nunn, and other councillors of a decidedly more conservative persuasion back in the 1970s, have made of a bloke dressing up as a woman, and no matter how fabulous the frock? Come to that, what would Timothy Hackworth?

The term "conservative", it should be noted, has a decidedly small 'c'.

There's also talk of an outfit called Symphonic Ibiza, booked for a two-day park run in the summer of 2025, and that those living in the vicinity will be warned about noise levels. Not akin to the Northern Sinfonia, then? "Probably not" says Coun Reynolds and subsequent googling reveals that Symphonic Ibiza "fuses a thrilling live orchestra with high-tempo beats from world club DJ Andy Joyce."

Whatever happened to "Who needs Presley when you've got Nigel Gresley", or to the British Railways band?

Then there's the real, ripe, scandal. For years it's been supposed that the S&D's bicentenary celebrations would have three separate launches, in Stockton and in Darlington from which the line took its name and in Shildon, from where the world's first public railway began. The assumption was mistaken. The launch will take place on March 29 2025 in Bishop Auckland, which didn't get so much as a whiff of steam until 17 years later, taking place on the site of the annual Kynren night shows.

The programme talks of a journey through time and place and of "distinctive combinations of technology, live performance and drone shows – a celebration of the bold innovation, creative thinking and ingenuity that led to the world changing opening of the Stockton and Darlington Railway."

But in Bishop?

Dave Reynolds, at the heart of so much that's vigorous and reviving in Shildon, insists that he'll boycott the event. The mayor, who'd hoped that the launch might wholly appropriately have been in Timothy Hackworth Park, speaks diplomatically of "real disappointment", of the event very likely being "ticketed and expensive" and of Shildon folk being seriously disadvantaged. Coun Reynolds talks of the behest of Bishop Auckland's "local philanthropist", by which he means Jonathan Ruffer – cited in an earlier chapter – the munificent mastermind behind the reimagining of so much in Bishop Auckland and of Kynren, too. But what's that to do with the Stockton and Darlington Railway?

Dave says he wouldn't be quite so aggrieved if they were doing something at Witton Park, the village from which the first train was hauled by gravity – "but Bishop" he adds, followed by several words unspoken and about three dozen invisible exclamation marks. It's subsequently announced that the launch event will cost just £5 a head – which these days would barely buy a pie and a pint, not even in Shildon – and that, of all things, it'll be called *All change*. Debate may ensue over who thought of that one first but, as they say elsewhere, beware of imitations.

A final civic retrospection before once more heading out of town: when first I dipped a quill into the inky trade, or in vain inveighed at Shildon Urban District Council, the area was covered by four different newspapers, and a dozen or more reporters, all based on Bishop Auckland (qv). Now, save for the *Town Crier* and other community newspapers delivered free, there's nothing. The press bench is bare, as it is for every meeting and at almost all councils. Local journalism wastes away, democracy and accountability the collateral damage. A meeting which reveals how Bishop Auckland has monstrously been allowed to steal its neighbour's crown jewels could pass without comment and for all sorts of reasons that's awful.

Chapter thirty

Independents' day?

One-and-a-half thousand leaflets have been pushed through letter boxes promoting a public meeting in the Civic Hall. Half-page advertisements have been taken in the *Town Crier*, social media saturated. Broadly it's to discuss the town's future and to seek potential candidates for the Shildon and Dene Valley Independent Group – is "Independent Group" not an oxymoron? – at the Durham County Council elections in May 2025.

The guest speaker's Jamie Driscoll, former elected Mayor of North Tyneside who, standing as an Independent, had come second in the North-East mayoral election in 2024.

Unless you count the kids who sneak in beforehand, send the Christmas tree crashing to the ground and return to the depths whence they came, the total attendance of members of the public is four, with another four or five already signed up.

Mr Driscoll does his best. He's also a jiu-jitsu black belt and gave up driving as a gesture towards saving the planet, preferring to turn up to mayoral meetings on his bike. How he's got from North Shields to Shildon on a late November night is unclear but if his bike's been parked outside the Civic Hall then it's not there any longer.

The meeting divides into what apparently are known as break-out groups, four or five in each, anchored in negativity. A lady wants to talk about housing conditions in Birmingham. Further distracted, I'm reminded of what became known as the Serenity Prayer, ascribed to Magi for about 700 years: "O God, give me the serenity to accept what cannot be changed, the courage to change what can be changed and the wisdom to know the one from the other."

The meeting's been called by 75-year-old Fred Langley, a son of Shildon with a fascinating cv and some innovative and imaginative aspirations for the old town's future. They include a memorial to Shildon's miners. "They've been forgotten" says Fred. "There are memories of the railwaymen, rightly so, but what of the pitmen? I still remember as a youngster seeing old miners helplessly coughing their lungs out, and that was just the ones who survived. We've spent a lot of money on railway heritage and forgotten the miners."

He puts the memorial cost at about £25,000, hopes for grants, envisages a site opposite the historic coal drops just up the line from Locomotion and has sounded out a sculptor.

He also owns a collection of around 10,000 books – "the storage probably costs more than they're worth" – many of which he hopes to sell in coming weeks in order to help fund his ambition.

We again meet a few days later at Locomotion, seemingly the town's coffee shop of choice after Costa decided that they could no longer afford Shildon (or, possibly, vice-versa). Fred in turn is joined by his mate Kevin Bibby, whose model railway passion includes a layout of Shildon station on which the track had added rust for authenticity. "It's pretty standard practice" says Kevin, anti-corrosively.

The museum's gained a couple of Christmas trees, happily un-vandalized, but not many visitors. The gift shop has little that's Shildon-specific, though great sheds of Thomas the Tank Engine and mementoes of Flying Scotsman, the great locomotive

Independent minded: Fred Langley

now immaculately if impatiently stabled a few yards away.

There are also a great many books. Oh crumbs, might there yet be room for a little one – a different one, anyway – a bicentennial stocking filler, Christmas 2025?

Fred's early years were spent in the Elm Road prefabs before the family moved to Coronation Avenue, on the post-war council housing estate. "There were three sets of police houses up there alone" he recalls. "Now the town has half a sergeant."

He left the Boys Modern school at 16 with few qualifications, worked at the Randolph Coke Works at Evenwood and then at BXL, formerly Bakelite and later Ineos, at Aycliffe. "It wasn't a very good start" he concedes, though like the Scotsman stuck behind a goods train, he sharp made up for lost time, gaining two science degrees and enjoying a lengthy teaching and education career in Africa – often working with black youngsters excluded from mainstream education - before 11 years as head tutor to the peripatetic cast of the musical *Billy Elliott*, based mainly in London and Hamburg.

He'd been a Billy, too – William Frederick Langley – but sought upon leaving school to be known as Fred. "Billy didn't seem masculine enough" he says, though there are manly Shildon lads, not silly Billies in the least, who'd doubtless disagree.

So was Shildon the one he had to come back for? Fred pleads necessity. "I was divorced for a second time. If you want to lose a fortune get married and then divorced. If you want to lose an even larger fortune, do it again. I'd bought some property in Shildon and when I finished *Billy* didn't have a lot of money left. Shildon it was.

"When I was growing up you could buy anything you needed

in Shildon, no need to go to Darlington or anywhere else, just by going up the street. No one called it Church Street, you just went up the street. Look around now, the centre's almost dead, no footfall. I couldn't believe what I was seeing, it was disheartening, awful. Ideally I think it would have to be knocked down, a lot could be rebuilt around it."

Nor were things helped when in January 2025 a devastating fire destroyed the street's motor bike shop, on the road for 22 years, physically and figuratively leaving a gap which may never be filled. A few days later, however, it was announced that Shildon and Newton Aycliffe would be the centre of a National Lottery funded £10m "Heritage Places" initiative with a focus on children and young people. Having Shildon recognised as a World Heritage Site would also be a Durham County Council "priority". It didn't say how much of the £10m would be targeted towards Newton Aycliffe and how much the other place.

Fred won a seat on the town council, standing as an Independent and topping the poll in his ward. Now he hopes others will join him in tilting at Durham County Council, where power and influence reside. "You have to be accessible, you have to be visible. Some of these councillors aren't and they're well paid for it."

He's also working with Newcastle University dental hospital in the hope of setting up an initiative under which, ferried by the community bus, Shildon kids might get specialist treatment. "When I was a student I tried opening a bottle with my teeth, as you do, and ruined them. I know how important dental health can be. A lot of people tell me that I'm wasting my time, but because it's difficult doesn't mean it's impossible",

Eleven days to Christmas, day one of Fred's quid-a-book sale at the Railway Institute. His back's gone through all the humping, his mood's anxious. "Shildon just doesn't seem to be a book town" he says. "Even when I tried to give away children's books, I think I managed two in four hours."

Dave Reynolds, in his role as Institute chairman, is upstairs in the McNay Room – effectively the Institute's own library – cataloguing a growing and important collection. Though the morning's bitter, Dave wears shorts. "I got into the habit when I was a postman" he says and at once triggers thoughts of Matt Bendelow, another Shildon lad – Foundry Street, memory suggests – who'd been a miner before himself becoming a postman.

Matt had been married in 1914 when just 17, enlisted in the Green Howards a few days later, lost a leg and suffered serious arm injuries on the Somme in September 1916. Discharged, he returned to the pit but when the miners went on strike became village postman at Bowes, in Teesdale – his six-days-a-week delivery round embracing nine moorland miles for getting on 40 years, all weathers and every step on crutches.

Postman Matt also covered the village telephone exchange – Bowes 1 – at night, met the mail train at the little village station at six o'clock every morning, bred prize-winning rabbits, was saddler, shoemaker and swimmer, castle custodian, cartoonist, billiards champion, poet, chimney sweep and accomplished cook, St John Ambulanceman and the first Bowes resident to volunteer for the Home Guard. Someone really should have written a book about Matt Bendelow, though none ever did.

Fred's collection is extraordinary, and eclectic, nonetheless. Almost all are hardback and in pristine condition; many are what the leisured call coffee table books and they're going a little faster than he'd anticipated. Biographies and autobiographies embrace everyone from Michael Palin to Kerry Packer, from Gary Sobers to Sidney Poitier and from John Humphrys to Elton John. An *Oor Wullie* annual – braw – is among those which comes home with me.

None haggles, some pay over the modest odds. A chap with a pound shop carrier bag picks up several dozen books, disdainfully examines each and leaves the literary love feast with his bag as empty as it had been when he arrived, headed home to his second hand copy of the *Daily Star*.

The early interest has faded, Fred's back's buggered, his concerns resurfaced. "There are still an awful lot of books where these came from" he says. "I think we may still be a few bob short of a memorial."

Round figure: Matt Bendelow

Chapter thirty-one

House of Yorke

Rob Yorke is one of those movers and shakers of whom it may unanswerably be wondered how 24 hours can accommodate all that daily he essays. Successful and entrepreneurial businessman, prominent and purposeful member of Durham County Council, chairman of the South Durham Enterprise Board and of the Trustees of the Auckland Project – Jonathan Ruffer's blue-blood baby – he is also a passionate supporter of Newcastle United, where he has a sumptuous executive box, and a hands-on president of Bishop Auckland FC.

Born in 1971, effortlessly charismatic and greatly magnanimous, he has recently spent a great deal of time and money creating his ideal home.

His ideal home is in Shildon. It's there that we spend a couple of December hours supping coffee and scoffing his mum's fruit cake. "There's so much that's lovely around here" he says at once. "I take the dog for a walk and marvel at it, not least the park. Shildon people are lovely, too; they mightn't know who you are but they always stop to say hello. They're so friendly; that's worth a million dollars."

Doesn't it sometimes seem, though, that Bishop Auckland – not least since Jonathan Ruffer's improbable arrival – is getting a disproportionate slice of that moreish fruit cake? Might not the burgeoning Auckland Retail Park, barely two miles down the road, be the final nail in Shildon's shopping coffin? Isn't it a bit unfair to champion the Stockton and Darlington bicentenary launch on the Kynren site at Bishop?

Rob, county councillor for the West Auckland ward and involved with much in Bishop Auckland, insists not. "I don't believe in boundaries, I don't look at Shildon as separate, I look at it all as one. We want Bishop Auckland to be a visitor destination but there's no reason why Shildon can't be, too. I try to help anyone, no matter where they live. It doesn't take long to send an email to County Hall. Job creation doesn't have borders. Our own job is to ensure that people have aspirations, no matter where they are."

He was born in Witton Park, crucible in the 1960s of the ultimately successful county-wide fight against a Category D policy which sought to condemn 121 Durham communities to death by no development. As the village declined, his parents – like many more – were moved to the post-war Woodhouse Close council housing estate three miles away in Bishop Auckland.

"Witton Park was where I learned about a real sense of community, a sense of belonging. You knew everyone, you felt involved, but when my mam and dad moved to Woodhouse Close it was like they'd won the Lottery. They had an indoor toilet, they had electricity, they had a garden, not water running down the walls.

"My dad wasn't really interested in politics, though he loved to watch Question Time on television. I was fascinated by Robin Day. Margaret Thatcher did some good things, but I was drawn to the Labour Party." He remains a member, or chairman, of several community groups in the reborn village and in nearby Escomb, lived in a smart four bedroom house in Bishop, jumped at the chance in 2019 to buy Enfield Lodge, beautifully situated but half-hidden from the rest of Shildon at the back of Central Parade and with 1.3 acres of imaginatively and vividly landscaped gardens.

One of those gnomic sculptures of Laurel and Hardy stands on the front door step, pictures of the comic couple – Stan Laurel lived briefly in Bishop – hang on the walls. "I love them, I think I've got every film they made" says Rob.

Immediately inside the house there's a large coat rack but, a little surprisingly, no sign of a hat stand, no milliners' row. Councillor Yorke wears an awful lot of hats, hopes (with well-founded optimism) that the Labour Party will regain control of the council in May 2025.

The house was built in 1878 for Dr Samuel Fielden, suitably juxtaposed, long Shildon's medical officer of health and (as we have said) owned from the 1960s by George Romaines, the Shildon lad who became an early singing star of Tyne Tees Television. There's still a photograph of George beside the Tyne Tees helicopter, landed on the lawn and a framed illuminated scroll presented by townsfolk to Dr Fielden and his wife Jane – "gentle and sweet" – on their golden wedding.

Born in Shildon in 1871, their son Edward became a doctor ("and public vaccinator") in Bracknell, remembered particularly for his care for the "impoverished" – the more affluent paid sixpence a week – and honoured still by the Fielden Clock in that Berkshire town centre. Sir Edward Hedley Fielden, Samuel's grandson, became an aviator, was appointed personal pilot to the Duke of Windsor when the future Edward VIII bought himself a Gipsy Moth in 1927, flew through the ranks, became an air vice-marshal and piloted the new Queen Elizabeth and her husband home from Kenya after news of her father's death in 1952.

While junior ranks doubtless called him "Sir", others knew him as Mouse – "because of his discretion and self-effacement"

Enfield of dreams: Rob Yorke

211

says Wikipedia, though what's so discreet or self-effacing about mice is not immediately obvious.

Sir Edward died in 1976, aged 72, 13 years after his son Mark had been killed in a motor racing accident at Silverstone.

Rob bought a nine-bedroomed house and has converted it into four. There's now an indoor swimming pool, a spacious bar and games room, a wonderful stained glass window of Timothy Hackworth and S&D history created over 18 months by the artist Bridget Jones. The conversion tried to be faithful to the original, he says. The garden attracts tawny owls – he's installed hidden cameras to film them – and ducks to one of the water features. There are family trees, too, planted by the good doctor and flourishing yet.

The tour's accompanied by his dog, Ted – named after Ted Henderson, his boss when he began work at Teescraft Engineering at South Church near Bishop Auckland, just the fourth employee, as a 16-year-old in 1967. Having spent nine years studying and making money by buying and selling property, he bought the company for £80,000 20 years later. Now there are around 250 employees, another base at Alston in Cumbria and four foundries across the north.

"I called it the back-to-front house but I'd never been through the gate until I expressed an interest in buying it" says Rob. "I fell in love with it immediately. I love to sit in the garden to do some green sky thinking."

Doesn't he mean blue sky thinking? "Oh no" he says at once, "these days it's all about green energy, isn't it?"

Even in winter the garden's truly lovely but on the other side of the wall, out of sight but by no means out of mind, Shildon's problems remain. What's to be done? What of the decrepit main street, the crime rate, the tumbling population and the tide of homeless and rootless from London and elsewhere? What of the decision to launch the bicentenary at Bishop Auckland – Rob would quite have liked it to have been at Witton Park (which, goodness knows, has a better claim than Bishop.) Times change, he says. "Main streets can't just be retail any more. There has to be a mix, that's the same everywhere, many people prefer out of town shopping."

Unwelcome visitors? Houses in multiple occupation? "The same company is buying up cheap housing all over the area, we're aware of that and looking at how to address it. At the moment it's not really working for anyone."

Crime? "Three fantastic Ofsted reports for Shildon's schools don't just reflect really well on headteachers and their staff, they say a lot about the kids. There are some wonderful kids in Shildon and they're the majority. Locomotion's brilliant and will grow still further, the town council does a fantastic job on the park and other green spaces and just look at Shildon Alive. There's still a real spirit about the place.

"The town could do with a better bus service but that could be said for the whole of Co Durham, and it could do with more good quality executive housing because we don't want it to become a dormitory town. Shildon still has a lot going for it; I look forward to walking the dog and finding out more. I know the other man's grass is always said to be greener but I don't envisage living anywhere else. I'm very lucky to be here."

Chapter thirty-two

Christmas present

Christmas was always special when we were bairns, Christmas Day just about the only day of the year that we used the little bay windowed front room – the sitting room – and certainly the only day on which the coal fire was lit. On other not-quite-so-special occasions the room was electrically warmed by something called a Berry's Magicole, though "magic" only in a Tommy Cooperish sort of way.

There was Mary's Boy Child not Band Aid, chicken not turkey, figs in syrup not pigs in blankets. Then there was Christmas cake, succeeded a week later by New Year's cake to the same fruitful formula, though the greater thrill was to run sticky child-like fingers around the bowl in which merrily they'd been mixed.

And all of it was lovely (save, laxatively, for the figs.)

Back then the decidedly deciduous Christmas tree came up from Joe Birt on Alma Road and municipal festive illumination was unknown. When the council did finally light up the main thoroughfares it called to mind nothing more greatly than Mrs Cratchit, poor Bob's triumphant spouse, who (it will be recalled) was "dressed out but poorly in a twice-turned gown but brave in ribbons which are cheap and make a goodly show for sixpence."

These days the lights show is luminously improved. Two handsome trees twinkle near the King Willie and on the Town Square, happily having survived the onslaught from Storm Bert a few days earlier, though Bert blew away the planned Christmas concert at the parish church. Probably the storms were just as bad in the 1950s but the Met Office didn't see need to christen them and, if they had, it probably wouldn't have been Bert.

It's December 12, the night of the town mayor's carol service in the Civic Hall. Maybe eighty are gathered, few under 50 save for the choir from St John's primary school, of whom we shall hear a little more in a moment.

Shirley Quinn, mayor for a second term, welcomes other mayors and leaders from the town's principal churches – Anglican, Roman Catholic, Methodist, Salvation Army, Amanda Smethurst, the Salvation Army officer, gives a short talk in which the children are asked what they'll be having for Christmas dinner (as always it should be called, whatever the hour of its serving).

One says turkey, another chicken, a third pork. "A parmo" adds a fourth, a child of the 21st century. "I think you're on your own there" says Amanda.

The carols are mostly traditional, *Come and join the celebration* a relative though jolly newcomer. The St John's bairns venture something to the tune of *Jingle Bells* though with rather more spiritual content followed by another to the tune of *Alleluia* as sung by the lugubrious Leonard Cohen who they probably think plays full back for Newcastle United. They're terrific.

The Salvation Army band plays *While shepherds* and to the traditional tune – none of this Ilkley Moor nonsense north of the Tees – though it still recalls the innocent merriment when, aged about nine, we first heard the variant about washing socks by night, all seated in the pub.

Afterwards I confirm attendance at St John's Christmas Eve "midnight" service with Carol Harris, the vicar, ask if the organist might be persuaded to play *Joy to the world*, Christendom's greatest Christmas song. Carol says it won't be possible for the very good reason that it's many years since the church has been able to find an organist, accompaniment now provided via something computerised called Spotify.

All change? Spotify the difference.

Had good King Wenceslas looked out on Christmas Eve 2024 – and how old were we before realising that the monarch wasn't King Wences who'd last looked out? – he'd have found Shildon unseasonably warm and uncommonly quiet. In the King Willie at 10 30pm a sole punter is propping up the bar – possibly vice-versa – while all around him chairs are piled upside down on tables. Lads more sensitive than Shildon's might have taken that as a hint.

Still for sale, the Fox and Hounds appears never to have opened, no room at the inn. The Red Lion's half-empty, most of the takeaways steel shuttered. Chisholm the best-bet bookie offers Christmas gift vouchers and "festive forecasts", Godfrey Card has branded his pork and chilli sausages as "Rudolph's revenge" for reasons which might little tax the imagination.

It doesn't feel a lot like Christmas. They can't all be at home watching Gavin and Stacey, surely?

Around the town, however, many homes are fittingly, festively festooned. Were there a prize it would go to the folk on Sterling Way, still misspelt but gloriously decked. That there are relatively few lights in what we must suppose New Shildon may be because there are so many abandoned houses, and it's hard to illuminate a boarded-up window.

On the nearby bypass a cacophonic convoy of police vehicles offers discordant reminder that not all may be peace and good will this Christmas.

Back in the 1960s, the blessed season at St John's parish church didn't begin until 4pm on Christmas Eve, the tree at last lit up for the children's crib service with the seeming reluctance of a latter day Scrooge faced with a soaring electric bill. Canon Corden took the view that Advent lasted until midnight on the 24th and that Advent, if not as haggard and as hairshirted as Lent, should be prim and penitential, nonetheless.

Were *O Come all Ye Faithful* to be sung, even with just eight hours to go, the last verse – the exultant "Yea Lord we greet thee, born this happy morning" – was strictly and canonically omitted, the more lustily to be bellowed in the infant hours of the following morning.

Back then the midnight church would overflow – hundreds of them, side aisles, too – and little matter that many had spent contemplative hours in the similarly packed pub beforehand. It was still an important part of Christmas. The pews have long since been replaced by more comfortable chairs, the whole church imaginatively and thoughtfully re-ordered. It looks lovely, made yet more attractive by three twinkling trees.

But the "midnight" congregation on Christmas Eve 2024 numbers precisely 17.

Compulsive reading, two or three parish magazines from the mid-1960s sit on a table in the church foyer. In the January 1967 issue the new vicar, Canon Corden, addresses the need – perhaps for the first time, by no means for the last – for

Glad tidings: St John's church

"planned" giving to the church substantially to increase. St John's needs £80 a week and gets £30, he says, urging the flock to give sacrificially. "It is an insult to God to put Him off with a tip. It seems to me that 1967 is going to be a highly critical year for St John's. Obviously something drastic will have to be done."

Unlikely wholly to address the deficit, the price of the magazine was to go up from fourpence to a tanner.

John Wraight, a curate in charge of the parish between vicars, had the previous March written of some of the excuses for not attending church – "I don't like the vicar/curate", "Sunday's the only chance we get of a lie-in", "Nobody spoke to me when I came" – and in that respect suggests that, more than half a century later, little may have changed.

Back then St John's had three Sunday services, Holy Communion and Evensong every day of the week and twice a month was also responsible for a service down the bank in Middridge. Almost every Saturday there were weddings, often two and sometimes three. For better or worse, how many church weddings today?

Advertisers included D&A Foskett, long at the top of Main Street – "your Murphy dealer, television installation a speciality" – Coxon's in Church Street ("big selection of bras, girdles, underwear and nighties") and Hackett and Baines, bless them, advising of a 30 shilling part exchange deal on old mattresses for new.

In 1968 the magazine transmogrified into a tabloid parish newspaper, the first of its kind in the Durham diocese, the price indeed rising to sixpence and with complaints addressed to the new and wet-eared editor. I ignored them, of course.

Carol's as welcoming as ever. The service is led – enthusiastically, almost passionately – by Emma Harte, the South Shields-born curate who bears a marked resemblance to Helen-Ann Hartley, the Bishop of Newcastle, in the Christmas news for reasons which speak little of peace and good will to all.

"Emma's so keen we almost have to batten her down" says oner of the churchwardens. "Some parish is going to get a brilliant vicar when she leaves here."

Apart from anything else, it's joyful to be back in St John's for an occasion other than an old friend's funeral, among the other changes that hymn books and prayer books have been replaced, hanging above the chancel, by the biggest screen seen in Shildon since the Hippodrome bowed to bingo and took Cinemascope with it. Everything's writ large on this one, so blessedly large that even I can (just about) make it out.

The churchwardens are manifestly sober, no chance of local ecclesiastical history repeating itself or of a 1am game of knocky-nine-doors – exuberantly, egregiously – down a snowy front street. Emma speaks of the "absolute privilege" of being there, tells of a time of peace, hope, love and joy, prays for the poor, the homeless and for the sadness of the world.

Spotify's fine, if occasionally a mite obstreperous, but will never replace one of Messrs Harrison's finest pipe organs giving it, as they used to say hereabouts, what fettle.

The service has begun at 11 15pm. Though the church clock doesn't chime, it's barely a minute after midnight when the last hymn – *O Come all Ye Faithful*, of course – is announced, the last verse in particular effervescently addressed. That's when

you know it's Christmas.

Carol and Emma greet the departing congregation in the foyer, the vicar eager to point out that they'd had 100 for the crib service at 4pm and 45 for the midnight service the year previously. She proffers an open Quality Street tin, holding all manner of sweeties.

Another thing that's changed is that they no longer take a collection, though a twinkling little gizmo in a corner of the foyer invites electronic donations. Perhaps it's the lateness of the hour, more likely innate incompetence, that I find myself trying to proffer a Christmas gift with a North Yorkshire County Council codger's bus pass. Clutching for just the second time in 70 years a little tube of Love Hearts, we head for hearth and home, a memorable start to the season.

Chapter thirty-three

Beginning and end

New Year may be old hat. Never midnight's children, not as nippers, we were allowed after breakfast on January 1 to go banging on neighbours' doors – "Happy new year, bottles of stir, please can I have my new year's gift" – an effrontery usually rewarded with a small value coin and perhaps a sliver of shortbread. A little older, I was in demand as a first foot, always bearing a bit of stick and a lump of coal, the tradition that the first across the threshold should be tall, dark and handsome and two out of three deemed on a dark night to be acceptable.

Aunty Betty was always the first, followed across the back street cobbles by a call on old Mrs Stephenson in Alexandra Street and thereafter next door to Tom and Violet Roberts (whose grandson Ben was another with Shildon roots who made a successful living as a professional footballer.)

At each house there'd be fruit cake, shortbread, maybe a bit of cheese and, inevitably, a little glass of port or sugar-sweet sherry, quite likely the only occasion in the succeeding 365 days in which alcohol was poured in those abstemious homes and with the sole saving grace that it was marginally less gruesome than cherry brandy or, nadir, advocaat. How greatly I loathed it all, how greatly I longed (then as now) for a pint of bitter, how heroically I quaffed the stuff and wished them, with sincerity, all that they wished themselves.

St John's church bells would peal away, the ubiquitous George White doubtless calling the tune, the welkin ringing simultaneously with New Year greeting and, on one memorable occasion, a pie-eyed piper outside the King Willie. These days he might play a lament for the licensed trade, the papers on December 31 2024 reporting that another 412 English pubs had closed in the previous 12 months. We shall return to that solemn statistic shortly.

First footing finished, we'd then catch up with the lads – maybe even the lasses – another of those rarefied occasions when the parental front parlour might be thrown open to the uninitiated, like the Masonic Hall on wives' and sweethearts' night. It was always boisterous, always bibulous, always benevolent and usually home in time for breakfast.

On the last day of 2024, the dawn of one of the most crucial years in Shildon's heavy metal history, it seems appropriate to return, to roister and once again to raise a glass.

Andrea Savino had been happy in Sorrento until a Shildon lass called Marilyn came for a fortnight's sunshine. The attraction was happy and mutual, the proposal of holy matrimony swiftly forthcoming but for Marilyn terms and conditions applied. Never mind coming back to Sorrento, as Dean Martin or someone suggested, they had to live in Shildon.

In time for the Stockton and Darlington sesquicentennial in 1975, Andrea opened a restaurant at the top of Main Street in what probably had been Arthur and Dorothy Foskett's record, television and pedal cycle shop. He was a delightful chap, a brilliant chef and a glad-handing host. It took off. The soups were sensational, the fish fabulous, the tiramisu terrific and the garlic bread so wondrous that it was possible seriously to question the scripture that man shall not live by bread alone because this man could have done, or tried to, quite happily.

As warm as a Sorrento summer evening, Andrea – "vibrant,

eccentric, charismatic and irresistible" I once wrote – offered seemingly endless, and always gratis, refills of limoncello, a liqueur so liberally poured that it was possible to suppose that he'd discovered a bottomless limoncello well somewhere out the back, where the car park now overflows on match days. To say that Andrea was colourful was a bit like Pharoah supposing Joseph's dreamcoat to be a bit on the gaudy side.

Far too early, greatly mourned, he died in the summer of 2007, his funeral in the Methodist church directly across the road. After a while the restaurant was re-opened by Salvatore, his son, named Maralena's in salute to Marilyn, though Andrea proved a hard act to follow. "One woman told me that my roast potatoes weren't as good as my dad's because they weren't burned" said Salvatore. "Sometimes you can't win"

A third incarnation was short lived. It's now Santinni and it's there on a stormy winter night that we gather for the last knock-ings of 2024.

Fully booked, by 7pm it's chocker. The deal's that £15 gets admission, prosecco on arrival, several shots – limoncello re-mains top of the shots, there really must be a subterranean stash in the vicinity of Primitive Street – a turn (quite a good turn), "party games" and nick-nacks like party poppers and glow sticks. Food from a fairly standard Italian menu is additional.

We're seated beneath a big picture of a Vespa motor scooter, which should not be taken as a suggestion that we represent the Mods. Very likely we're the oldest there. "Did you know that 'vespa' means little wasp?" asks Sharon, who learned such erudite things at university.

The atmosphere's vibrant, the feel factor good, the age range extensive. Since this is Co Durham there are those who order pollo (and pizza, and pasta) with chips; since this is Co Durham the womenfolk head for the loo in twos and threes, as if scared of being mugged for their glow sticks. Updated somewhat, it's a bit like Hogmanay hoolies of old and all the better for that. When the turn reprises *Dancing Queen* – "having the time of your life" – for many it may seem a pretty fair summary.

At ten o'clock they come around with the free bingo cards – when in Shildon, see above – but we need to explore elsewhere. Coats on, bill paid, tip abundantly earned, we're on the way out when intercepted by the barman. "Would you like another limoncello" he says. The shocks, the real shocks, are about to begin.

The main streets are almost deserted, the rain incessant, the town surreal, somnolent, almost silent. The front door of the Red Lion, party central all those dancing queen decades ago, is steel shuttered. The Fox and Hounds remains closed, so does the Locomotive, opposite where the wagon works once whirled. Church Street's so quiet you can't even get a haircut.

Old Shildon Workmen's Club is almost directly across the road from the restaurant. In the days when licensed premises didn't open until six o'clock there'd be New Year's Eve queues half way down the street, such the anxiousness to find a seat. At 10 20pm on New Year's Eve 2024 the big main bar has precisely one customer, a gentleman who looks (shall we say) like he's been there quite a long time. At 10 22pm the barmaid comes around with the vacuum cleaner, an action which those of a more sensitive nature – as at the King Willie a week earlier – might suppose to be a suggestion.

The hint having fallen on stony ground, she tells him that they closed at ten o'clock. On New Year's Eve? In Shildon? On the telly the Music Channel's churning out something indeterminate, but it sure as eggs isn't Auld Lang Syne.

Down in the Railway Institute, the main lounge is locked. Four elderly chaps, quietly talking around a table, are alone in the Hackworth Room; maybe 25 are gathered, merrily enough, in the bar. There's a nice pint of something called Santa's Little Smelter, a product of the Consett Brewery which likes to keep the ferrous wheel turning.

At 11 55pm they play *It's the final countdown*, at midnight we welcome 2025. No church bells ring, none seems in search of bottles of stir.

At noon on Wednesday January 1 locomotive whistles across the land, including at Locomotion half a mile from the Institute, will with some sort of synchronicity welcome the great year of the bicentenary, a year of potential renaissance, a time of unique and perhaps never to be repeated opportunity but with the barely suppressed fear that, for the old home town, it may be too late.

So at the end of the book we're back to where it all began. Welcome the world, Shildon. Go for it – and a very happy New Year.

Acknowledgements

For better or worse – opinions may vary – *All change* has been very much all my own work. Numerous other written sources have been consulted, however – some even read. Many have been Shildon-oriented, sometimes quirky, others more general and perhaps more academic. The list below embraces many of them, sometimes simply by way of acknowledgement, sometimes as possible suggestions for further reading.

It's also important to thank local historian Alan Ellwood, a mainstay of the Shildon Recall History Society – now sadly defunct – for his invaluable help in sourcing many old photographs, including the wonderful cover picture. Some of the more recent pix, probably those out of focus, are mine; others come courtesy of *The Northern Echo*.

Warm thanks, too, to all who so happily gave of their time, or who let me by a fly on their wall, or who occasionally got the beers in. Thanks also to the guys at County Print, Middlesbrough, for their accustomed professionalism and patience and for designing the book.

The most improbable of the written sources, and perhaps the least accessible – he only produced 20 copies of each - are the seven compendious volumes about his home town, written and privately published by the late Frank Lawson BA MLitt, a particularly long distance love affair because he'd for many years lived in Harpenden, Hertfordshire.

Frank grew up in Simpson Street, near the wagon works, and could remember his grandfather selling paraffin from a horse and cart. Like me he attended Timothy Hackworth primary and King James I grammar schools – the former when lessons would be interrupted by evacuation drills - but had several months absence through illness, during which time, unlike me, he'd read Encyclopaedia Britannica from cover to cover. Unlike me, he also attended All Saints church where the pie and pea suppers – and especially the mushy peas – were eagerly anticipated.

"I can still remember going to a friend's house one Christmas Eve and eating mushy pea sandwiches" he wrote in one of the magnificent seven.

Though there's little else of a personal nature he does somewhat sheepishly admit that he was a member of the Young Conservatives – the highlight when a Rolls Royce dropped him outside his parents' terraced house – and that he once appeared on stage with George Romaines, Shildon's singing son. "I didn't give up the day job" adds Frank.

Some of his research is exhaustively academic, some anecdotal, some improbable and some perhaps a little irrelevant. What, it's possible to wonder, is the relevance of the note that they used to keep llamas in Romaldkirk or that Shildon station's first porter was called Barney? The library may hold copies; they're abundantly worth finding. Further reading….

Shildon Wagon Works: a working man's life by Ron Spedding. Durham County Library (1988).

Stockton and Darlington Railway: anniversary celebration by K Hoole. Dalesman (1974).

Timothy Hackworth and the Locomotive by Robert Young (Hackworth's grandson). The Hackworth Society (reprinted 2000).

Spirit of Locomotion by Anthony Coulls. PiXz Books (2012). The story of the National Railway Museum in Shildon.

North-East by Rail: Railway Development Society (1986).

Shildon: Cradle of the Railways by Robert Corkin. Frank Graham (1977).

Memories of Shildon. Co Durham Books. Old photographs. (2003)

An insatiable first by Dave Reynolds. Amazon (2024). The story of the Railway Institute.

The Wizard and the Typhoon by Dave Reynolds. Amazon (2022). The story of Shildon's two musical geniuses.

Shildon coal by David G Snell. Fund raising booklet (1995) for the Salvation Army.

Shildon, the world's first railway town by Gerald Slack (2021). One of several Shildon histories meticulously researched and privately printed and published.

A railway history of New Shildon by George Turner Smith. Pen and Sword (2019). Hardback.

Memories of the LNER: SW Durham by Allan W Stobbs. Privately published (1989).

The Peases and the Stockton and Darlington Railway by Bernard McCormick. MacDonald Press (2008).

Rail 150: the Stockton and Darlington and what followed by Jack Simmons. Eyre Methuen (1975).

Platform souls: the train spotter as 20th century hero by Nicholas Whittaker. Victor Gollancz (1995).

Timothy Hackworth Primary School: a century of learning. Published by the school (2010).

Shildon Coronation souvenir brochures (1937 and 1953). Rich in adverts for local retailers before and after the war.

Shildon: official guide and industrial handbook - at least three local authority publications down the years.

Around Shildon by Vera Chapman. Nonsuch publications 128 pages, nostalgic old photographs.

The Globe quarterly journal of the Friends of the Stockton and Darlington Railway.

Souvenir booklet to mark the centenary of Timothy Hackworth's death. Published in 1950 by the centenary committee.

Shildon 150 official souvenir booklet, just 25p at the time and with a foreword by the Queen Mother.

Mike Amos was born in Sedgefield in October 1946, in turn delivered to the parental home in Shildon a week later and lived there – pretty much – until 1973. He was an urban district councillor, churchwarden, parish newspaper editor and Church Council secretary. A journalist since leaving Bishop Auckland Grammar School, mostly on *The Northern Echo*, he was named North East Journalist of the Year seven times in sixteen years, won many other regional and national awards, was an inaugural inductee into the Provincial Journalism Hall of Fame and in 2006 was appointed MBE for services to journalism in North-East England. He was made redundant, aged 73. For 20 years chairman of the Northern Football League, he remains a committed supporter, and vice-president, of Shildon FC.

Other books include *Unconsidered trifles*, an autobiography, *No-brainer* – combining the life story of former Middlesbrough footballer Bill Gates with the campaign for greater awareness of the dangers of repetitively heading a ball – and *Prairie stories*, about life and gusty times on Stanley Hill Top, above Crook. He has also written or edited several books about the Northern League.

Married with two adult sons and four grandchildren, he now lives in North Yorkshire but throughout 2024 seemed never to have been away from Shildon.

Contact: mikeamos81@aol.com

Mike Amos